Praise for *Sacred Land*

'A wonderful read – intensively researched and inspirationally written, it offers a fascinating insight into our sacred history. Martin's incredible knowledge and storytelling ability shine through – you will never look at a landscape or building in the same way again!'
Miranda Krestovnikoff, television presenter, natural historian and author

'The modern world has followed the path of secular materialism for a considerable time. Now we have reached a cul-de-sac. Here comes Martin Palmer as a guide to show us a new way to see the world and develop a sense of the sacred. Nature is not there just for our use, it is a sacred gift to celebrate. *Sacred Land* is informative, enlightening and inspiring – I read this book and saw the earth in a completely new light. Unless we develop a sense of the sacred, our environmental, economic and social problems will continue to intensify and humanity will find itself increasingly dissatisfied, whereas a sense of the sacred brings joy and delight in everyday life. Martin Palmer's beautifully written book is a companion to help us at a great turning point.'
Satish Kumar, Editor in Chief, *Resurgence* magazine

'Martin Palmer makes a first-rate and unusual tour guide. *Sacred Land* leads us through the broad sweep of centuries, even millennia, of historical analysis, as well as along gentle and reflective strolls, on trails to be found in places from cities to hamlets. Along the way, clues to the spiritual significance of the sites and features are identified, enriching not only this journey but also providing the foundation for discovering our own insights when we go walking ourselves.'
David Nussbaum, Chief Executive, WWF-UK

About the author

Martin Palmer is a writer, broadcaster and prolific translator of Chinese classics, as well as being secretary general of one of the world's most unusual environmental charities – ARC, the Alliance of Religions and Conservation. He lives in Somerset, very close to one of England's most impressive Neolithic long barrows.

Sacred Land

Decoding Britain's extraordinary past through
its towns, villages and countryside

MARTIN PALMER

piatkus

PIATKUS

First published in Great Britain in 2012 by Piatkus
Reprinted 2012

Copyright © Martin Palmer 2012

The moral right of the author has been asserted.

A CIP catalogue record for this book
is available from the British Library.

ISBN 978-0-7499-5292-1

Typeset in Palatino by M Rules
Printed and bound by CPI Group (UK) Ltd, Croydon, CR0 4YY

Papers used by Piatkus are from well-managed forests
and other responsible sources.

MIX
Paper from
responsible sources
FSC® C104740

Piatkus
An imprint of
Little, Brown Book Group
100 Victoria Embankment
London EC4Y 0DY

An Hachette UK Company
www.hachette.co.uk

www.piatkus.co.uk

This book is dedicated to Victoria Finlay, my companion and my wife, who has walked every page and mile of this book with me and brought her own insights, wisdom and passion to it. Here's to the continuing journey.

Contents

Acknowledgements

I am grateful to the research team who worked with me on this book and continue to work on the Sacred Land Project: my brother Nigel Palmer, whose encyclopaedic knowledge of buildings and sites across Britain never ceases to amaze me. Jay Ramsay, who over one summer walked and talked with me and then wrote his poem *Summerland*, which runs through this book. He was, as ever, a delight and joy to work with. Philippa Moss started work one day and was found walking across rugged landscapes the next, interpreting the landscape and exploring the core themes of this book. Her contribution to this book is immense. Joshua Newton walked urban landscapes and discovered that once you do that it's hard to walk quickly through a city like Bristol. His enthusiasm was infectious. Michael French gave time from his PhD studies to research and, most importantly, to come and debate ideas, movements in history and all the details which make working on a book like this such fun. Oliver Walter has really done the work on the Gazetteer and now claims that he cannot stop 'reading' places as a result. To all of them I owe a huge amount.

Melvyn Bragg and I have appeared together on *In Our Time* on numerous occasions over the years, discussing everything from the intricacies of Christian theology, through Hell, Satan and Daoism, to Shintoism and the Muslim rule in Spain. I am honoured that he agreed to write the Foreword.

Apologies should go to my son and daughter, James Palmer and Lizzie Miller, for the many, many occasions when we turned off the road to visit yet another church, burial mound or Roman site.

Gill Bailey and Jillian Stewart at Little, Brown have wrestled with this book for far too long and with unimaginable patience. It is the better book precisely because they were always right in their comments and criticisms.

Susan Mears, my agent, has kept me on her books for reasons I suspect of charity but I am grateful to her belief in this book and in the Sacred Land Project.

Finally, in words which are inadequate, a Thank You to my wife and companion Victoria Finlay, for the many walks, explorations and discussions which lie behind the best of this book.

Foreword by Melvyn Bragg

Martin Palmer is a man for whom the spiritual aspect of life is palpable. He has made himself a connoisseur of the great world religions and radio audiences have been enriched many times by his fluent erudition.

He has an enviable facility for interconnecting different faiths – Judaism, Islam, Taoism, Confucianism, Hinduism, Buddhism and the many branches of Christianity. Martin Palmer seems at times to stride across these massed mountains of knowledge like a giant in magic boots.

Now he has set himself the task of uncovering, explaining and listing what he calls the 'sacred places' in Britain which are still there to be found and in his view to be felt, even today. He begins by laying out his cards:

'I am often asked "what do you mean by sacred?". To my mind there are four kinds of sacred place, and I believe that they capture four kinds of sacred experience that run through time and through all faiths. Most people are familiar with the first type, as they are all around us. Communities decide upon a site that will be holy to them and then build their local church, chapel, synagogue, mosque or temple on that piece of ground . . . it becomes a holy place . . . The second type of sacred place might be a raging sea, viewed from a cliff top, or a giant redwood forest that stretches to the horizon . . . or a peaceful grove where the sunlight seems to dance through the branches. It is somewhere that overwhelms us with the sheer beauty or magnificence of nature . . . The third type . . . has been made holy by history or legend . . . a small cave that has been worn into the cliffs by the sea in Whithorn, Dumfries . . . in the fourth century St Ninian would come here to be alone with God and nature . . . or Stonehenge . . . or Clifford's Tower in York . . . or Tyburn . . . or Lindisfarne . . . Finally there are those sacred places that mean something special to individuals . . . for me the Quantock Hills in Somerset are sacred because I used to go there as a child with my magical godmother . . . They are all sacred because they link us to the Divine and give us a sense of meaning . . .'

I quote at some length what I trust you will soon be reading, because I want to emphasise the core of the author's mission. It needs to be held onto. Such is his enthusiasm that he is perfectly happy to whirl us through geological ages, to skim across centuries of historical time, to expand in detail on the placing of an altar, to flourish the miracles that made saints and above all to raise the dead of all ages into the light of today.

A substantial portion of this book is devoted to lists which tell us where sacred places can be found: the ruins of abbeys, long barrows, henges, parish churches, battlegrounds, springs, rivers, forests, walls and what he refers to as the 'sacred environment'. His position on this is clearly stated in his opening paragraph. He helped launch the Alliance of Religion and Conservation (ARC), whose aim is 'to protect as many of the world's sacred places' as it can.

He wants people to 'rediscover the heritage of wisdom, spirituality and respect for nature that was built into the landscape for generations and which we are in danger of losing for ever'. So this is an act of reclamation and also an alarm call. We are provided with compendious guides at the end of each sweep of a chapter. The chief purpose of the book is to persuade us to visit these places and learn from them. It is boldly at odds with the prevailing culture of reason. He loves what appears to be out of reach, that which is as much myth as history, those largely invisible tracks of the growth of mankind made visible only to those who seek or try to understand the remains of their day.

There is much to disagree with. He seems to hold that unless you have a religious sense you can have no true sense of beauty or harmony or peace. There are many who claim their experience disproves that. And some will doubt the outer range of his 'sacred places'.

But there is much to relish. He swings through from 1.5 million BC to the present day with such zest that at times the book trembles on the edge of a stream of consciousness as the author spirals into ever increasing layers of information that he cannot bear us not to know. We have cycles and collapses of nature; the sacred in every field, in language, in places names, in country houses . . . There is almost an infestation of sacredness here which the author passionately wants to draw to our attention. And it is full of rich information.

Why is the Severn referred to as 'She'? How did Sanskrit influence the naming of the Celtic sea gods? How does Torpenhow Ridge near Plymouth translate into 'hill, hill, hill, hill' in four different languages? Why are All Saints and All Souls and All Hallows collectively the second most common dedication of Churches in Britain (St Mary is the first)?

On we go to local saints and the church as a sanctuary, to the market place made sacred by its proximity to the church, to the myths in the streets of Canterbury and Carmarthen and on we go, ever more inclusive, town halls and commercial buildings.

One great theme focuses on the customs through the ages of burying the dead. This is a fascinating strand.

He fears that unless we take account of all this then the civilisation that we have today will implode for lack of essential spiritual sustenance. This is his case. He makes it with panache.

Introduction

In the summer of 1996, I travelled to a retreat centre in North Wales with two friends – one from India, the other from Japan. Our wives were visiting their families, so we were in charge of keeping seven small children entertained for a week. As if that were not enough, my two friends and I were also hoping to make a start on devising reli- gious–ecological programmes for our respective countries based upon ancient understandings of the sacred nature of the land. This was the task I had set myself the previous year, when launching the Alliance of Religions and Conservation (ARC) with the Duke of Edinburgh. Our ultimate goal was to protect as many of the world's sacred places as we could.

One day, on the recommendation of our host at the retreat centre, we packed two cars with the children and went to visit an ancient valley in mid-Wales – Pennant Melangell. After several wrong turns, we finally arrived beside a tiny medieval church that seemed to have grown organically out of the ground itself. However, the church was a relatively recent addition to this site, which also contained a four-thousand-year- old burial mound and an ancient yew tree. Once inside the building, we learned the beautiful story of St Melangell, a woman who became a hermit here in the seventh century. She chose this spot for its remote- ness from the rest of humanity and for its closeness to nature. She prayed, meditated and became trusted by the local wildlife. Then, one

morning, a pagan prince rode into the valley with his hounds and followers. They flushed a hare out of the woods and began the hunt. The
hare fled across the meadows and through the hedgerows, with the
prince and his hounds in hot pursuit. Then, just as they were closing in
for the kill, to their astonishment they were confronted by a very angry
young woman – Melangell. The terrified hare had stopped running and
was quivering at her feet. Deeply moved by the hermit's compassion,
the prince became a Christian that day. He donated the valley to
Melangell and to Christ in perpetuity, saying it should become a sanctuary for all creation. To a large extent, it still is today.

As we listened to this story and stood before the tomb of the saint,

© Mary Evans Picture Library/Francis Frith

Ancient yews, many over 2000 years old, have survived in churchyards, a sign of
continued spirituality from pre-Christian to Christian times.

both of my friends asked the same question: 'Why did you not tell us before that there is a sacred Britain? Why have you never told us about your sacred land?' Their confusion was understandable. In spite of increasing environmental pressure over recent years, Japan and India have never lost sight of the ancient tradition of sacred land. Britain, by contrast, very nearly had – to such an extent that my friends had been unaware of its existence in this country.

Thus was born one of the most successful programmes in ARC's history. A year later, in partnership with the World Wide Fund for Nature (WWF), we launched the Sacred Land Project to protect, revive, restore and even create sacred sites across Britain. Our remit was broad – from holy wells that had been covered or lost, through to pilgrimage paths, sacred gardens, groves and woods. The plan was to revive a sense of the sacred throughout Britain. This was more than nostalgia or merely prettifying the landscape. For millennia, Britons had been acutely aware of their role in a great story that had given their lives and the rest of creation meaning. Over the past few centuries, we had lost that connection with the land and that sense of the sacred. Now it was time to rediscover it.

SACRED PLACES

I am often asked, 'What do you mean by sacred?' To my mind, there are four kinds of sacred place, and I believe that they capture four kinds of sacred experience that run through time and through all faiths. Most people are familiar with the first type, as they are all around us. Communities decide upon a site that will be holy to them, and then build their local church, chapel, synagogue, mosque or temple on that piece of ground. Whenever a site is chosen, marked out, blessed and therefore made special, it becomes a holy place. It is a place which, over time, has become redolent with prayer, celebration, mourning and the cycle of the religious year. It might be as old as St Martin's,

Canterbury, built in the fourth century AD, or a new church on a housing estate; it might be a converted terrace house which is now a
mosque or it might be the oldest mosque in Britain, purpose built in
1889 in Woking, Surrey. We create sacred places for our everyday lives
and they become more sacred as we use them.

The second type of sacred place might be a raging sea viewed from
a cliff top, or a giant redwood forest that stretches to the horizon, or
a stream that reflects the flash of a kingfisher's wings, or a peaceful
grove where the sunlight seems to dance through the branches. It is
somewhere that overwhelms us with the sheer beauty or magnificence of nature. That sensation might last for only a moment or for
hours, but it allows us to understand that we are part of something
much greater and grander than ourselves. Moreover, these places
generate a sense of gratitude to whatever or whoever we understand
to be the origin of all this beauty – what many people call 'God'. For
those who believe in a creator, the word 'creation' has a special definition. It means that everything has been created by love, so
everything should be valued for its own sake. St Francis of Assisi
encapsulated this by writing that we are all 'part of God's family',
whether that is sun or moon; birds or animals; fish or human beings.

The third type of sacred place has been made holy by history or
legend. I love a small cave that has been worn into the cliffs by the sea
near Whithorn, Dumfries and Galloway. Here, in the fourth century, St
Ninian would come to be alone with God and nature. Crosses have
been carved into the cave's walls, testimony to centuries of pilgrimage,
and visitors and pilgrims still search the beach for stones with crosses
created by veins of quartz. Millions of years of nature thereby contribute to the holiness of the place. For many of us, visiting an ancient
site, such as St Ninian's cave or Stonehenge, can evoke awe at the idea
that this is a meeting place between the past and the present; and even
between heaven and earth. Not all such places are to do with joy, however. For instance, Clifford's Tower is a gaunt building in the medieval
part of York. In 1190, more than a hundred Jewish men, women and
children took refuge there from a rampaging mob. Hoping for

protection from either the archbishop or the king, they were failed by both. Realising the mob was about to break into the tower and would probably tear them apart, all of the Jews committed suicide. Today, this is a terrible holy place. The same is true of those places where people were burned to death for their faith, such as Tyburn in London, where many Catholics were brutally executed in the sixteenth and seventeenth centuries. In 2010, Tyburn was honoured as a holy place by Pope Benedict XVI during his visit to the United Kingdom. Other places are considered sacred because someone is said to have had a vision there, or simply because they generate a sense of holiness among visitors. One such place is the holy island of Lindisfarne, Northumbria, where St Cuthbert found peace through prayer in the seventh century.

Finally, there are those sacred places that mean something special to individuals. They might be places where you go to think; or you might have experienced great happiness there with friends and family; or perhaps you made a decision there that shaped the course of your

Clifford's Tower, York, site of the 1190 mass suicide of Jews in the face of an anti-Semitic mob.

life. For me, the Quantock Hills in Somerset are sacred because I used to go there as a child with my magical godmother. I still return there now whenever I feel the need to recover or reflect. We each have our own sacred land map, even if we have never called it that.

All four of these types of sacred place tell us something about ourselves in relation to a greater story, a greater purpose than merely our individual lives. They are sacred because they link us to the divine and give us a sense of meaning. They add significance to what lies around us, to our work, to our families, to our community and to our histories. Believing that some places are sacred means that we do not see ourselves only as selfish genes or as random acts of procreation but as parts of a greater narrative within which we have the opportunity to play a part. It is this combination of the sense of the sacred and of meaning which has literally shaped our landscape and which I invite you to join me in exploring through this book.

THE SACRED ENVIRONMENT

For the past half-century, the environmental movement has been trying to persuade us to protect the natural world, largely through a rather crude combination of fear, guilt and blame. Although various organisations have succeeded in putting the environment on local and national agendas, it remains quite far down the list and is still seen as politically expendable. One of the reasons for this is that many of us have forgotten – or never knew – how to connect with nature. So we are unable to see ourselves as participants in something infinitely greater than human history. We have reached the stage of arguing that a wonder of nature such as the Amazon is important only because it absorbs billions of tons of the carbon dioxide that we produce each year. This is a frightening example of losing sight of what really matters. The Amazon is worth preserving because it houses a vast proportion of the world's plant and animal species; because it is beautiful and terrifying at the same time; because it has as much right to exist as we do; *and* because it absorbs carbon dioxide. By rediscovering our place within a greater story, we might start to develop the mindset that will enable us to save the planet from ourselves. So, while this is a handbook that provides techniques on how to read the human landscape, it is also a guide for to how to live in nature and find a path through the confusion we have created by forgetting that we are all parts of creation.

I grew up in a family where faith was vigorously debated. My father was an Anglican priest, while my mother had been an agnostic before she met him, and she always retained a healthy dose of wariness of organised religion and an awareness of its problems. For much of my childhood, we lived in the vicarage on a vast housing estate on the outskirts of Bristol. It was a tough place, devoid of any human-created beauty. But above us rose the fields and trees of Dundry Hill, so I learned early on that it is possible to find beauty and meaning in the harshest of places.

I also had the wonderful blessing of a godmother who lived in rural Somerset. She was an artist with a vivid imagination who took me on innumerable adventures through her gift of storytelling. 'Who do you think those people are in the car in front?' she would ask. 'Where have they come from? Are they spies? Or lovers running away from home?' We would concoct all sorts of wild versions of their lives. Sometimes she was more historical in her stories: 'Why do you think this road has such an odd name?' 'Who built that hill fort?' 'What does the dedication say about when and why this church was built?' 'What do you think we'll find when we go inside?' We would look for fossils in limestone uplands, flint arrowheads in farmers' fields, and medieval glass fragments – smashed out of windows by the Puritans – in churchyards. She taught me that most people used to live in a world of faith and belief that shaped and informed everything they did. As a result, I learned to look at the landscape of Britain in much the same way as she and they did. Yet, it took two friends – one from India, one from Japan – to help me understand that people have viewed Britain as a sacred landscape for millennia.

Over the past thirty years, I have tried to help various faiths engage with the environmental movement. For much of that time, I have been the religious adviser to WWF, working alongside the Duke of Edinburgh, a man whose compassion for nature has helped shape the conservation movement for decades. Through this work, I have also had the privilege of working with the Russian Orthodox Church. One day, I was chatting with two Russian Orthodox professors and two bishops in Moscow. Suddenly, they all started talking about the damage that had been done to the sacred layout of the city by the communists. I asked what they meant, so they unrolled a huge map on the refectory table. First, they began running their fingers along the streets, tracing symbols of the Unity of God (circles) and the Trinity (triangles). Then they indicated where churches and monasteries had been given specific names either because they brought a special kind of spiritual protection or because they were related to sacred directions. For example, 'St Peter's' was usually in the east – the direction of paradise – because of his connection with the pearly gates.

When I expressed surprise at the amount of thought that had gone into the planning of the city and the naming of its buildings, they were taken aback. 'Surely you know all about this?' they said. 'After all, we got these ideas from the West – from Constantinople and from the wider Church of Europe in the Middle Ages and even before.' They told me to go and look at maps of Britain's towns and cities, and confidently predicted that I would find that they had been laid out according to the Bible, and especially according to the Book of Revelation with references to the special powers of the various saints and the belief in the Trinity and the Unity of God.

THE SACRED LAND PROJECT

On returning home, I soon discovered that my friends from Moscow were right. Most of our old cities, towns and even villages had been laid out not only to express an understanding of the sacred but to bring that sacred element right down to earth, where we lived. This new understanding fed into the Sacred Land Project and initially attracted considerable scepticism. But as the project developed and more people began to look for an underlying sense of the sacred in our environment, more evidence emerged. Before too long, we were able to convince at least some of the sceptics that urban design could be sacred.

The Sacred Land Project has achieved many notable successes. In recent years, we have created the popular 'Sacred Bristol' walk and map in association with the ancient parish church of St Stephen's. We have restored and updated pilgrimage routes – for example, pilgrims visiting Britain's most famous shrine of the Virgin Mary, at Walsingham in Norfolk, now walk the last mile or so on a disused railway line, because the road is too busy. We have preserved and protected a holy well in Kendal, Cumbria, and have assisted in the development of the longest sacred walking route in Britain: the Cistercian Way in Wales.

I am constantly impressed by the revival of interest in the sacred landscape. For example, the Scottish government is considering creating a new pilgrims' path between St Columba's holy island of Iona in the Hebrides all the way to the ancient sacred city of St Andrews on Scotland's east coast. In England, the Two Saints Way, linking Chester and Lichfield (and their two saints, Werburgh and Chad), is a brand-new route that has come into being with local government and church support. Walking our sacred land is back in fashion.

Overseas, the project has helped protect sacred forests and mountains in Mongolia, China, Mexico, Lebanon, India, Indonesia, Papua New Guinea and many other places. A new network of Green Pilgrim Cities – from Amritsar in the Punjab, to St Albans in Britain, to Kano in Nigeria – is linking pilgrimage with ecology in new ways. An important component of this is the *Green Guide to the Muslim Hajj*, a handbook for Muslim pilgrims, which helps them make their journey gentle upon the earth. A reawakening is even taking place in lands that we in the West view as inherently sacred, such as India and

Egypt. All round the world, communities are rediscovering insights and lifestyles they had almost forgotten. They are learning that possessing a sense of the sacredness of the land is invaluable when instituting community-based programmes to protect nature and enhance our understanding of our place within it.

Now, though, ARC is turning its attention back to Britain by launching a new foundation that is dedicated to helping local communities uncover their own sacred landscapes and to encouraging an ecological perspective and practice. In particular, I want people to rediscover the heritage of wisdom, spirituality and respect for nature that was built into the landscape over generations and which we are in danger of losing for ever. (This book is the guide to that new movement, and we hope that if you enjoy it you might think about becoming part of this new movement across Britain and beyond – please see our website at www.sacredlandproject.org.)

This is not to say that we always used to live as thoughtfully as we should have done. As we shall see later, Britain has experienced four major collapses over the past five thousand years, and on each occasion the dominant religion collapsed, too. But then faith and our understanding of the sacred landscape always helped us rebuild. If we allow ourselves to lose that understanding, as we almost did in the second half of the twentieth century, we might not be able to recover next time.

THE BOOK

This book is divided into two distinct parts. In Part One, I explore how we arrived where we are today by looking at our sacred history. Then I suggest some of the tools that will help us rediscover what we have almost lost. In Part Two, I explain how to read the sacred layouts of religious buildings and façades, towns and cities, fields and woods. I hope this knowledge will allow you to look again at where you live, see it in a new light, and perhaps think about the potential that lies around you. Then, if you wish to venture further afield, at the end of chapters three to nine you will find the gazetteer (complete with post-codes where helpful), which gives examples of everything from stone circles to market crosses, and from sacred city layouts to ancient field systems across the country.[1]

I have had the great delight of exploring all of these topics in two of my earlier books – *Sacred Britain* and *The Sacred History of Britain* – and in several radio and TV programmes for the BBC. But this book goes much further. Not everyone has an inspirational godmother to reveal the hidden stories of our landscape; nor do many people have the chance to meet Muscovite bishops who are able to explain the urban landscape as a theological journey. So I have written this book to share the good fortune that allowed me to develop a particular view of the world, and to show that we are in very real danger of destroying that world if we do not fully appreciate and understand its sacredness. Planet Earth is a source of enormous joy, but we must never forget that looking after it is a tremendous responsibility.

Finally, I have written this book for the sheer fun of learning how to read our rural and urban landscapes. Once you crack the code, every building, every field, every street becomes more significant, more fascinating, more revealing. And with each new discovery, you learn more about yourself.

PART ONE

BRITAIN'S SACRED HISTORY

Innumerable physical, spiritual and psychological forces have shaped the landscape of Britain over the past eight thousand years. Beliefs, traditions, stories, legends, hopes and fears have driven the people who have lived here to design their towns and cities in particular ways, to settle in certain places, and to mould the rural landscape into specific patterns. But this has not been a seamless process. On several occasions the whole of society has collapsed, leading to deserted villages, derelict towns and abandoned burial sites. We can learn much from these ups and downs of life in Britain. They can help us work out where we are, where we are going and whether we should change course.

This part of the book explores the great stories that have

shaped the landscape, and the great collapses that have concluded each of those stories. Chapter 1 examines eight millennia of human success and failure, strength and weakness, triumph and disaster, all of which is still reflected in the landscape of Britain today – if you know where (and how) to look. To help with the latter, Chapter 2 provides some of the basic tools and information you will need to start exploring Britain's sacred land. Chapter 3 then gives practical advice on using those tools to gain an understanding of how our ancestors' beliefs impacted on the landscape. Finally, Chapter 4 focuses on Britain's natural features – our rivers, hills, springs and islands – and explains how their ancient names reveal the sacred nature of the natural environment.

1

The sacred world around us ... and how to see it

There's always a story
That's bigger than you and me[2]

Every generation has had prophets of doom who have predicted 'The End of The World'. I used to think that this was because we, as a species, like to feel simultaneously important and vulnerable. We seem to enjoy the sensation of living on the edge. Meanwhile, those doing the preaching have the bonus of basking in a sense of superiority, a 'we know better than you' state of mind. However, as I have delved deeper into the past and have explored the catastrophic collapses of societies around the world, I have come to a rather different conclusion. Buried deep within us is the knowledge that everything we take for granted can be swept away in an instant. We share a collective ancestral memory of ice caps advancing across the landscape time and time again over the past hundred thousand years; and of the equally alarming melting of those ice caps, which submerged vast areas of land where people used to live. These facts have been elements in our

collective psyche for millennia. Sometimes, they have also become
integral parts of our folkloric tradition. For instance, ancient stories are
still told of lands disappearing under the sea, such as the lost city of
Cardigan Bay and the drowned forests off the Cornish coast. And, of
course, let's not forget the story of Noah and the Flood.

Over the past five thousand years, there have been four major collapses (these are discussed in detail in Chapter 3). Each of these
apocalypses has literally left its mark on the landscape of Britain (and,
I would argue, on our collective memory), and each tells a story of the
collapse of not just certain ways of life but specific beliefs. The British
landscape was created by people who believed that they were part of
a greater, sacred story. Their way of life and impact on the land around
them were founded on a sense of faith derived from this story, which
gave direction to everything they did and created. Initially, far back in
prehistory, the story honoured ancestors who first farmed the land
and thus became its venerated protectors. Later, it was dominated by
a small elite who believed that their power was divinely authorised.
This often resulted in the building of grandiose structures, such as
Stonehenge or medieval cathedrals and castles. Another story
involved those who turned their back on such sacred power models
and instead found the sacred within the small, local details of the natural world. This happened among the tribes in pre-Roman Britain,
and to some extent it is happening again today in the organic and
local movement, which itself is rooted in the simple religious traditions of such groups as the Quakers.

Until the end of the eighteenth century, Britain's sacred story –
whether we call it religion, or faith, or beliefs – was about having a
world view that gave the people a sense of purpose and belonging. For
example, for hundreds of years, every local church in Britain was built
to be a miniature model of Jerusalem. Simply by walking through one
of these buildings, you could join Jesus on his journey to the hill of
Golgotha where he was crucified. The drama of this story was literally
built into the fabric of each church, and it therefore became each wor-
shipper's story as well. In addition, fields themselves manifest the

particular understanding at the time of their creation – they show how humanity saw itself in relation to the rest of creation that lay all around them. (As I will show later, the model for farming comes from one of the most beautiful books of the Old Testament – Ruth.) Moreover, the names of mountains, hills, rivers and springs usually have a sacred dimension to them, filling the physical world that surrounds us with meaning and spirituality. Right up to perhaps two hundred years ago, even the layout of our towns and cities reflected the sacred story that we believed at that time.

Then, around the start of the nineteenth century, we very swiftly lost this sense of seeing the sacred in everything and our perception of our role in a greater story. After millennia of looking at the land-scape and our place within it in a certain way, over the course of just a couple of generations we started to view life very differently. Britain was the first industrial, and the first majority urban, country in the

© Akg-images/Interfoto/Winifried Wirth

The famous circle stone of Men-an-Tol (meaning stone with a hole) in Cornwall. Originally probably part of a burial mound from the Neolithic period, the current arrangement is much more recent.

world. By 1851, over 50 per cent of the population was living in towns and cities, and many of these people had already lost their roots. Industrial ways of seeing and thinking, fused with the inexorable march of science and its challenge to religion, meant that by the mid-to-late nineteenth century, there was a distancing from faith and tradition. It became embarrassing to mention local legends or to praise old customs. However, embedded deep within those were the experiences of collapse and failure which had been learnt the hard way. The rejection of anything which spoke of the sacred, or which told a story which did not fit with the prevailing scepticism of the age, led to a loss of collective memory and an inability for many people to see that there was, or could be today, any other way of seeing the world other than a reductionist, economic or 'factual' way.

However, all around us, there are still clues that we once thought and lived differently. If you know where to look, you might see six-thousand-year-old long barrows on hills, built to venerate ancestors; or four-thousand-year-old stone circles, which were sacred trading and meeting areas; or the divine cosmology of medieval churches that face the rising sun and were built to resemble ships of faith carrying us through the storms of life. Theology and ancient stories shaped everything from farmers' fields to Georgian country houses, whose architects believed that symmetry was not just good design but how the universe worked and how God – the Great Architect – intended life to be.

We need to learn how to read these clues and start to see what lies all around us once again. A road might seem to bend for no apparent reason, but perhaps it was constructed to bypass an ancient burial ground; a town might have been designed to create a heavenly city on earth; a church might have been aligned in a certain way to show that those who built it believed they were loved by God; a natural feature might have a name that links us back to ancient India; place names, street names and even pub names might reveal much about how our ancestors lived and how they viewed their place in the world.

THE STORIES AND WHY WE NEED THEM

Human beings have always used stories and beliefs to give their lives meaning. Without such beliefs and stories, as Carl Jung put it, we would be 'crushed by the sheer awe-fullness of the universe'. In other words, without a story to give us a place in the greater picture, we will become lost or, even worse, think that *we* are the story. To some extent, this is exactly what has happened over the last two centuries. The loss of confidence in narrative and its role, not just in entertaining us but in helping us to understand ourselves and our world, is a severe one. It has led us to be obsessed by data rather than by the significance of knowledge and to be determined to prove things, rather than to experience and risk experiencing things as part of an adventure of faith, coupled with uncertainty. Yet the truth is we live just as much in stories as we ever did and we believe many things which are not 'true' but are about the truth of being human and making our way through life without being crushed by its 'awe-fullness'. We all live mythologically, even though we might not know it, because, to us, it is simply the way things are.

In 1543, the Polish clergyman Nicolas Copernicus published a book which explained that the earth orbited around the sun, rather than the other way round. Prior to this, people had believed that the earth was the centre of the universe and therefore the centre of God's cosmos. Copernicus therefore started the modern revolution in thinking. Now we know that we live on a planet that circles around a quite insignificant star in a minor galaxy somewhere in the suburbia of a universe that contains billions of similar solar systems.

Theoretically and scientifically, then, we have moved a very long way from the idea that the earth and therefore we, the human race, lie at the centre of the universe. However, in spite of what we know to be 'true', almost all of us still adhere to a pre-Copernican world view and belief system. If you woke up every morning thinking, 'I live on a minor planet, circling an insignificant sun, in a secondary galaxy, somewhere on the edge of the universe,' you would find it pretty hard to get out of bed. After all, what would be the point? But we do get up, get dressed and get on with our lives, because we still truly believe that we are the most important things in the universe, and that the earth is the centre of our universe. And we support this deeply unscientific primary belief with a myriad of secondary beliefs – some rooted in the great faiths of the world; some, paradoxically, based on science; some based on economic or political models; often a mixture of all of these and more.

In the West, there is a widespread belief that time is linear; yet about half of the world believes that time is cyclical. We believe that human beings are the most important species on the planet; yet about a third of the world thinks that we have meaning only because we are elements in a complex web of life. We believe that each person has one life; yet more than half of the world believes that we each have many lives.

It is easy to patronise the beliefs of those who came before us. However, if looked at objectively, some of our beliefs are as weird as those of our ancestors. Of paramount importance in the Western world is an unshakeable belief in the supremacy of human beings. It doesn't matter if your personal belief system is based on the Book of Genesis or *On the Origin of Species*, because each of these puts humanity at the very pinnacle of life on earth. We were either placed here by God or have evolved to the highest level of development of any species. Either way, our current situation is good for our egos. But this has led to our reckless abuse of the resources of the natural world, with almost no consideration given to the needs of the rest of nature. We believe in 'the need for growth', yet we live in a finite world. We adhere to the tenets of such ideologies as capitalism, consumerism, Marxism and democracy, all of which prioritise the advance of the human species. Then we construct grand narratives – such as battling against the 'Axis of Evil' – to give our lives meaning. We seem to believe that if something cannot be

The beliefs of our time shape our actions. In this seventeenth-century engraving, one of the men burying victims of the Plague of London is smoking: the commonly held belief at the time was that tobacco smoke not only covered the stench but could prevent the spread of the infection.

quantified, it means that it does not exist. Most of the rest of the world thinks this is just plain ridiculous because how, for example, do you quantify love?

No one lives without beliefs, even in the modern, 'developed', Western world. These beliefs shape everything we do and why we do it. It has been that way since time immemorial, and the consequences of successive layers of belief are still all around us, exactly where our ancestors left them.

THE FOUR APOCALYPSES

The opening of *The Romance of the Three Kingdoms*, one of the greatest of all Chinese classical novels, says, 'Empires come and empires go; everything falls apart and then arises again.'[3] It is appropriate that a great novel should open this way, because humanity lives by narrative. We give ourselves a place within the universe through our stories, and we live within those stories for as long as we can. Eventually, though, each story collapses, to be replaced by a new one. As I mentioned at the start of this chapter, this cycle – rise, peak, collapse, then rise again – has occurred four times in Britain over the last five thousand years. On each occasion, it shattered the core beliefs of the people who remain. It seems that we are currently on the brink of a fifth such collapse, so this is a good time to pause, reflect and appreciate that we have been down this path before, and it has cost us dear.

We can trace these rises and falls of faith in our landscape. Each cycle starts simply, with a focus on local sites and shrines. Over time, these are absorbed into ever-larger conglomerates and more self-aggrandising systems. The cycle progresses from the local to the regional, the national and even the international. Eventually, though, the system becomes too vast and unwieldy to survive, so it collapses. Then the cycle starts again, once more at the simple, local level. Each time this happens, a new religion – a new story – emerges from the ruins of the old; new ways of living and thinking rise from the chaos; and new ways of seeing and understanding the landscape develop, providing new points of contact with the sacred and the divine.

This cycle also has another theme: the move from people thinking they are part of nature, towards thinking (as we tend to do today) that we are apart from nature. As societies move from the initial simple, local stage, they also move from this 'part of' way of thinking to the now much more common 'apart from' way of thinking. Nature becomes something against which humanity struggles or which humanity exploits. Instead of blending in, we try to stand out and as a result our buildings – and societies – grow in scale and ambition. This in turn brings us to the edge of what nature can provide. Complex societies are far more vulnerable to swift collapse simply because they have become so cumbersome and disconnected from reality. Decisions cannot be made locally or logically, and the whole edifice falls.

Modern commentators are increasingly recognising this cycle and the dangers of separating ourselves from nature. In 2009, a group of writers, artists and poets launched a manifesto that offered a succinct appraisal of our current situation:

> The myth of progress is founded on the myth of nature. The first tells us that we are destined for greatness; the second tells us that greatness is cost-free ... Both tell us that we are apart from the world; that we began grunting in the primeval swamps, as a humble part of something called 'nature', which we have now triumphantly subdued ... [O]ur separation from it [nature] is a myth integral to the triumph of our civilisation.[4]

This dichotomy between being 'part of' or 'apart from' nature features throughout our exploration of the past and also brings us forcefully into the present. One major aspect of each historical cycle has been the move from 'going with the flow' to trying to impose order and control over nature – over the land itself.

DISCOVERING THE STORIES

As Neal Ascherson puts it his book *Stone Voices: The Search for Scotland*:

Everything done on that thin, stony ground from the beginning –
from the retreat of the ice to the advance of the motorway – leaves its
scar or its pock on the surface. A cultural landscape is very much what
Scotland is: something showing marks from all periods and land-
uses of all kinds, an artefact whose art is human and inhuman at
once, a picture which is paint, frame and National Gallery together.[5]

The same is true for Wales and England. This book is designed to be
a journey, perhaps even a pilgrimage, through the environment we
have created. The aim is to discover the stories and beliefs that have
formed this extraordinary landscape. It is a journey both to actual
places and through time and meaning.

If you leave your home on foot and then just keep walking, looking around you and using some of the clues in this book, then
regardless of whether you live in a town or the countryside, whether
your neighbourhood is wealthy or poor, whether it is obviously
ancient or seems entirely modern, you will find a hidden world. This
world is made up of layers of human cares, concerns and faith (or
sometimes lack of faith), which have created the landscapes that we
take for granted today. To see it, you need to become an adventurer
in your own land. You need to know how to spot the clues. You need
to know where to look, how to look and – perhaps most importantly – which questions to ask. Later, I will explain how to find the
hidden meaning in medieval town planning; how the name of a
church can help you read a landscape; what makes a market square
as sacred as a great stone circle; why we bury the dead where we do;
and how to read the layout of fields to discover when they were created and, even more importantly, to gain an understanding of the
vision of God, humanity and nature that they enshrine.

On the journey, we will unearth evidence of Britain's four apocalypses, and hopefully find a way to pull back from the brink of the fifth
that we are nearing today. As we discover how our ancestors' belief
systems shaped the landscape, we will also explore how our own
beliefs are shaping the world today. Our forebears' sacred visions cre-

ated our landscape, our urban settlements, our fields and our buildings, and we should honour their achievements and learn from their
mistakes so that we might plan a better future for ourselves and our
descendants.

Four major belief systems have come and gone. We are in the fifth,
and we urgently need to rediscover the sacred in the ordinary, the
divine in nature, and the transcendence that gives us a sense of our
role in the great story. Until we know our past, we cannot begin to
understand the present or prepare for the future. Let the adventure
begin!

2

Tools for the journey

This is our story
where we all have a place
in how we live and choose
and move through every day

beyond you, me and she – we
unfolding this tapestry
that is all we can be
in truth and beauty.[6]

To help us find Britain's stories and beliefs – and in the process redis-cover the sense of the sacred in everything – we need some basic tools to help us see what lies all around us.

GOD BLESS THE OS

One of the greatest resources we have to help us discover Britain's hidden sacred landscape is the Ordnance Survey (OS) map. Its very existence tells a story. In 1800, the first OS map – of Kent – was drawn to assist in the defence of Britain against a seemingly inevitable Napoleonic invasion. Kent was chosen because it was assumed the French would come across the narrowest part of the Channel, just as William the Conqueror had. In the event, of course, Napoleon never launched an invasion, but thankfully the Ordnance Survey has kept going ever since. Today, it offers a magnificent window on Britain's layers of history.

There are two main ways in which we can use the OS. The first is obvious. Each map specifically marks every church and chapel and often other religious buildings, too; many ancient sites; Roman towns; and ancient roadways. It also provides a bird's-eye view of the key features of the landscape – rivers; the contours of hills and plains; inlets; cities, towns and villages – along with their (sometimes very significant) names. I am always thrilled when I see the Gothic script that the OS uses to mark most historic sites, and the particular font

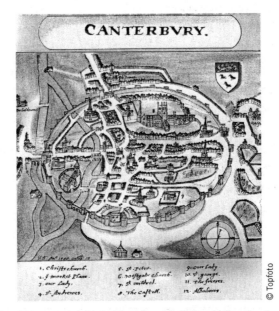

This sixteenth-century map of Canterbury shows both its old Roman street pattern and the overlay of a Christian street pattern, including the circular city wall and road.

it uses for Roman sites. The more detailed the map, the greater the number of features it will show; so if you are truly inspired to discover your local area, go for the largest-size maps. They will show you all sorts of exciting things that the ordinary (1:50,000) maps omit.

The OS also produces maps of ancient Britain that highlight the main prehistoric and historic sites. There are detailed maps of such cities as York, Canterbury and Bath, which can provide a huge amount of information about how these places have developed over the centuries. For instance, you could compare Roman Canterbury with medieval and then modern Canterbury to reveal the town's layers of history. These maps also contain details of buildings or fortifications that have long since disappeared, albeit with evidence of their existence preserved in place or street names.

GOOGLE EARTH AND SHAPES IN THE LANDSCAPE

Google Earth allows the user to zoom in on any part of the landscape, or zoom out to gain a wider perspective. This is a fantastic tool for the historical adventurer, allowing you to see the outline of an Iron Age hill fort; a medieval town layout that has clearly been superimposed on an earlier Roman settlement; or a field system that dates back to the Middle Ages. When used in combination with an OS map, Google Earth can also reveal the patterns and shapes that allow us to pinpoint sacred elements in the landscape.

PLACE NAMES

The place names of Britain also reveal much about the layers of our sacred history (see Chapter 6). For example, in Manchester, there are two areas, within a mile of each other, called Rusholme and Withington. We know that the former must have been a Viking settlement because of its *holme* suffix (as in Stockholm), whereas the latter must have been an Anglo-Saxon settlement (its *ton* suffix indicates that the community developed around a farm). An ancient defensive barrier, called Nico's Ditch, was dug around AD 900 to keep these two antagonistic communities apart.

The sheer range of prefixes and suffixes means it is worth investing in a good dictionary of place names. However, don't just go by what the experts say. It's fun to try to work out what a name might mean for yourself. Even if you get it wrong, the process will be worthwhile, because it will teach you how to explore and interpret the physical evidence of a site. In the countryside, look out for unusual place names, such as Gallows Hill. And remember to make a note of the names of rivers and streams, as these often date back thousands of years.

LOCAL GUIDEBOOKS

Local guidebooks often contain information you will not find anywhere else. While some are rather pedestrian and focus on formal history, others are far more entertaining. They might be full of local legends and ghost stories that shed unexpected light on the area. Walking guides can also be excellent sources of local information, not least because they often take you off the roads and across fields, through woods, up and down hills and across streams that you would otherwise never visit or notice. Avoid those that concentrate solely on getting you from A to B and search instead for those that contain snippets of local knowledge alongside the route maps.

WHAT TO LOOK FOR

The unusual

Having consulted an OS map and noted down its ancient sites, place names and basic layouts, look again – this time much more closely – to see if there is anything out of the ordinary. You are looking for the hidden Britain, for the layers that lie just below the surface; for the slightest hint of something unusual; for odds and ends that don't seem to make sense. For example, there might be a seemingly unnecessary bend in an otherwise straight road. This might well indicate that it once went round something that is no longer there – a house, a Roman fort, even a palace. Or it might bend because it was once a ditch between fields, dug to separate two estates, possibly going back to Anglo-Saxon times.

The straight

Look for straight roads. As most people know, these may well have been constructed by the Romans, such as the Fosse Way. However, they might equally be military roads of the eighteenth and early nineteenth centuries, when Britain feared invasion from France and embarked on a frenzied upgrading of its infrastructure. If they are in Scotland, they might have been built to aid suppression of the Jacobites. In short, it wasn't only the Roman army that appreciated the value of straight roads. Every military force needs to be able to march as quickly as possible from its headquarters to a series of strategic points. Follow a straight road to its end on the Kent coast, and you will be able to identify exactly where the British army expected Napoleon's forces to land. Meanwhile, in the Highlands, two 'Old Military Roads' head north-east and south-west from Fort William: the first goes alongside Loch Lochy to Fort Augustus and

Ricknild Street, Gloucestershire, a Roman Road said to have run from Derby to Bourton-on-the-Water, where it is joined by the Fosse Way.

then alongside Loch Ness all the way to Inverness; the second runs alongside Loch Linnhe and then heads spectacularly up Glen Coe and across Rannoch Moor. These military roads, built to enable the British army to march deep into the Highlands, were created to enable the army to suppress rebellion in the Highlands after the defeat of the Jacobites in 1745. They run as straight as a die, except where nature forced a bend or change of route.

FOSSE WAY

The Fosse Way, which cuts across England from Exeter (Isca Dumnoniorum) in the south-west to Lincoln (Lindum Colonia) in the north-east, follows a route that has been in use since prehistoric times. It was the first major Roman road in Britain,

▶

providing an important trading route and opening up communications. Its name comes from the Latin word for ditch (*fossa*). Before the road was constructed, a defensive ditch running along its entire length marked the north-western boundary of Roman Britain. When the road was built, it therefore ran alongside the original markings in the landscape. It is the only Roman road in Britain that has retained its original Latin name, as many were given Saxon names following the fall of Rome in the fifth century. Many villages took their names from the road, such as Lydford-on-Fosse and Stratton-on-Fosse in Somerset, and Fosscross and Fossebridge in Gloucestershire.

Shapes

In towns and cities, look for odd-shaped houses, the edges of estates, or the remains of an old path running through a new housing development. These can all tell you a great deal about what was there in the past and why what is there now assumed the shape it did. Look at the core shapes of old towns and cities to see what they reveal of earlier settlements and how they reflect the builders' and planners' beliefs.

Orientations

The way a place is laid out on the ground – the orientation of a building, settlement, church or burial mound – does not usually occur by accident. For example, look at where the poorer houses were built in a town or city and you will immediately discover the prevailing wind direction. The working-class houses were invariably built downwind from the factories, mines and mills, while the more privileged middle classes lived upwind, away from the pollution. For example, in

Birmingham, the prevailing wind is from the south-west, so the traditional middle-class areas of Edgbaston and Selly Oak occupy that part of the city, while the old working-class areas of Aston and Newtown are to the north. The much smaller town of Saffron Walden reveals a similar pattern. In the past, the noxious fumes of the town collected in the dip of High Street, right in the town centre. Consequently, small, cheap houses were built there. However, as you follow the steep road south, up and away from the centre, the houses become grander with almost every metre.

As we will see in Chapter 5, churches have very significant sacred orientations, but so do many other buildings from our past. In all cultures, certain directions are considered more auspicious than others. In Christianity, for example, the north is always the direction of spiritual threat – the source of evil or the devil. That is why churches with the name St Michael tend to be found to the north of towns and cities, because Michael fights the devil in Christian mythology.

There are even older sacred orientations to be found in Britain. For instance, there is increasing evidence that Neolithic and Iron Age settlements, homes, stone circles and burial mounds were built facing the south-east. This probably had something to do with the aforementioned prevailing wind direction: obviously, it was logical to face the opposite direction from the south-west because otherwise the wind would tend to blow straight through the front door. However, it also seems that the west was considered a sacred direction from at least the fifth century BC. Many legends relating to the Isles of the Dead being located to the west of Britain survived into early Christian times. It is possible that this sacred direction of death was an inauspicious direction for the houses and buildings of the living.

Some orientations, such as churches facing the east and mosques facing Mecca, are obvious. Others are less so. For instance, Knights Templar churches are all round because their design is always based on the Temple Mound building in Jerusalem, where the Order had its headquarters. And early Nonconformist chapels do not face east because that direction was associated with Catholicism.

3

Our sacred history

These buildings and all
the land has been
age after age distilled
in this moulding of clay
and in the same hands
pressed palm to palm in prayer
that is older than its name[7]

If the landscape has been created by stories, by faith, by a sense of the sacred, then how do we uncover those stories and learn when they were first told? This book is designed to reveal the physical signs of the psychological and spiritual layers of narrative, religion and vision. In this chapter, I shall outline the most momentous events in Britain's history and explain how to find evidence of them in the landscape that surrounds us and lies beneath our feet. Learning about these events will help us understand our own times and our own environment. History is not all about dates (although the most significant dates of major events will be provided when necessary). The root of the word is the Latin for 'enquiry', so history should be a search, an exploration of the stories that have brought us to where we are today.

A great deal of conventional history focuses on the particular but neglects the wider narrative that gives individual events significance and meaning. For example, archaeology textbooks often simply state that the 'long barrow' style of burial mound was abandoned around 3000 BC, then move on to the next topic. But to a religious historian, a historian of ideas, this abandonment prompts numerous questions that demand answers. It is the search for these answers, this enquiry into a greater narrative, that provides the framework of this book. That journey will reveal the process that created the British landscape, by which I mean not only the physical environment of fields, forests and buildings but the internal, spiritual landscape of the people whose beliefs shaped that world.

UNTOLD APOCALYPSES: 1.5 MILLION BC TO 5000 BC

Ever since human beings first appeared on Planet Earth, Britain has been subject to astonishing extremes of weather and conditions. During several ice ages, the land was covered by up to a hundred metres of ice, and the British Isles (including Ireland) formed part of the European mainland – with dry land in place of the Channel, the North Sea and the Irish Sea. At other times, the ice melted and water flooded into those channels, while the land turned to tundra. In even warmer periods, Mediterranean-style landscapes of broad rivers and lush woodland developed.[8]

Each succeeding ice age ground its way across our landscape. In the warmer periods, such as the Hoxnian Interglacial Stage – between 420,000 and 360,000 BC – people moved north into Britain. We know this because a couple of thousand sites featuring Hoxnian-era flint tools have been identified. The most famous are Jaywick Sands at Clacton-on-Sea, Essex, and Swanscombe, Kent, where some magnificent handaxes have been found. However, while there are many

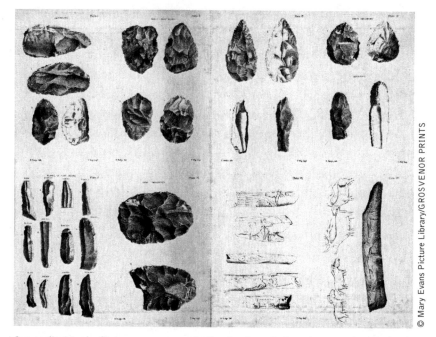

Our earliest tools: flint arrows, axes and other implements have been made in Britain for at least half a million years.

sites, it is likely that only a few scattered groups of hunters lived in Britain during this period. These hunters created tools from the stones of Britain, but they had negligible, if any, impact on the landscape. The same was true of all of those who followed them, at least until Britain emerged from the last of the great ice ages around eleven thousand years ago.

Thereafter, humans in Britain started to shape the natural world and started to tell their stories through it. Then, as soon as they began farming, they launched the great cycles of history, the first four of which each culminated in a dramatic collapse – and Apocalypse.

THE AGES OF HISTORY

These are the generally accepted periods of British prehistory and history. The great cycles and collapses are highlighted in bold.

- Palaeolithic (Old Stone Age): c. 500,000 to c. 10,000 BC

- Mesolithic (Middle Stone Age): c. 10,000 to c. 5000 BC

- Neolithic (New Stone Age): c. 5000 to c. 2000 BC

- **First Cycle:** c. 5000 to c. 3000 BC. Ancestor worship, ending with the collapse of upland farming and the abandonment of long barrows.

- Bronze Age: c. 2000 to c. 750 BC

- **Second Cycle:** c. 3000 to c. 1160 BC. Stone circles, ending with the eruption of a volcano off Iceland.

- Iron Age: c. 750 BC to AD 43

- Roman period: AD 43 to 410

- **Third Cycle:** c. 1160 BC to c. AD 400. Celtic and Roman traditions, ending with collapse through environmental abuse and the impact of plague on the Roman Empire and in Britain.

- Anglo-Saxon period: 410 to 1066

- Medieval period: 1066 to 1485

- **Fourth Cycle:** c. 550 to the early 16th century. Monastic and Catholic Christianity, ending with the rise of the Renaissance and the Protestant Reformation, triggered by the Black Death.

- Tudor period: 1485 to 1603

▶

- Stuart period: 1603 to 1714

- Georgian period: 1714 to 1837

- Victorian period: 1837 to 1901

- Modern period: 1901 to the present

- **Fifth Cycle:** Early 16th century to the present. Protestant individualism and the Enlightenment, leading to the Industrial Revolution and urbanisation.

THE FIRST GREAT CYCLE: ANCESTOR WORSHIP AND THE NEED FOR THE SACRED

Throughout history, sacred places have been built to last. In Britain, there are still hundreds of stone circles, thousands of burial mounds and tens of thousands of ancient churches. All have long outlived the domestic dwellings of the people who created them.

The placing of sacred sites is also crucial. For instance, many Neolithic sites are on the edges of hills or raised land. In part, this was probably done for pragmatic reasons: for defence; because the lowlands were wetter and marshier than they are today; because the valleys were more densely forested. However, it was also a statement to anyone wandering past that this area had already been claimed, or that there were people up there who might be willing to trade. In a world where law courts and legal codes did not exist, the authority and legitimacy of the dead, of ancestors and of semi-divine beings were the only certainties. Many ancient sites are therefore believed to be sacred zones within which safety could be assured and agreements had to be honoured.

As far as we know, Britain's earliest form of religion was ancestor worship. This was why the great long barrow burial mounds were built. Between approximately 4500 and 3000 BC, Neolithic families would revere their dead ancestors at these places. With the dead watching over their fields and settlements, they could be relatively confident that their land rights would be respected. In Britain, we abandoned that practice many millennia ago, but in China the rural dead are still buried alongside their fields and venerated as protectors of the crops and the land itself.

Understanding the siting of the long barrows on ridges near the tops of hills requires us to make a psychological leap. Most of us now dwell in the lowlands, in valleys, so when we visit a Neolithic site, we generally have to walk up to them. But that gives a false perspective of how they were viewed by those who created them. We need to understand that they were built primarily by people who lived on hill-tops, so they would not have been overlooked by these tombs. Rather, they located them on the edge of their world, so that their ancestors looked down and away to the valleys. They were built as landmarks of boundaries – both physical, in terms of farmsteads, and possibly also spiritual, marking the border between the world of humans (up here) and the world of nature and wilderness (down there). Once you see them as outposts that look down, you get a very different sense of why they are located where they are. They mark a danger zone between the hilltop communities and the perils below, with the dead acting as guardians for the community.

Many prehistoric tombs performed a similar variety of functions to today's parish churches: rites of passage, weddings, newborn cele-brations and wakes were almost certainly held there. This makes sense, as there would have been little point in building such huge construc-tions merely for burial rites. Moreover, if your ancestors are your deities, then you would surely want to celebrate with and beside them.

In addition to their typical location on hillsides, most long barrows seem to have been sited very carefully, with the builders paying par-ticular attention to the view, the shapes of natural features around the site, and their orientation to certain solar or lunar phenomena. We still have little idea how these various elements contributed to these people's great story, but they surely did. Nothing ever happens randomly. Everything has a purpose and meaning beyond the mundane. One example of this may well be the invention of pottery.

The sacredness of the ordinary: farming and pottery

Hunter–gathering – essentially all human activity in Britain prior to the development of farming – has very little impact on the landscape, because people are constantly on the move. Nowhere is 'home'. Farming changes that, and changes our relationship with the land. We start to build structures in which to live, and places we see as sacred and powerful.

The most enigmatic Neolithic enclosures, with their distinctive ring of ditches crossed or broken by causeways, often have ritual objects buried at each end. Sometimes these are skulls, but more often they are simply pots that have been buried upside down.[9] In many cultures, the invention of pottery is viewed as a divine gift. It is considered miraculous that the simple act of mixing earth, clay or mud with water and baking it in a kiln can create a pot. This sense of wonder and the semi-divine nature of the skills involved echo down through time. For example, in Chinese mythology, both pottery and agriculture are revealed to the people by the ancestral semi-divine being, Sheng Nu. And in both the Old and New Testaments of the Bible, God is cast as a potter who moulds the clay of humanity as He wishes.[10]

Pots, often containing seeds or food, are the main objects found in burial sites from the Neolithic period onwards. Of course, we treat our cheap, mass-produced pottery casually, viewing it merely as a means to contain or hold foodstuffs. But it seems likely that pots served a much more important function to Neolithic people. They may well have been seen as vessels of communication between the human and divine worlds. If the knowledge of how to make pots was believed to be a gift from the gods, then placing them in tombs and other sacred sites would have been highly significant. These were not merely vessels that were used to contain other items. They, themselves, were important offerings to the gods. This explains why they were buried with the dead or upside down in the enclosure ditches. It was not the function of the pot that was important, but the pot itself.[11] This was not just a useful consumer product, but a sign of divine significance and meaning.

While we now have a very different relationship to our everyday crockery, we have not entirely lost sight of that sacred significance. Think, for instance, of the enduring mythology of the Holy Grail. Or even of the passion and prayers that are generated every year by the FA Cup – a pot by another name. These are faint echoes of the sacred aspect of something we now usually take for granted. Neil MacGregor, in his radio series *The History of the World in 100 Objects*, has pointed out that the fruits of agriculture were deified in both Central America (maize) and ancient Egypt (the cow). Things we take for granted were in the past revered as life changing, gifts of the gods and thus sacred. This is what I am arguing for the pot. It was not just a useful consumer product but a sign of divine significance and meaning.

If 'simple' pottery was capable of such numinous significance, we have to start looking differently at everything that was made – from artefacts to fields to settlements. All of these things might indicate a sense of the immanence of the sacred – a sense that we now find almost impossible to imagine.

However, if our earliest settlers did have this intimate connection with the sacred, it didn't help them. They cut down much of the upland forest, created farms across huge swaths of Britain, and then fled, never to return, leaving their dead behind them. They did this because something went catastrophically wrong.

The first great collapse and the end of the First Cycle

Around 3000 BC, Britain's environment collapsed. The Neolithic period was initially characterised by small-scale farming and modest settlements, but just before it ended it was much more complex. It had shifted from being part of nature to being apart from nature, and the people were trying to impose 'order' on the natural environment. Tragically, for them, their efforts started to have significant impacts on the land, but not in the way they must have hoped.

We know that Neolithic people deforested the hills because the land altered from wildwoods to woodland managed for its products, such as fruits, nuts and fodder for cattle. As a result, the extent and the diversity of the woodlands changed because of human pressure and activity.[12] Inland communities lived primarily on higher ground, exploiting the thin, less heavily forested upland soil with their arable and livestock farming. This was the land that their venerated ancestors had given them, ancestors who were still present and worshipped in their long barrows and tombs. Although this land was easily exhausted, it was also relatively easy to prepare for agriculture as the trees and shrubs were shallow rooted.

Whether because of this over-exploitation of the thin soil, excessive deforestation or some other reason, the climate changed, the uplands dried out and the population declined, with many settlements on the now-exhausted uplands being abandoned. Tree-ring evidence indicates that there was also a widespread reduction in the growth rate of trees around 2911 BC. Mike Ballie, Emeritus Professor of Palaeoecology at Queen's University, Belfast, attributes this to some extraordinary environmental changes triggered by a passing comet. This, coupled with farms' increasing inability to feed the population, resulted in the collapse of the traditional culture and the rejection of the prevailing belief system. The ancestors had failed the people – or vice versa.

This was a radical break with the past. The abandoned settlements had been tribal homes for centuries, maybe even millennia. To leave those homes and resettle somewhere entirely new must have been traumatic for these people, especially as they were also abandoning their sacred long barrows and their ancestors. At the time of the collapse, those long barrows were sealed, with huge rocks placed in front of the openings.[13] The people who did this might have been

The blocked entrance to the Neolithic long barrow of Wayland's Smithy in Oxfordshire. It was sealed c.3000 BC when the ancestor religion collapsed.

protecting themselves from something that they now feared rather than revered, or perhaps they were simply closing the door on a once sacred place that they felt had lost its power. Either way, they shut in their ancestors and left. The old agreement – that our ancestors will look after us and ensure the fertility of the land if we respect and honour them – had been broken.

Surprisingly, we still have legends that reflect the trauma of this period, especially in areas that have a wealth of long barrows. The best example is the legend of Wayland Smithy on the ancient Ridgeway, close to the ancient White Horse of Uffington, Oxfordshire. Wayland was a magical blacksmith. It was said that if you left your horse at the tomb overnight, along with a payment in silver, he would shoe your horse and those shoes would last for years. But woe betide anyone who tried to catch a glimpse of him at work, or tried to short-change him. If you did, you would either die instantly or be so terrified that you would have nightmares for the rest of your life.

However, the Neolithic tomb that now bears Wayland's name was built about 5500 years ago, long before anyone was forging iron. Wayland is the Scandinavian god of blacksmiths, and stories about him arrived in Britain with the Vikings, in the ninth century AD – more than four thousand years after the long barrow had been sealed with huge stones. So is this tale a revised version of a much earlier one, passed down over millennia, about the dangers of offending the ancestors who are buried in the sacred site? Wayland's story certainly makes little sense without such a link to the long barrow's past. The discovery of iron and the skills of the blacksmith were long considered divine gifts that were tinged with danger. Of course, this site originally had nothing to do with any of that, but it would have been associated with similarly dangerous divine forces. People would have met there – it is on a major ancient roadway – and they surely would have exchanged stories. Over time, it is likely that the 'modern' myth of Wayland was worked into far more ancient legends, and eventually he gave his name to the place.

When the first British religion died, a particular way of seeing the land disappeared along with it. This created a spiritual vacuum and allowed the next great cycle to emerge. What came next has been the subject of more contemporary speculation and controversy than any other era in the sacred history of Britain.

THE SECOND GREAT CYCLE: THE MYSTERY OF THE STONE CIRCLES

We know very little about the beliefs that led to the construction of Britain's stone circles. What we do know is that, over the centuries, this faith drove its adherents on to ever more ambitious building projects. Moreover, this pattern was echoed around the world at this time. From the pyramids of Egypt, through the vast buildings of the Cycladic cultures of ancient Crete and Greece, to the first great city states of northern India, humanity made its first truly monumental impact on the landscape in the form of grander and greater buildings.

In Britain and northern France, the stone-circle culture represented the most dramatic human adaptation of the landscape up to that point. Large tracts of land were redesigned to accommodate not only the circles themselves, but stone avenues, henges (ditches with embankments), standing stones, burial mounds and other extraordinary features. Prime examples are Silbury Hill in Wiltshire and the lesser-known Merlin's Mound, just seven miles East of Silbury, which now lies in the grounds of Marlborough College. We still have no idea why they were built, but they were certainly designed to be impressive. At thirty-seven metres high, Silbury Hill is the largest man-made prehistoric object in Europe.

It is estimated that there are still over a thousand stone circles in Britain today, with many of them dating back to the mid-Neolithic period (3000–2500 BC), although some were built as late as 1400 BC. Given how many must have been lost through changing land use, destruction by farming or demolition to provide building materials, it has been estimated that maybe three thousand stone circles once adorned the landscape.

We do not know whether the British people 'converted' to the stone-circle faith as soon as they abandoned ancestor worship or whether there was a century or more of religious confusion. But the new faith certainly incorporated elements of the old, at least initially. Mock tombs – they usually did not contain any bones – were constructed in the centre of some of the earlier circles. They took the form of support stones topped with a lid stone – which is what remains when the soil topping of a long barrow has been eroded. One of these 'coves' was built in the middle of the northern ring at Avebury, and two of its stones still remain. Perhaps the missionaries of the new faith – which spread rapidly along the Atlantic coast from Spain right up to Scandinavia – felt the need to make the transition to a very different religion as gentle as possible for the local people by permitting (maybe even encouraging) nostalgia for the old belief system. That seems likely, especially as continuity has tended to go hand in hand with innovation in Britain ever since.

Nevertheless, the major stone circles were fundamentally different from the long barrows. They were brash, dominant intrusions into the natural landscape that were proudly man-made. They were markers, signifying power, territory and the separation of humanity from the rest of nature. If they had a reference point, it was to the cosmic realm of sun and moon, time and seasons, not to the everyday nature that lay around them.

To understand the stone-circle phenomenon, it is helpful to look beyond the mega-sites, such as Avebury, Stonehenge and Callanish, all of which were later developments. It is better to start somewhere like Sunkenkirk, also known as Swinside, a well-preserved stone circle near Swinside Fell in southern Cumbria. This is a near-perfect, medium-size circle, some twenty-nine metres in diameter. There were once fifty-five stones, but only thirty-two remain today. They range in size from knee high to above head height. The circle was clearly a major focal point for the local area, and it is still visible from several miles away. It is designed to be entered from almost any direction, as the stones touch to make a wall at only a few points around the perimeter.

In an earlier book, *The Sacred History of Britain*, I argued that the most likely use of most stone circles, including Sunkenkirk, was as a sacred meeting place. In a tribal society with few laws and probably few leaders, the people needed to have a safe trading and meeting place. In later millennia, monasteries and churches in Europe and mosques in the Middle East would perform the same function. Their violation, as when Thomas Becket was murdered in Canterbury Cathedral by agents of King Henry II, was considered an affront to God Himself.

Excavations at stone circles have occasionally revealed signs of burials and maybe even sacrifice. But usually archaeologists find no such evidence, so it seems that most circles' importance lay simply in the fact that they designated a certain place as sacred. Sunkenkirk is a good example of just such a sacred marked space. Furthermore, it is only the later major stone circles that appear to have specific astro-logical/cosmic and calendrical significance by indicating key moments in the year, such as mid-winter or mid-summer.

Many stone circles are quite small. For example, on Stapeley Hill in Shropshire, the remains of three circles stand within a mile or so of each other. Most of the stones are less than knee height and the circles themselves have modest diameters. All three might have been erected over the course of a week or so by a gang of local lads. But these circles were important. Near by, there was a major production centre for axe-heads, among the most highly prized objects in Britain at the time. One theory is that the three circles were rival trading centres that sold these valuable items to dealers.

Such commercial activity does not rob the stone circles of their sacred, religious role. Far from it. As we shall see, market squares later fulfilled the same purpose – and they were always centred upon a market cross. In many parts of the world, trading still involves vowing in the name of God that you will honour the deal. It is only our de-sacralised, Western world that finds it difficult to link commerce with the sacred, and it is this that has led us to fantasise about ritual sac-rifices, Druidic rituals and even alien spaceships using these holy places as landing strips. Specific religious practices undoubtedly occurred within the confines of the circles, but they formed only a small part of their overall function, and they were probably as mun-dane as the various rites of passage, discussions and meetings that most religious buildings have hosted over the millennia.

The second great collapse and the end of the Second Cycle

After maybe eighteen hundred years of almost continuous construc-tion, the building of stone circles in Britain stopped almost overnight. The story here is one of the most dramatic ecological and social catastrophes that these islands have experienced over the last ten thousand years. It was a collapse that eclipsed human faith as well as human livelihoods.

Around 1160 BC, a volcano erupted off the coast of Iceland. It threw so much ash into the atmosphere that the sun was obscured for a decade. No crops could grow in that time, animals died in their thousands in the freezing winters, and death and decay visited Britain on an unimaginable scale. It is estimated that at least half the population perished during this literally dark age. Unsurprisingly, given the extent to which it had failed them, their faith, and its associated stone circles, seems to have died with them.

The stone-circle culture had been on the wane for at least a couple of centuries anyway. Most of them were created before 1500 BC; and all of them, as far as we can tell, were abandoned after 1100 BC. Moreover, Stonehenge had become so powerful that it seems to have slighted all other stone circles within a radius of 150 miles. The power politics – the probable use of force and violence that must have accompanied the elevation of this mighty henge – speaks also of the political ambitions of its sponsors. This surely must have discredited the whole stone-circle religion in the eyes of many ordinary people. Then, when the sun did not appear for ten long years, their last remnants of faith were extinguished altogether. How could they be expected to continue to believe in something that had failed them so dismally?

There are hints of this collapse, and the reasons for it, in many legends associated with stone circles. These myths tell of greedy, ambitious kings who paid little or no heed to warnings and mocked the sacred. Often they involve people dancing on a Sunday and being turned to stone as punishment. At the major stone circle of Stanton Drew in Somerset, the local story is of a wedding party that asks the devil to continue playing for them once their regular fiddler has retired for the night. As dawn breaks, the whole party is transformed into the standing stones. (There is a wonderful folk song about this.)

Other stories tell of failed attempts to build a church. At Sunkenkirk, the story goes that the site was chosen for a church

Rotrich the great circle of stones in Oxfordshire.

The Rollright Stones, Oxfordshire – a complete stone circle from the Neolithic Age. This depiction is from the eighteenth century.

building, but at night the devil came and caused the stones to sink into the ground, thus stopping them being used as the planned building's foundations. The story is captured in the circle's name, because 'kirk' is the Scandinavian word for 'church', while 'sunken' of course refers to the fate of the stones. (It is thought that the name dates from the time when Vikings settled in the area.)

Some places might have retained even older names that tell stories of power and abuse of that power. For instance, the name of the Rollright Stones in Oxfordshire might come from an old British phrase meaning 'the place of the king'. This would fit with the fact that the stones are known locally as the King's Men, and that just across the road stands a single stone known as the King Stone.[14]

These legends tend to share a common theme: that the stone circles were built by people who could not restrain their pride, stupidity, greed and ambition. As punishment, a divine power sent down a disaster that destroyed their world and caused them to abandon everything they had held sacred for almost two thousand years – above all, their stone circles.

THE THIRD GREAT CYCLE: UNCERTAINTY, DRUIDS AND THE COMING OF THE ROMANS

What comes next, in terms of both religion and landscape, is most peculiar. It seems as if Britain was agnostic for at least half a millennium. There are no burial mounds from this period; no great stone edifices; nothing that echoes the previous three thousand years of performing rituals within and, latterly, apart from the landscape. The few burials that have been identified are so few and far between that they are archaeologically insignificant.

So what did the people of Britain do with their dead for five hundred years? Did they cremate them and throw the ashes into rivers? Did they scatter their bones after birds and animals had been allowed to pick the bodies clean, as Tibetan Buddhists still do today? Or did they simply bury them in their farms and settlements in unmarked, unadorned graves?

No places of worship from the period 1100 to 500 BC have been identified, either. Furthermore, we know of only about fifty sacred places that were constructed between 500 BC and the arrival of the Romans in the first century AD, and all of them are small, modest and usually hidden beside streams or springs, or in woods. One is now underneath Heathrow airport but two thousand years ago it was in the midst of a heath – a wild landscape.

In short, it seems that the people of Britain turned away from grand plans that were designed to dominate and alter the landscape – such as Stonehenge – and instead started to venerate the landscape itself. Trees, water and specific plants, such as the oak and mistletoe, all became sacred to them and were appreciated in a modest, almost invisible, manner. If the late Neolithic to Bronze Age was characterised by megalomaniacal building projects, the people of the next millennium seem to have been revolted by such ostentation. It is possible that the volcanic 'nuclear winter' was such a shock that it brought about a sense of communal humility in the face of the power and wonder of nature.

This is the foremost example of the shift from 'grand and controlling' to 'simple and modest' in the cycle of the rise and fall of beliefs and lifestyles. The stone-circle culture, especially towards the end, was determined to stand apart from nature. Strikingly, the Third Cycle opens not only with a wholehearted rejection of the previous era's great construction projects, but with a renewed respect for the ordinary yet essential elements of nature – rivers, land, forests and so on. Even the dead are not isolated from nature – hence the absence of burial mounds from this period and the increasing veneration of lakes, rivers and streams, presumably because the remains of the dead (and perhaps ritual objects) were scattered in these watery places.

Between 500 BC and the start of the Roman era, the most sacred places in Britain seem to have been springs, holy wells, pools and rivers, all natural features upon which agriculture also depends, of course. The custom of dropping a coin into a well for good luck seems to date back to the Iron Age tradition of placing iron offerings – swords, coins, helmets, breastplates – into water. Many of these were deliberately broken before immersion, as if to kill their power, and human bones are often found alongside them. These were all items of considerable value, so it is likely that they were thrown into pools to honour or appease some very powerful deities. This is a prime example of the sacred being located within, rather than above, the natural environment. We know that a particular body of water was sometimes associated with and named for a specific deity because the city of Bath was known to the Romans as Aquae Sulis, after the Iron Age deity Sulis. (As we shall see in the next chapter, many of these natural features have retained their ancient names to this day.)

From roughly 500 BC onwards, the dominant cultural style of Britain was Celtic. There is currently great debate over whether this was due to the migration of Celtic tribes into Britain or the adoption of Celtic ideas and styles by existing British tribes. Either way, under the Celts' influence, religious activity seems to have resumed in Britain, but it was markedly different from anything that had gone before. The veneration of nature culminated in the rise of the Druids, whose beliefs were focused on trees and forests, as is noted by several Roman writers. However, they seem to have fused this respect for the natural environment with a tradition of sacrifice, including human sacrifice, which is why the Romans banned them throughout the Empire. It is this Celtic world of nature and the sacred that the Romans discovered when they arrived in Britain in the first century AD, while its influence led to the creation of a distinctive local religion and also shaped early British Christianity.

Paradoxically, the Druids are now frequently associated with Stonehenge, even though, as we have seen, they could not have been further apart (ideologically and chronologically). The forest and water worship of the Druids was the antithesis of the arrogant belief system that had imposed the great stone circles on the landscape a thousand years earlier.

The sacred in every field

Rather than building great sacred monuments, the post-apoca-lyptic people of the Third Cycle created fields and settlements that followed the ebb and flow of the land. In this period, we begin to see the development of a rural way of life that continues to this day. Where the land has been little disturbed (because poor soil has made modern farming impossible or because it is protected), it is still possible to see demarcations of fields and homes from the late Bronze Age and Iron Age, as if they were made only a century or so ago. For instance, on Dartmoor, you can barely travel for a few hundred metres without encountering field boundaries or marks of Iron Age homesteads. And just outside Glossop, in the Peak District, I once spotted an entire field system, revealed by the low January sun.

So what allowed these farms and homesteads to spring up suddenly all over Britain? One factor was certainly the rise of metalworking. We are so familiar with the terms 'Bronze Age' and 'Iron Age' that we sometimes overlook the seismic impact that the discovery of these metals had on human development. Their true significance is revealed in old legends that turn metalworkers into deities, such as Thor, the Norse god of war, and the aforementioned Wayland. These gods possessed the seemingly magical ability to create weapons and tools from lumps of rock, and their fiery furnaces spoke of dangerous, powerful forces that might be tapped, but only at great spiritual risk. It was hardly surprising that ordinary people held mortal metalworkers in such high regard, especially as they provided the tools that made felling trees and digging the earth so much easier and quicker.

It is possible that this led to agriculture becoming the dominant form of spiritual expression. Farming, along with metalworking, might well have been perceived as a manifestation of the sacred for Iron Age people (and for many generations thereafter). If you no longer believe in the power of stone circles and henges, then what is the focal point for your spirituality? These people must have felt a need to identify their place in the great narrative, and perhaps they did so through their farms and fields. Britain had recovered from a major environmental collapse. The sun had disappeared for a long time, but it had finally returned, as it did on a much smaller scale every day. The people must have had great respect for the regenerative powers of nature, for the coming of new life that springtime always brings.

In many ancient cultures with written records, we know for certain that farming was seen as another gift of the gods. And even today we can see traces of something similar in Britain. On Rogation Sunday, the fifth Sunday after Easter, parishioners might walk the boundaries of their parish and witness the blessing of fields and farms, streams and woods, in the hope of securing a good harvest. For example, the parishioners of Burnett, near

Keynsham in Somerset, still beat the bounds, as they have done for centuries. Meanwhile, at Kinton in Kent, the tradition was revived as recently as 2004. Similarly, Lammas Day, in early August, celebrates the first loaf made from the new grain, while Harvest Festival, in early autumn, combines many different aspects of Britain's farming tradition – religious and secular – to remind people of the importance of the harvest and the land.

The sacred pact with the land is still particularly evident among farmers. When the European Union first paid them to set aside land in the 1980s, many asked their local church to hold a simple service in the fields. This enabled the farmers to say thank-you to the land through prayer and quiet reflection. If such gratitude towards the land is still alive today, imagine how powerful it must have been three thousand years ago.

In our own time, the simple honesty of agriculture is often contrasted with the superficiality of urban life. This theme is particularly strong when we are shocked into acknowledging the degree to which we have damaged nature through our urban materialism and extravagance. Perhaps this sensation first entered our consciousness three thousand years ago. That would certainly explain why so few sacred places were built in the first millennium BC. If everything you do as a farming community is sacred, then a designated sacred place becomes much less important. And if the myths and legends tell you that your ancestors were abandoned twice by their gods, why would you place your trust in some great religious site and its associated rituals, power structure and ideology? By comparison, trusting in nature must have seemed far more logical and rewarding.

Nevertheless, the forces of order and control were merely biding their time, and before long the grand would once again sweep aside the simple and the modest. This time they came in the form of the invading boats and commercial lifestyles of the Romans.

The return of order and the separation from nature: the Romans

The Romans tried to invade Britain twice: first under Julius Caesar in the middle of the first century BC, when they had a brief look around before leaving; and then a century later, when they established strongholds, subdued local rebellions, and began four centuries of occupation. They also had a profound impact on the landscape, building famously straight roads and founding numerous towns. The Fosse Way, as we saw in Chapter 2, was originally built to serve the same purpose as the Romans' later defensive walls, such as Hadrian's Wall and the Antonian Wall: to mark a boundary and to provide protection against attack. Once the roads had been built, the towns and villas swiftly followed, signalling the dawn of urban culture in Britain and shifting the focus from countryside to town for the first time. Hundreds of contemporary place names still reflect the Romans' impact on Britain. Lancaster and Ribchester in Lancashire, Caister-on-Sea in Norfolk, Caerleon in Gwent, Cardiff and Carlisle were all Roman *castra* – fortified towns.

The Romans were history's ultimate pragmatists, and by the time they arrived in Britain they had learned the value of giving a nod of respect to local deities. They tended to do this by associating the native gods with their own deities. For example, when Julius Caesar described the religions of Gaul, he simply used Roman religious terminology and names: 'The god they worship most is Mercury and they have many images of him.' He then mentioned that the Gauls also worshipped Apollo, Mars, Jupiter and Minerva.[15] Of course, this would have been news to the Gauls, who were totally unfamiliar with these names until the Romans arrived. Across Britain, statues of the classical Roman gods – such as Jupiter and Mars – stood side by side with local deities, including the Three Mothers of Celtic tradition. The best example of this fusion came in Bath, where the temple and springs were dedicated to Minerva while the town was named Aquae

Sulis. As has been mentioned, though, the Romans drew the line at human sacrifice to the gods, which led to the disappearance of the Druids by about AD 100. Consequently, the British had to abandon their tradition of hanging the heads of captured enemies over wells and holy springs, making carvings of them instead.

While the Romans were happy to incorporate many local British customs and traditions into their belief system, of course they had their own great story, which was largely derived from an earlier Greek tradition. They felt that the gods had given them power and might because they were a chosen people. They also believed that their role was to build a world that combined control and order with skilful management of the natural world. They certainly did not see them-selves as part of nature. Rather, they felt that the gods had created nature for their use and sometimes even their amusement. The

© Topfoto

This illustration of the palace of the Roman Governor of London shows the classic fascination with order and symmetry, which returns with the Georgians.

games, which took place in hundreds of amphitheatres across the Roman world – including those at Dorchester, Caerleon and Chester – often included hunts of wild animals.

Even though Roman mythology was a reworking of the Greek belief system, the Romans despised the Greeks, as is clear from one of their favourite legends. The story goes that Aeneas, a close relative of King Priam of Troy, escaped the terrible destruction of his city by the Greeks at the end of the Trojan War. He and his companions eventually made it to Italy and founded Rome. Thus, the Romans saw themselves as descended from Trojans and therefore as the implacable enemies of the Greeks, rather than their spiritual descendants.

The Greek and Trojan theme continued all the way to medieval Britain. In his epic saga *The History of the Kings of Britain*, written in the twelfth century AD, Geoffrey of Monmouth tells of Aeneas's great-grandson coming to Britain with other Trojan refugees and giving his name to the origin of the name 'Britain'. This provided the British – and especially the Normans, who were still in the process of cementing their control of the country – with a grand narrative that linked them back to the greatest feud of antiquity, and the greatest Empire – Rome – that they knew about.

The Roman world was ordered, powerful and controllable, all of which is reflected in their buildings, which were invariably symmetrical. Think of classic Roman temples and amphitheatres. Their symmetry is one of their most striking features. Think of their forums and shopping centres, which are always perfectly regular. Meanwhile, Roman power was displayed in the sheer scale of what they built. Their buildings were grander and larger than anything Britain had seen before.

Like Greek buildings before them, all Roman construction

projects – from individual villas to towns and military camps – were designed to reflect the divine order and perfection of the world and the universe. These people believed that the world around them could be managed, and that they had the honour and responsibility of being its managers. This is the message of every Roman town and every perfectly straight Roman road. To them, the immutable rules of nature and the world – both physical and spiritual – were based on order, structure and security. These were the core elements of the Romans' great story, and there are echoes of them in Britain to this day. They comprise one of the Romans' greatest yet most troubling legacies.

The third great collapse

Some four centuries after its legions had set up camp in Britain, the Roman Empire collapsed. Partly, this was due to increasing attacks and then invasion by Anglo-Saxon tribes from areas that were beyond the control of the Empire. Scandinavia was never conquered by the Romans and it was from Denmark, Norway and Sweden that hordes of invaders came in their long boats.

However, while the collapse was partly due to invasion, as well as corruption and inflation, there was another cause: environmental crisis. This was the result of the Romans exhausting the land to the extent that there was not enough food to feed the towns and cities. It is only recently that this aspect of the ecological collapse of Rome has come to be understood. The work of writers such as Jared Diamond and Clive Ponting has drawn attention to the ecological stages of collapse of empires throughout history. Rome was no exception.

Over-farming, deforestation, intensive industrial development and pollution all meant that by the early fifth century much of the farmland of Europe was exhausted. The grain fields of Egypt were turning to desert and huge areas of France and Britain were abandoned and turning into scrubby wasteland. Populations fell and invasions increased because there was no money or food to supply the troops. The great villas also declined, meaning the rural infrastructure suffered too. Combined with the arrival of the yellow plague, which may have killed as much as half the population of Europe and the Middle East, this scenario meant that Britain and much of Europe was on the edge of disaster.

This physical decay was accompanied by the collapse of the local religion (or religions) of the time. Once again, the covenant between the people and their deities – be they Roman, British or, more commonly, a fusion of the two – had seemed to fail, which led to rising scepticism and eventual abandonment of whole belief systems. The fusion religions were especially vulnerable because once the legions withdrew, and took most of the civil structure with them, there seemed little point in worshipping the gods of the Roman Empire. Meanwhile, the Celtic deities – most of which were meant to guarantee fertility, bountiful harvests and health – had surely failed the people, too.

THE FOURTH GREAT CYCLE: THE RISE OF THE CHRISTIANITIES

While all of this was going on, a new religion that had been quietly growing now emerged, becoming popular precisely because it offered a theological, psychological and material response to the crises. The new religion was Christianity. Theologically it explicitly linked ecological and cultural collapse to God's punishment of the people, but it also offered a belief – based on the story of the death and then resurrection of Jesus – that through times of trouble come times of redemption. It offered psychological help by creating new communities who broke with the past spiritually and, just as importantly, structurally, by creating new worlds of meaning and belonging which lay beyond the traditional bonds of Roman society and crossed cultural and class boundaries. Materially, this new religion helped in a most dramatic way, still visible to this day. It deliberately built religious communities in the most ecologically desecrated areas and brought them back to fertility and productivity. Think of the largest old monastery sites near you and many of these will be set in dramatic but wild countryside. In part this was because of the desire to meditate on God and nature, but in part because this was where the struggle to rebuild the land had to take place in order to inspire others. Yet again, an ecological and spiritual collapse was followed by a return to being part of nature, not apart from nature. The cycle had begun again.

When the Roman legions left Britain in AD 409–10, Christianity was already widespread across the country but not yet in control. For instance, there were religious centres as far afield as Whithorn in southern Scotland, Hinton St Mary in Dorset and Lullingstone in Kent. Through first the Empire and then Christianity, Britain was firmly linked to the political and religious systems of mainland Europe. For example, the word 'diocese' – which is now used to describe both Catholic and Anglican church divisions in Britain – derives from the Greek word '*dia-oikein*', meaning to manage a settlement. Later, the Latin term '*dioecesis*' was used by the Romans for the political division of a country. At the end of the fourth century, Britain had four dioceses – administrative areas of the government, each of which was ruled by a political appointee. It also seems to have had three religious divisions, also known as dioceses – probably London, Lincoln and either Carlisle or Caerleon. Furthermore, recent research has shown that our existing parish boundaries – which were probably first designated as such in the late seventh century – almost exactly follow the boundaries of former Roman estates.

The Church therefore retained many aspects of the Roman system, but it combined Roman order with the concepts of simplicity and working within rather than apart from nature. It was this fusion of two seemingly antagonistic ideals that enabled Christianity to become the principal religion of Britain.

The new religion's mission was exemplified by the work of the West's earliest monastic Order – the Benedictines. The word 'order' is important here: of course, it echoes the Greek and Roman belief systems, but the Benedictines gave those systems a dramatic new twist. St Benedict founded his Order in the mid-sixth century with the aim of repairing the damage done to the landscape by the late Roman Empire. He instructed his monks to seek out the most devastated areas and then told them to live by the three key elements of his rule: pray, study and work. The last of these involved reviving the land through composting, letting the fields lie fallow every seven years, planting trees to restore watersheds, diverting streams, creating fish ponds, and building and maintaining dovecotes to generate guano to fertilise the fields. Over the centuries that followed, the monks led the revival of Europe's ecology and created the agricultural societies and traditions that endured for over a millennium. They also laid the foundations for the emergence of village Britain.

A specific form of Christianity emerged in these islands – Celtic Christianity. This arose especially among the Romano-British populations that fled into the more remote parts of Britain when the Anglo-Saxons started invading in the late fourth century. So Celtic Christianity developed in Wales, Cumbria and Cornwall, and in two areas where Roman influence had been marginal, at best – Ireland and Scotland. It was a rural faith that shunned the urbanism that was in the process of collapsing, and its adherents viewed that collapse as God's judgement on a corrupt society.[16] It was also monastic and quite closely mirrored the Benedictine model, as it stressed dedication to the spiritual life and the importance of restoring a proper relationship with the natural world. However, whereas the Benedictines chose where to site their monasteries and were able to utilise the remains of Roman civilisation, the Celtic Christians had often fled from their old lives in Roman Britain and viewed their communities as places of refuge as well as restoration. They were closely tied to the land and nature, and developed a much more sustainable agricultural system than had been practised by the Romans. Like the Benedictines, the Celtic Christians saw the sacred in nature and felt that they were seeing God in action. This helped them survive the collapse and led to a new understanding, a new story that allowed them to rebuild.

However, to sustain this new story, Christianity had to endure a massive assault in the form of invading Anglo-Saxon tribes. For a couple of centuries, the Celtic Christians and the 'pagan' Anglo-Saxons struggled for supremacy. But then, with the conversion of the Anglo-Saxons from the late sixth century onwards, the Christian story became the pre-eminent shaper of Britain's landscape over the next millennium and beyond.

The revival of the local

On any journey to find hidden, sacred Britain, you will almost certainly pass through a village or a small town. Perhaps you live in one. If so, you live in the landscape gifted to us by the Anglo-Saxons. While the Romans loved the grand and the imperial, the Anglo-Saxons preferred the small and the local. From them, we have inherited the archetypal English village, with its church, market place or green and manor house. Their love of the local is reflected in the names of our villages and towns, almost all of which date from the time when Britain was being invaded and then settled by the Anglo-Saxons and their great foes, the Vikings. In effect, Britons returned to the system that had been crushed by the Romans. Once again, they revered holy wells and local deities, only this time those deities were known as saints. This tradition originated with the Celtic Christians, who passed it on to the Anglo-Saxons.

An interesting example of an early Anglo-Saxon Christian settlement is London. It grew from the sixth century to the ninth and
lay outside the Roman walls, to the west of the River Fleet. At the
time, it was called Lundenwic – meaning London market – and it
is remembered to this day in the name Aldwych – meaning the Old
Market (see Chapter 6).

Many of the Anglo-Saxon and Celtic saints who lived between the
sixth and the tenth centuries were highly local, known perhaps in
just one valley or even just one village, where the parish church
might still bear their name. This is particularly true of Scotland,
Cumbria, Wales and Cornwall. Writing in the early twelfth century,
the Norman monk William of Malmesbury noted that, before the
Norman Conquest in 1066, every village had its own local saint. In
addition, there was a proliferation of holy wells, springs, pools, and
churches erected on high hills and at river crossings, all of which
indicates that people were keen to re-sanctify their local landscapes.
Anglo-Saxon and Celtic Christians always displayed respect for
nature when they chose the locations for their sacred buildings, with
rivers, hills and even particular trees, such as the yew, often having
roles in their decisions. But now, for the first time, all of these local
elements were part of a much wider picture, a more cosmological
story – the story of God, Jesus Christ and the Holy Spirit, and God's
plan for all of creation.

The threat from the north

However, just as that story was becoming firmly established in
Britain, it was very nearly destroyed. The first hint of the terrible times
that lay ahead came in a short entry in the *Anglo-Saxon Chronicle* for
the year 793:

Here terrible portents came about over the land of Northumbria, and miserably frightened the people: there were immense flashes of lightning, and fiery dragons were seen flying in the air. A great famine immediately followed these signs: and a little after that in the same year on 8th January the raiding of the heathen men miserably devastated God's church in Lindisfarne island by looting and slaughter.[17]

This was the point at which the Vikings erupted into British history, and over the next three hundred years they had a dramatic impact on the landscape, the culture and even the place names of Britain. Vigorously and aggressively anti-Christian, at least at first, they were an even greater threat to Christianity than the Anglo-Saxons had been. Traces of their gods are still to be found in many place names, and of course they also survive in several of our days of the week. For a while, it looked as if the Christian story would be overwhelmed but slowly Christianity converted the Vikings and brought them within the Christian story, albeit that the Vikings themselves helped create, once again, a distinctly British version of Christianity.

The Vikings' conversion did not begin until the late ninth century, when the Anglo-Saxons, under the inspired Christian leadership of Alfred the Great, started to fight back against the raiding parties that had been assaulting Britain for a hundred years. Alfred built new towns – known as burghs – which were fortified to protect the people against the invaders. These towns, such as Wallingford in Oxfordshire, were laid out in a very specific pattern that revealed their defensive purpose but also a clear sense of order and faith. At the centre was a church, and each town was surrounded by walls. A particularly impressive example can be seen in the surviving walls around Wareham, Dorset, which included a church over the main entrance. Located safely inside the walls were the market place and designated areas for various trades, all laid out on a grid pattern, such as Barnstaple in Devon.

Alfred prevented the total conquest of England by the Vikings, but he was unable to regain those areas that had been lost before he came to the throne – the land to the north of Wessex and Mercia that became known as Danelaw. The Vikings ruled England to the east of a line stretching roughly from just east of London, past Northampton, to the coast near Liverpool. Much of Wales was also under their rule, as were the Scottish islands and Caithness. Meanwhile, the Scots ran their own kingdom north of Edinburgh. As we will see later, many Scandinavian names are still to be found in the areas that were once ruled by the Vikings.

There was constant warfare, civil wars, invasions by other Viking leaders from Norway and Denmark, as well as the struggle by the Anglo-Saxons to regain control. But that was all changed by the final and most comprehensive Norse invasion – the Norman Conquest. For, while William the Conqueror was the ruler of a region of northern France, just a few generations earlier his ancestors had been Vikings.

Rome and the Normans: power, order and the Church

After their somewhat surprise victory over the Anglo-Saxons at the Battle of Hastings on 14 October 1066, William's forces swept through England and seized power. They then invaded much of Wales and formed political and dynastic links with Scotland. The Normans, victorious but also fearful of the mass of Anglo-Saxons, then set about changing the landscape. They greatly extended the urbanisation projects begun in the late Anglo-Saxon period. At the same time, they planted maybe seventy new forests and enclosed thousands of new parks. This pattern of urban development combined with designated rural areas remains the dominant model for the British landscape today, and it reflects a peculiarly British way of viewing land and the relationship between town and country. The baronial estates of the Norman lords were the forebears of the housing estates of the twentieth century. In fact, the latter came to be known as estates because of the association with the countryside and comfort that the word has enjoyed since Norman times.

William and his followers' delight in their creation of forests and towns can be seen to this day. It seems that they especially enjoyed the fact that these places were totally 'new', so they incorporated that word into many of the names – such as the New Forest, in Hampshire, Newcastle-upon-Tyne, and Newport, in Shropshire. Anywhere with 'Forest', 'Chase' or 'Wood' in its name is likely to have its roots (literally) in Norman times, when the whole of England and much of Wales and lowland Scotland were divided into vast estates, and specific hunting zones were created for the lords and their retinues. This passion for hunting eventually contributed to the barons' rebellion against William the Conqueror's great-great-grandson – King John – who was thought to have created too many new forests.

When the Normans laid out their new towns, they often offered 'burbages' to potential inhabitants. These were near-identical plots of land running at right angles to the main streets, sometimes up to a hundred metres long. Nowadays, such a Norman town can be identified by looking at the width of the buildings' façades on the main street. If they are all almost exactly the same, then you are probably looking at the result of Norman town planning, with is emphasis on order and uniformity. In many towns, these original plots have endured to this day. Marshfield in Gloucestershire and Pembroke in South Wales are perfect examples of the medieval town plan that was pioneered by the Normans.

Every Norman lord also wanted to create his very own park, and over the next two centuries they did so with relish. The Domesday Book (compiled in 1086) lists thirty-five such parks; by 1300, there were three thousand of them.[18] Their shapes and the spaces they created, entirely free from buildings and villages, were often visible until very recently. Indeed, many modern housing estates were built on old parks precisely because they had been kept as open spaces for centuries. So, if you live on a housing estate with 'Park' in its name, the chances are that its boundaries were first drawn by a Norman lord. In addition, most of the National Trust grand houses and landscaped grounds and parks have their origin in this Norman movement.

The Normans also brought castles to Britain. Of course, there had been fortifications here before, but the scale and type of Norman castle-building was unprecedented, and these buildings dominated the urban and rural landscapes for centuries. A prime example is the White Tower in London, still the core of the Tower of London complex. Elsewhere, entire towns came into being simply to supply the new castles, such as Castleton in Derbyshire. The town of Stirling, in Scotland, also developed rapidly after 1100, when its huge castle was built on a craggy outcrop. Across the countryside, hundreds of smaller castles – known as 'motte and baileys' – ensured that the vastly outnumbered Normans maintained control over the peasantry (see Chapter 7). A very good example can be seen from the M6 motorway at Junction 38 for Tebay, in Cumbria. Here, the motte (central part) of Castle Howe towers some nine metres above the flat bailey.

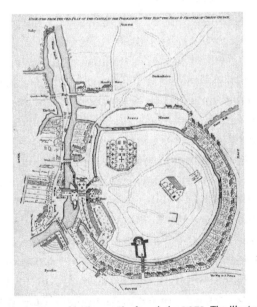

A good example of a motte and bailey castle, founded c.1071. The illustration shows the ditch, surrounding houses and their gardens, the tower and the keep.

Clearly, once the Normans started to put their stamp on Britain, the now-familiar cycle turned again, and the simple succumbed to the grand and the domineering. The secular rulers of the landscape were determined to bend it to their will. However, from the thirteenth century onwards, there was a countervailing force in Britain: the great monastic orders. By 1200, they controlled much of the land, and they had very different ideas about how it should be treated. For the monastic movement, the land was God's and they were its custodians, responsible not just for its productivity but also for the welfare of those who were sick, homeless and poor. While both the Church and nobility were powerful land users, the latter did so purely for their own military benefit. The church, in contrast, especially through the monasteries, continued the Benedictine rule of restoring damaged landscapes and helping those who were damaged by the brutal power exercised by the nobility. Two parallel stories were now being told, each based upon an almost identical belief in an all-powerful God, but each with a very distinctive view of what God required of them, as well as of humanity's place and role in the natural world created by God.

Before the Normans arrived in Britain, most churches were small, wooden and thatched – local, simple buildings. William the Conqueror changed all that, as big, stone-built parish churches and even bigger cathedrals became awe-inspiring statements about order and control. These buildings were as much celebrations of the Normans' secular power as they were sacred places in which to worship God.

The Normans also launched the great era of pilgrimage in Britain. This was when the national and even international significance of saints became central to the power of the Catholic Church. Local pilgrimages had been going on for centuries, but the major ones – to Canterbury for Thomas Becket; to Santiago de Compostella for St James; to Rome for St Peter; and, of course, to the Holy Land itself – became increasingly significant as the Normans sought to link English Christianity with continental Catholicism. It was pilgrimage that created the Canterbury we know today, in terms of the street layout, the churches and the cathedral. Meanwhile, St Andrews, in

Scotland, was laid out as a pilgrimage route to and from the town's great cathedral – now in ruins – where a relic of St Andrew was held.

Anglo-Saxon pilgrimage sites were often given make-overs that transformed them from very simple buildings to vast edifices. Meanwhile, the routes to them boasted ever more pubs and inns to cater for the growing numbers of pilgrims. Iona in Scotland (St Columba), Durham (St Cuthbert), Crowland in Lincolnshire (St Guthlac), St Davids in Pembrokeshire, Winchester (St Swithun) and Westminster (St Edward the Confessor) all bear witness to the Norman drive to consolidate their power by recruiting the saints of the land. Pilgrims and supplicants traipsed to all of these centres and many more to offer up their prayers. Scores of today's roads still follow the old pilgrimage paths, such as the A55, which runs from the shrine of St Werburga at Chester Cathedral, to those of St Winifred (at Holywell), St Asaph, St Deniel (at Bangor) and St Beuno (at Clynnog Fawr) before becoming the A499 and heading down to Aberdaron and the boats to Bardsey Island – the Island of the Ten Thousand Saints.

Many of the great pilgrimage centres were run by the monasteries, but the influx of pilgrims and their money often turned centres of simple spirituality into power centres of economics and politics, mirroring the nobility and their power rather than the monastic model of simplicity and humility from which their care of the poor came. There was a striking difference between the wealth and attitude of say St Andrews or Canterbury, with their huge numbers of pilgrims, and the small hard-working monasteries looking after leprosy victims or the remote meditational monasteries such as Strata Florida in Ceredigion, Wales.

It is possible that the medieval obsession with pilgrimage ultimately helped to undermine the power of the Catholic Church. In his *Canterbury Tales*, Geoffrey Chaucer made it abundantly clear that priests and the Established Church were not held in high

▶

regard, and it may well be that he simply wrote down stories that were being told and retold up and down the pilgrimage routes of Europe. Interestingly, Henry VIII banned pilgrimage in 1536 as one of the earliest of his reforming acts.

The Norman combination of piety and power finds expression wherever they held control – from the lowlands of Scotland, in the border regions, and throughout England. For they developed a strong sense of the village or town ruled by the feudal lord, who controls and runs an area in which the church is one of the main status symbols. This led to the building of some ten thousand parish churches that are still standing in Britain as well as the introduction of new agricultural practices that shaped the fields and the countryside around the villages (see Chapter 4).

The fourth great collapse: the Black Death and the rise of uncertainty

In 1348, a cargo ship arrived at Melcombe (now Weymouth). In the hold were black rats, carriers of the fleas that bore the Black Death virus. Over the next eighteen months, just under half the population of Britain died from the disease, with some towns and villages losing 70 per cent of their people. The impact on the landscape was both apocalyptic and revolutionary. Possibly as many as three thousand villages were abandoned and never reoccupied. For instance, in Leicestershire alone, more than fifty were deserted.

Sometimes you may see a solitary church on an Ordnance Survey map. The chances are that it used to stand in the centre of a plague village. While the people's homes will long since have fallen into ruin, the church – one of those solid, stone-built demonstrations of

Norman power – will remain as a silent witness to those who died and are possibly buried in its graveyard. Villages can be abandoned for any number of reasons: a river might change its course and leave a once-thriving port landlocked; the coast might advance or retreat; some places are even overwhelmed by windblown salt. But in the Middle Ages, far and away the most common cause was the arrival of the Black Death. And it wasn't only communities that were destroyed by this catastrophe. Once again, people started to question everything. Neither the secular powers of king and local lord nor the spiritual powers of the Church seemed capable of halting the advance of the terrible disease. Many concluded that God must be angry and was punishing them.

Where villages did survive, the social order changed radically. In some parts of the country, there were not enough peasants to work the fields, so the feudal lords had to start buying in extra labour. Market forces ruled, and the labourers started pitting rival lords against each other to secure the best deal for themselves. This undermined secular feudal society at its most vulnerable point, but the parallel religious order fared little better.

And so, once again, the religion of the time of crisis began to die. The old Catholic Order of loyalty to the Church, had been marked through payment of tithes and the giving of service, leading to a place in heaven through the kindness and intercession of the Church and the saints. It was also increasingly marked – as ever in these great cycles – by a separation of the people from nature. Now that system began to fall apart. Faith in the Church was understandably shaken to its core because it had proved so impotent in the face of the Black Death. Even bishops began to question what was happening, as can be seen in the illustrations that adorn their tombs.

In Wells Cathedral, Somerset, you will find the tombs of a number of Anglo-Saxon bishops, all carved around 1220 as part of the new, impressive Norman cathedral. Each man is shown lying in his bishop's robes with his hands clasped together in prayer, clearly confident that Catholic Christianity is the one true faith and that through membership of the Church, the bishop is on his way to heaven. Likewise, Bishop William de Marchia, who died in 1302, also lies resplendent and confident in his robes. However, Bishop Beckynton's tomb, carved in 1440, shows something very different. There are two levels to this tomb. The upper level is elaborately carved and the bishop seems in fine fettle. But on the lower level his naked body is depicted half wrapped in a shroud and decaying. The old certainty has gone or at the very least now has to be balanced by an element of fear and apprehension.

Almost a hundred years after its arrival in Britain, clearly the Black Death was still shaking confidence, even among the highest echelons of the Church. It brought about a more reflective and uncertain age. It also sowed the seeds of one of the greatest cultural upheavals in British history – the Reformation.

THE FIFTH GREAT CYCLE: THE INDIVIDUAL, THE ARCHITECT AND THE EMERGING NEW ORDER

Britain's post-medieval story includes two very different perceptions of humanity's relationship to God. On the one hand, many people come to believe that God is deeply concerned about the salvation of each and every individual, and they start to have a very personal relationship with Him. On the other, many feel that they are now standing alone, because the Church that replaces the old Catholic model does not seem as relevant to them or as powerful.

The largest single transfer of land in British history took place in the late 1530s, following King Henry VIII's dissolution of the monasteries. Henry claimed that he embarked on this because of the corruption of the monasteries and convents in England and Wales.

© Author

The Dissolution of the Monasteries from 1536–1560 meant that not a single one survived intact. In most cases, the destruction left little standing.

However, in truth, he feared that the monastic orders would remain faithful to the Pope, who had refused to sanction Henry's divorce from his first wife, Catherine of Aragon, leading Henry to take power over the church away from the Pope and into his own hands. Henry demanded that the church swear allegiance to him and it was clear that the strongest resistance would come from the monasteries, with their direct links to Rome. That would undermine Henry's authority, the status of his new queen and the potential succession of any children they might have. Of course, he also wanted the Orders' land and wealth for himself.

It was not only church buildings that were destroyed. The very fabric of Catholic, traditional Britain was systematically ripped apart. Roadside crosses were smashed into pieces and scattered. Almost every shrine, little chapels on hilltops and holy wells were dismantled or vandalised. Holy trees were cut down. People were told that sacred pools were now nothing more than water sources. Almost every statue in the land was ripped off its plinth and either burned (if made of wood) or smashed, with the fragments used to repair walls. Only the local parish churches were allowed to remain. But the empty saints' niches in almost every one of them bear mute witness to this iconoclastic rage. Murals that told the Christian story to illiterate worshippers were whitewashed over. Even ritual items, such as altars and fonts, were often thrown out. The veneration of saints, especially the Virgin Mary, disappeared almost overnight, as soon as their statues were destroyed and could no longer provide the focus for festivals. Under Henry's even more ardent Protestant son, Edward VI, chapels and shrines in the parish churches were broken up and chantry chapels were abolished.

Before the Dissolution and the similar movement to destroy the monasteries in Scotland, there were thousands of monasteries throughout Britain – from Melrose Abbey via Scone Abbey in Scotland, past Rievaulx in Yorkshire, Tintern in South Wales and Canterbury in Kent. Beautiful churches were destroyed, hospitals closed, schools ended – all in the name of Henry's authority. After 1539 not one single monastery remained in England and Wales and by 1560 not a single one existed throughout Britain. Their great estates were broken up; some of them were taken by the aristocracy but most were sold to the rising merchant classes. In later years this turn of history made this class even stronger and more powerful than they could otherwise have been. The abbeys that had dominated the landscape, both spiritual and economic, were destroyed.

This had enormous impact on our landscape. The physical journey of faith and humour, which Chaucer's Catholic pilgrims made in the fourteenth century through a sacred landscape, had to become a protestant inner journey of the lone soul seeking God, reaching its finest and most stark expression in John Bunyan's *The Pilgrim's Progress* of the late seventeenth century.

Melrose Abbey in Scotland survived the Dissolution of the Monasteries more intact than most and its scale and beauty is a reminder of the significance of these sacred places.

The loneliness of the individual soul

Ordinary people were suddenly cut off from their own landscapes. The old pilgrimage routes had provided fun, adventure and spirituality, all bundled into one epic journey. Now woe betide anyone who tried to take such a trip. People also had fewer opportunities to meet up and swap stories closer to home. Under the Catholic Church, the year had been measured by many widely celebrated saints' days and special festivals for the Virgin Mary and the local saint. Almost all of these were swept away, leaving just Christmas, Easter and Whitsun. (In Scotland, even Christmas was banned and dropped from the approved list of festivals.) Many local rituals and traditions – especially those associated with holy wells, sacred hills and special trees – went with them. In most communities, only one sacred place remained –

the parish church. And even that was much more drab and uninteresting than it had been a few years before.

All understanding of the sacred geography of towns and cities, and even the sacred geography of churches, disappeared. Every visit to a church in medieval times was a metaphor for the spiritual journey; and the same was true of every trip to a town centre. Now the saints who were linked to these sacred local landmarks were either gradually forgotten or denied any validity, mocked and destroyed. Britain's sacred pattern, established over centuries, was torn apart in a few short years amid a vast land grab and the destruction of all of the old ways of seeing and believing. Everyone now had to stand alone and make his or her own pact with God.

This happened because the new merchants and landed classes knew that they had a golden opportunity to destroy the authority and power of the old order, which had been so badly shaken by the Black Death. For the first time in British history, we are able to study the impact of a major disaster on the next great story. From this, we can draw some conclusions about what happened to the people, their faith, and their perception of their place in the world and the cosmos.

This was the period when economic rationalisation began to emerge. The moment of transition from a narrative landscape to an economic landscape is brilliantly captured by Daniel Defoe in *A Tour through England and Wales*, first published between 1724 and 1727. Defoe, a wonderful storyteller, visited most of the major towns and cities of these two countries. He revels in pointing out the oddities, silliness, strangeness and delights of these places and their people, but he also feels obliged to grade their value in modern, economic terms. Thankfully, he never lets the latter get in the way of a good story, though.

Building the new divine city

From the middle of the eighteenth century, Britain's urban development proceeded at an unprecedented pace and on an unprecedented scale. Of course, this was generated by mercantile, economic impulses, but it can also be read theologically and spiritually. For the fifth time in Britain's history, the population started to abandon the simple in favour of the complex. Unlike their ancestors, these people had never truly viewed themselves as part of nature, but eventually their separation from it was literally set in stone. Order and control, in both town layouts and the great parks and estates, came to be the norm.

The first stage of this period of urban growth – from the 1730s to around 1800 – was marked by a new theology that was widely reflected in the buildings. Thanks, in part, to the rise of scientific thinking, the Georgians cultivated a belief in God as the 'original architect' who wound it up and set it going but who has either then moved on or handed over responsibility to humanity. In some versions, there is a real sense of a God who wasn't interested at all in what happened to his creation. It was felt that He not only loved symmetry but was manifest within it. The Georgian style reflects this new form of belief, which is known as deism. The architects, designers and builders of the eighteenth century still believed in a deity – God – but not necessarily in the Trinity or other aspects of traditional Christianity. The 'Greek temples' of Stourhead in Wiltshire, the Circus in Bath and Edinburgh's New Town are all manifestations of a 'divine order' that gave the designers and owners of these buildings a sense of legitimacy. In stark contrast to the past, when the sacred was located in specific, designated places – long barrows, stone circles, holy wells, market crosses and churches – the town layout itself was now viewed as sacred, thanks to its symmetry, its regularity, its order. However, during this transformation, people lost the sense that God could help them in their struggles. They were on their own. Furthermore, the sacred Georgian urban layout was the preserve of the rich. The poor lived in slums – in the old, decaying and neglected parts of town or in new, cheap housing far from the elegant avenues and crescents of the wealthy.

The dislocation from nature and the lack of any sense of being part

© Topfoto

It was in order to protect the poor in such slums that the Victorians created sophisticated sewage and water systems – a sacred vision of health.

of a sacred community soon led to the horrors of the Industrial Revolution. As the slums of Glasgow, Manchester, Birmingham and London grew, living conditions within them deteriorated. It didn't have to be this way. Some industrial magnates – such as Samel Greg in Style, Cheshire, and Joseph Rowntree in York – showed compassion for their workers. But the spirit of the time stressed individualism and the lone soul making his or her own way through life. The vast majority of entrepreneurs simply had no time for compassion.

William Blake attacked this attitude in his famous poem 'Jerusalem':

> *And did the Countenance Divine,*
> *Shine forth upon our clouded hills?*
> *And was Jerusalem builded here,*
> *Among these dark Satanic Mills?*

Meanwhile, a series of visionaries – some inspired by religion, others by socialism – tried to re-establish a link with nature in utopian communities, such as New Lanark, Strathclyde, founded in 1800. The inspiration behind New Lanark was Robert Owen, an early socialist who dismissed all religion as nonsense. He urged others to follow his example and create similar environments where people could reach their full potential. New Lanark itself was, at best, a partial success, but Owen set standards – for example, not employing child labour – that were eventually adopted throughout Britain.

Over the next two centuries, these utopian communities fought against the prevailing culture, which is best described as 'utilitarian'. Some were far more successful than New Lanark, such as the Cadbury family's creation of Bournville, built in countryside on the outskirts of Birmingham (see Chapter 9). The often romantic, spiritual and lofty aspirations of these communities might seem quaint or even hippy today, but they kept alive a belief that humanity is more than an economic production unit. They understood that life is meaningful only if it has a deeper purpose. The essential role they played becomes clear when we look at the last great story that has shaped humanity, and especially the people of Britain, over the last two hundred years.

Mr Gradgrind and the rise of utilitarianism

In the first half of the nineteenth century, Britain's first non-religious tradition came to the fore. The people in charge were not primarily – or even remotely – influenced by a sacred vision of their role and place within a greater story. Instead, an economic and pseudo-philosophical tradition came to dominate and shape our landscape. This sought to apply two centuries of scientific endeavour and discovery to every aspect of life. If something could not be quantified, then science decreed that it did not exist. Hence, those who insisted that they were seeking reality and the truth started to view anything that was termed 'sacred' with deep suspicion.

Charles Dickens parodied this tendency in the character of Mr Gradgrind, the headmaster in *Hard Times*, written in 1854. This was Dickens's forthright response to the 1834 Poor Law Act – a classic statement of utilitarianism – which demanded that workhouses should be as unpleasant and dehumanising as possible, in order that poor people were dissuaded from seeking help from the state. Through Gradgrind, Dickens mocks the utilitarian approach that discounts all emotion, all generosity and any notion of the sacred. As Gradgrind says,

Now, what I want is, Facts. Teach these boys and girls nothing but Facts. Facts alone are wanted in life. Plant nothing else, and root out everything else. You can only form the minds of reasoning animals upon Facts: nothing else will ever be of any service to them. This is the principle on which I bring up my own children, and this is the principle on which I bring up these children. Stick to Facts, sir!

Elsewhere, Gradgrind asks one of his pupils to define a horse, and he is pleased with the answer: 'Quadruped. Graminivorous. Forty teeth, namely twenty-four grinders, four eye-teeth, and twelve incisive. Sheds coat in the spring; in marshy countries, sheds hoofs, too. Hoofs hard, but requiring to be shod with iron. Age known by marks in mouth.'

This narrow definition beautifully captures the limitations of utilitarianism. Yet it remains the dominant belief system in Britain today, and over the past two centuries it has been allowed to wreak terrible damage to the landscape, spirituality and our sense of human community. Utilitarianism is a deliberately unsentimental, unspiritual, pragmatic movement that values everything purely on the basis of its usefulness to humanity. It is the reason why we measure a country's level of development in terms of Gross Domestic Product rather than quality of life, the degree to which industrial production is damaging the natural environment or whether what is being produced is beneficial to the rest of the world. Utilitarianism sees no virtue in adornment, in beauty for beauty's sake, or in setting aside space for anything non-productive. Our towns and cities have become production units rather than visions of the divine or sacred places; our people are producers and consumers, and their needs are assessed almost exclusively by economic models. Housing has to be as 'efficient' as possible, with the maximum number of people crammed into the minimum space. Utilitarianism created the back-to-back terraces of Victorian northern towns and the tower blocks of the 1960s. And yet, up to now, no alternative has managed to overturn it.

I work with environmental groups around the world, and one of our major concerns is the development of sustainable agriculture. We support small-scale, organic, locally based, environmentally sensitive farming, and we have dealt with numerous communities who are very receptive to these concepts. Usually, this nurturing model of agriculture is already deeply embedded within their faith and their sense of belonging to a greater story that involves caring for all of creation. However, we are often opposed by major international organisations that want to abolish small-scale farming. These are the agents of utilitarianism. They point out that people are leaving rural areas and migrating to the cities anyway, and argue that this should be encouraged as it allows farming to be industrialised, with huge fields and orchards tilled and harvested by vast machines. Then the food can be easily transported to the few centres of population where almost everybody now lives. This will make the people happy, because they will still be able to purchase what they need, without having the hassle of growing it themselves. It's all so much more efficient and productive than the old way, the utilitarians argue. The reality is rather different: untold environmental destruction and the devastation of local communities and ways of life that have sustained people for centuries. But such non-economic considerations do not enter into the utilitarian way of thinking. And it is from the faiths that resistance to this dehumanising model is arising, as it so often has in the past.

As was mentioned earlier, a few influential people have challenged this dominant belief system over the last two hundred years. These were people who refused to accept that everything can be reduced to numbers and equations. The rise of the urban park, the creation of beautiful churches and chapels in deprived areas, the Arts and Crafts movement, the rise of trade unions – all of these were inspired by people who remained acutely aware of the sacred landscape and their relationship to it. Many of them were radical Christians – often Quakers – who also campaigned against slavery, child labour and urban poverty.

However, they were usually fighting against the tide. This even swept along other Christians, who viewed utilitarian progress as a sign of God's special grace and favour to Britain. The astonishing scale of the British Empire, combined with the sheer inventiveness and drive of nineteenth-century British industry, fuelled a genuine sense of being divinely chosen.

Faster and faster

Britain's acceleration in the eighteenth and nineteenth centuries was exemplified in the transport sector. It began slowly enough, with the canals, which allowed goods to be carried smoothly across the country without the need to brave the seas and the tides. Some early pottery entrepreneurs, such as Josiah Wedgwood in Staffordshire, inspired this development. Delicate plates and bowls could scarcely be transported on unsprung coaches and wagons on bumpy roads. It was far better to glide down a smooth sheet of water to your destination.

At first, some of the profits from industry were invested in improving the roads, but then someone had the bright idea of making the roads pay for themselves. Consequently, toll-roads became increasingly familiar in Britain from the late eighteenth century onwards, although their introduction was far from smooth. For instance, in

▶

South Wales in the late 1830s and early 1840s, the locals started smashing up toll-gates, having been inspired by a verse in the Bible: 'And they blessed Rebecca and said unto her . . . let thy seed possess the gate of those which hate you'.[19] The largely Methodist protesters – who disguised themselves as women – took this to mean that no one should be able to stop them travelling for free. Their campaigns came to be known as the Rebecca Riots.

The railways started to grow from the 1830s onwards. Suddenly, journeys that had taken several days now took only a few hours, and it was difficult to refute the widespread assumption that technology, industry and science were improving Britain. Such mastery of travel, the thrill of new inventions and power all fed the sense that man was in control now that God had handed all of His authority and knowledge over to us. God had established a good pattern, but humanity was improving it (see Chapter 7).

Next came the car and the aeroplane, which shrank the world, just as the railways had shrunk Britain. Speed, ease of access to anywhere you wanted to go and commuting all changed the way we lived and the way we viewed the landscape. They also changed our perception of what we could do to it. Now that we travel everywhere in cars, trains and planes, we have literally, metaphorically and spiritually lost touch with the ground.

The fifth great collapse?

Growth, development, progress and success have arisen as the core themes of our contemporary culture. Most of us live within the confines of that story, whether we want to or not. Yet there are numerous alternatives: the remnants of Catholic and Protestant Christianity; newer arrivals in Britain, such as Hinduism and Buddhism; Marxism and socialism; militant secularism – a belief system that is just as intolerant as any medieval religion. There is a plurality of choice among a diversity of stories.

Perhaps, as has happened four times before, the current system will collapse and pluralism will collapse with it. Perhaps utilitarianism will be abandoned, just as the stone circles were abandoned three thousand years ago. Certainly, the lesson from history is that when we lose touch with the earth, we lose touch with ourselves. The next collapse, if and when it comes, will be psychological as well as physical. On four separate occasions, our sense of purpose and our place in the world has disappeared along with our places of worship, our systems of agriculture and our communities.

So, might we learn enough from history to avert a fifth apocalypse? Are there clues not just to what went wrong but to how societies managed to rebuild themselves – including rebuilding faith and a sense of the sacred in nature? Before we attempt to answer those questions by exploring how humanity has shaped the landscape, we need to learn how the natural world has been viewed and interpreted over the last five thousand years. Before we started to channel rivers and streams and quarry hills and mountains, we respected those great manifestations of nature and gave them special, sacred names. We often still use those names today, but have forgotten their significance.

GAZETTEER

Prehistory

Southern England
- Jaywick Sands, Clacton-on-Sea, Essex (CO15): Palaeolithic hunting site
- Swanscombe, Kent (DA10): Palaeolithic hunting site and flint production

Long barrows

Scotland
- Blackhammer chambered tomb, Rousay, Orkney (KW17): example of distinctive Orkney-style passage long barrow
- Fettercairn, Aberdeenshire (AB30): a fine long, long barrow

Wales
- Giant's Grave, Park Mill, Gower (SA3): fully excavated, the roof has been removed so it is possible to see very clearly the internal layout of this typical long barrow
- Pentre Ifan, south of Nevern, Dyfed (SA41): good example of Clyde-style of long barrow

Northern England
- Deadman's Graves, Claxby St Andrews, Lincolnshire (LN13): a collection of long barrows in an interesting and unusual formation

Southern England
- Wayland Smithy, close to the White Horse of Uffington, Oxfordshire (SN6): splendid setting with a great legend associated, it is recorded in a Berkshire charter as early as AD 855
- West Kennett, Wiltshire (SN8): the oldest and longest long barrow in England
- Stoney Littleton, Somerset (BA2): superb and open example of long barrow

Stone circles

Scotland
- Callanish, Isle of Lewis (HS2): dramatic sacred landscape with some of the tallest stones of any circle in Britain
- Loch Buie, Isle of Mull (PA62): very fine example, with huge outlier stones, and set in a stunning landscape

Northern England
- Appletreewick, North Yorkshire (BD23): typical small-scale circle (six stones of very modest height)
- Druids' Circle, south of Ulverston, Cumbria (CA10): rare example of double-ring stone circle in beautiful setting
- Nine Ladies' Circle, Stanton Moor, Derbyshire (DE4): good example of medium-size circle
- Stapeley Hill, Shropshire (SY5): three small and now much depleted circles but typical of the scale and closeness of such circles to a major flint tool factory of the Bronze Age

- Sunkenkirk, Swinside Fell, southern Cumbria (LA11): a well-preserved, near-perfect circle that is 29 metres in diameter

Southern England

- Avebury, Wiltshire (SN8): after Stonehenge, the largest stone circle and sacred landscape in Britain
- Fernworthy, Dartmoor, Devon (TQ13): a fine and wide stone circle
- Stanton Drew, Somerset (BS39): after Stonehenge, Avebury and Callanish, this is Britain's fourth most important sacred landscape of circles and stones
- Stonehenge, Wiltshire (SP4): the most important sacred landscape of the stone circle era in Britain
- The Merry Maidens, St Buryan, Cornwall (TR19): the only complete circle in Cornwall
- The Rollright Stones, Oxfordshire (OX7): well preserved circle of weather-worn stones with the remains of a burial mound – the King's Men – nearby

Monumental sites

Southern England

- Merlin's Mound, Marlborough College, Silbury, Wiltshire (SN8): a smaller version of Silbury Hill and only eight miles away from it
- Silbury Hill, Wiltshire (SN8): the largest human-made prehistoric object in Europe

Hillforts

Southern England

- Uley Bury, Dursley, Gloucestershire (GL11): perfectly situated on a flat hill so you can see the original ditch and a secondary one built in c.200 BC

The Romans

Scotland

- Antonian Wall, central Scotland: built c.140 AD it runs from north of Glasgow to Queensferry and is visible at various points

Wales

- Caerleon, Gwent (NP18): major Roman military centre and probably site of one of the three bishoprics of the Church during the Roman period

Northern England

- Caister-on-Sea, Norfolk (NR30): remains of the Roman town and fortifications
- Carlisle, Cumbria (CA1): site of the major northern military base of the Romans with many fine objects on display in the museum
- Chester, Cheshire (CH1): major military base for control of North Wales by the Romans, with much still to be seen above ground and the street pattern of the Roman city still in use today
- Hadrian's Wall, northern England: built c.120 AD and the largest and most dramatic of all Roman remains in Britain – it runs between Carlisle and Newcastle

- Ribchester, Lancashire (PR3): now a village, the remains of the Roman fort and settlement have been in part excavated and there is a fine museum

Southern England
- Maumbury Ring, Dorchester, Dorset (DT1): Roman amphitheatre built into a huge Neolithic henge monument

Early Christian sites

Scotland
- Whithorn, Dumfries and Galloway (DG8): site of Scotland's oldest church, built c.397 by St Ninian; the remains have been excavated and there is a good museum

Southern England
- Hinton St Mary, Somerset (DT10): site of the find of an extraordinary early Christian mosaic, incorporating pagan deities as well; now on view in the British Museum
- Lullingstone, Kent (DA4): one of the country's most important villas, with a Christian chapel and pagan shrine. The frescoes of Christian worshippers is now in the British Museum but the museum on the site has a fine display of this fascinating site and its religions

Medieval towns

Wales
- Pembroke, south-west Wales (SA70): fine example of planned medieval town with castle and burbages

Southern England
- Marshfield, Gloucester (SN14): fine example of medieval burbages with every building on the main street still occupying the original burbage frontage and with the land behind running back to the back lane
- Wareham, Dorset (BH20): good example of a walled town of Alfred the Great, with most of the original earth walls still in place

Castles

Scotland
- Stirling, Scotland (FK8): the dramatic castle sits on its crag with the town nestling below

Northern England
- Castle Howe, Tebay, Cumbria (CA16): good example of a motte and bailey
- Castleton, Derbyshire (S33): a town that came into being simply to supply a castle

Southern England
- White Tower, London (EC3N): the largest Norman keep in Britain

Cathedrals

Southern England
- Canterbury Cathedral, Kent (CT1): the finest example of a church built on the proceeds of pilgrimage, and the classic gothic design

- Wells Cathedral, Somerset (BA5): my favourite cathedral and the finest West Front of any church in Britain

Monastery sites

Scotland
- Melrose Abbey, Scottish Borders (TD6): a fine range of remains and a good museum
- Scone Abbey, Perthshire (PH2): probably Scotland's most important abbey, and site of the coronation of kings and queens. Lost for many years, the site has recently been rediscovered

Wales
- Tintern, South Wales (NP16): a favourite subject of painters (Turner) and poets (Wordsworth), it is a fine ruin in a dramatic setting by the river Wye

Northern England
- Rievaulx, Yorkshire (YO62): dramatic setting and fine remains of the church

Southern England
- Canterbury, Kent (CT1): good remains around the cathedral and around St Augustine's monastery

Georgian style

Scotland
- New Town, Edinburgh (EH1): spectacular example of Georgian town planning telling a new story

Southern England
- Stourhead, Wiltshire (BA12): one of the best examples of Georgian landscaping in the Daoist natural style
- The Circus, Bath (BA1): built by John Wood the Elder c.1750, it is based on a romantic idea of Stonehenge and its iconography is deliberately 'pagan'

4

Uncovering the sacred in nature

Here, I said, here where you stand
And pause, and let everything go still
Feeling your breath as you glance down
Is the ground that is everywhere –
　　　　　　Nameless under our naming[20]

I was thirteen when I learned – to my astonishment and delight – that I lived near a river that was a goddess. I was walking with my family and friends along the banks of the Severn. We met an old fisherman who told us about the riverbed's secret pathways, which were revealed only when the tide was out. He took us along one of these paths and we saw the vast blocks of stone that form the bed of the river, seemingly laid there by a mighty giant. We found curious curled fossils, which the fisherman told us were the devil's toenails. And whenever he referred to the Severn itself, he called it 'she': 'She likes to roll down to the sea,' 'She can flood over a mile wide.' I asked him why he thought of the river as a woman. 'Because she was once a goddess,' he said, matter of factly. My jaw dropped.

I did some research as soon as I got home and learned that the

River Severn was first recorded by the Roman writer Tacitus in the early second century AD. He calls it Sabrina, and while the origin of that name is uncertain, it is likely that it was also the name of the goddess of the river. Nearly two thousand years of a West Country accent has softened the original name to Severn. I was most surprised by the fact that such a name had endured down through the millennia. It had survived the fall of Rome, the Anglo-Saxon and Viking invasions, the Norman Conquest – all the trials and tribulations of history. And its sacred meaning had survived, too.

Perhaps I shouldn't have been so surprised, as I already knew that the days of the week were named after ancient gods and goddesses. Their stories fascinated me back then, and they still do today. These were stories of mighty deities and their epic struggles with one another; stories of the primal forces of the planet and of a cosmic vision that was radically different from our own. It was through these tales that I first realised that a sacred imprint from the past lies all around us – even in the most mundane details of our everyday lives. Tuesday is named after the Norse goddess Tew; Wednesday after Woden; Thursday after Thor; and Friday after Freya. Saturday is named after the Roman god Saturn; Sunday after the sun; and Monday after the moon. That's seven full-blown pagan names and associations that are happily used by Christians and secularists alike without a moment's thought. Even our name for the most significant Christian festival – the resurrection of Jesus Christ – is pagan in origin: Easter was the Celtic goddess of spring. Furthermore, Britain has been a Protestant country for over 450 years, yet we still include the mass – the main service of Catholicism – in the name of our most popular festival, Christmas. It seems that we are unable to abandon our old belief systems completely. This is fortunate, because it allows us to learn more about the sacred beliefs of those who have lived in these islands over the past few thousand years.

It is in the names of major geographical features – rivers, hills, islands and springs – that the old beliefs are most likely to endure through the ages. The same cannot be said of the names of places we build, which are frequently changed (see Chapter 4). This distinction – between what we have built ourselves and what we feel we have been gifted by God (or gods) in the natural landscape – captures one of the key elements of how humanity thinks. Whenever we name a natural feature, we acknowledge that we are part of nature – and indeed an insignificant part in comparison with the mighty mountain or river that stands before us. We are humble before such vast forces of creation. The names we give them reflect this clearly, as they either incorporate the names of ancient deities (such as Danu) or describe the sacred nature of the features themselves (as in 'Brent', which simply means holy). By contrast, the names of our own creations – towns, fields, buildings and so on – reflect a sense of being apart from nature or even sometimes being co-creators with God.

By exploring the origins of names, it is possible to hear faint echoes of the voices, stories – even beliefs – of those who lived thousands of years ago. Those beliefs determined how these people viewed their place in the natural world, and they are embedded like flies in amber

© Topfoto

The beautiful Scottish Island of Iona had many different Gaelic names before *i Chaluim Chille*, meaning Island of St Columba. The abbey and its buildings have now been rebuilt and Iona is once again a major centre for pilgrimage.

within the names they gave the natural features of the landscape. For example, many islands to the west of Britain are associated with death and with the intercessory power of saints. But that link between the west and death long pre-dates the arrival of Christianity in Britain. Early Christianity simply absorbed and adapted the existing beliefs – or, one could argue, it was absorbed by them.

The natural world provides us with a record of Britain from a time long before writing existed here. To this day, our maps are inscribed with names that take us straight back to the Iron Age – such as Penzance, from the Old Cornish for 'Holy Headland'. It may be that some names have even earlier origins, although it is almost impossible to prove that any go back to the Stone Age. Nevertheless, many of the names that are familiar to us today have been passed down over millennia, and they speak of the sacred forces that were revered by our distant ancestors and their sense of being part of a much greater story.

In this chapter, I provide some clues as to what to look for; some examples of the astonishing survival of ancient names – and even beliefs; and show ways for you to read your landscape anew, as one of the oldest 'documents' in the world.

THE ANCIENT, SACRED POWER OF NAMING

The Bible is one of the world's oldest documents, yet it contains many clues as to how even earlier people thought and viewed the world. It also offers guidance on how to read an ancient landscape, and leaves the reader in no doubt about the power of names. God's very first command to Adam was that he should name 'all the creatures of the world'.[21] By doing so, Adam gained power over them because, in traditional thought, a name captures some essence of the creature. A name also allows a relationship to develop. For instance, think of how much easier it is to hold a conversation with someone if you know their name.

Genesis and the rest of the Old Testament's history books – including Judges, Joshua, Samuel, Kings and Chronicles – catalogue events that took place between approximately 1800 and 900 BC (the late Bronze Age to the early Iron Age). In this era, places were frequently renamed simply because something important happened there. For example, when Jacob was sleeping out in the wild, he dreamed of a ladder with angels ascending and descending it. When he awoke, 'he took the stone he had used as a pillow, and set it up as a monument, pouring oil over the top of it. He named the place Bethel [House of God] but before that the town was called Luz.'[22] It was around this time that specific tribes of people first arrived in the areas that they still occupy today – be they in China, India, the Middle East or Europe. It was also when written documents first started to record events and memories of recent events.

As with Luz becoming Bethel, or the Anglo-Saxon town of Monkchester becoming the Norman town of Newcastle, conquerors often cannot resist renaming towns and villages. But it is much less common for them to rename natural features. Many rivers, mountains and lakes in Britain still have names dating back to the Bronze or Iron Age, almost as if those names are integral to the natural features' spiritual power. Even more astonishing is that many of the divine names of Britain's rivers and hills are shared with an equally ancient sacred landscape – that of India. These shared names invariably evoke the same spiritual forces that were believed to be incarnate or manifest in the landscape.

RIVER RIVER

In 1085, William the Conqueror ordered an inventory of his new domains – the conquered lands of Anglo-Saxon and Viking England. He wanted to know the full extent of his new kingdom and, more importantly, wanted to assess its potential to be taxed. This mighty work, the first of its kind in England's history, later became known as the Domesday Book (because, like Christ's Last Judgement, it was to be the ultimate authority on who was responsible for what, and what dues they had to pay). To create this great work, William sent hundreds of officials to every corner of the kingdom. Whenever they arrived at a settlement, they ran through a series of questions: what was its name; who had owned it before; how many families comprised the community; what were its crops; how many ploughmen, freemen and livestock lived there? The king's men also noted down the names of important natural features, such as rivers.

It's easy to picture the scene: a rather haughty Norman civil servant hails a group of Anglo-Saxon peasants and loftily demands the name of a particular geographical feature. Quite often, the peasants, probably thinking that the Normans were rather stupid, would reply, 'It's a river!' The British/Anglo-Saxon word for river was *afon*, so the Norman researchers would carefully write 'River Afon' in their books – 'River River'. That explains why there are eight River Avons or Afons in Britain to this day.

The sacred rivers of Britain and their link to India

Astonishingly, the names of many of Britain's rivers have their origins over 5000 miles away, in a culture that also gave birth to the gods and goddesses of India, and they were first written down in that country's ancient language – Sanskrit. These names arrived in Britain long before the Roman invasion of the first century AD. Some believe that they came here as early as the fourth millennium BC, while others argue that they arrived with the Celtic influences of the Iron Age – from around 500 BC onwards. Either way, they are the oldest surviving names in Britain.

All Indo-European languages, of which Sanskrit is the oldest surviving written example, originated in the steppes and mountains of Central Asia. From there, around the second millennium BC, the various Indo-European tribes spread out, with some going south, into India, and others entering Persia before moving on to mainland Europe and eventually Britain. The links between Latin and Sanskrit are easy to spot in any number of common words and phrases: for example, 'father' is *pater* in Latin and *piter* in Sanskrit. The same is true of any terms relating to horsemanship, indicating that most tribes left the steppes on horseback. However, Latin and Sanskrit metalworking terms are not related to each other at all, so these skills must have arisen after the various Indo-European tribes went their separate ways.

I think it's most plausible that Sanskrit-related names arrived in Britain with the Celts. As we saw in Chapter 3, rivers and other elements of the natural world were revered in the simple Celtic religion, in marked contrast to the grand building projects of the preceding stone circle culture. The most powerful images of the Celtic world come from their amazing artwork in metal and stone. Often this is at its most magnificent on their weapons and armour – especially their helmets – which have been dredged from rivers across Britain. These items were probably thrown into the water as offerings because the rivers were viewed as so sacred. They were absolutely central to the Celtic belief system, so it is hardly surprising that their sacred names have survived to this day.

Fast flows the goddess Danu

Danu first appears in the *Rig Veda*, one of the oldest Indian religious texts and revered to this day in Hinduism. She is a fierce and terrifying river deity, with a name that translates as 'swift running' or 'powerfully flowing', and she is remembered in almost any river in Britain that begins with 'Da', 'De' or 'Do'. The pronunciation changed as she travelled with her tribes across the plains and mountains from Central Asia, but en route her name was revered in the naming of such rivers as the Don, the Dneiper and the Danube. In Britain, if your local river begins with the letter 'D', it was probably once sacred and revered (and feared) as a deity. This goes for all of the rivers that are named Don, Dene or Dane, as well as many others.

The awesome spirituality of Danu's name has echoed down the centuries, running like a swift river itself through our history. For example, the River Dane in the Peak District flows past the striking natural gorge known as 'Lud's Chapel'. Lud was the Celtic sky god and the husband of Danu. The medieval story *Sir Gawain and the Green Knight* is set here, and ends with a battle between the two pro- tagonists in Lud's Chapel. Clearly, this had been considered a sacred place and a source of power for millennia.

Dark River Thames

The Sanskrit word *tamasa* translates as 'dark river', and it is the name of one of the tributaries of India's most sacred river, the Ganges. In many belief systems, the notion of a dark river is associated with the underworld; and in the Vedic (Sanskrit) tradition, rivers transport the dead through the underworld and into the next life, hence the prac- tice of casting the ashes of the dead into the Ganges.

In Britain, rivers starting with 'Tam' or 'Ta' are linked to *tamasa*, but remember that the pronunciation has changed over the past few thousand years, so there are other variants, too – most notably the

The upper reaches of the River Thames. The name is linked to the Sanskrit word *tamasa*, meaning dark river.

Thames. The powerful symbolism of the word *tamasa* can also be seen in the fact that the Tamar has formed the boundary between Cornwall and the rest of Britain for hundreds, if not thousands, of years. Other important rivers in this group are the Tavy (Devon), the Tame (Staffordshire) and the Teme (Herefordshire).

Interestingly, the Roman writer Virgil would have known the meaning of such names because *tamasa* is also the root of the River Tiber, which flows through Rome and features in *The Aenead* as the 'dark river'.

The power of Stour
The Sanskrit word *sthavard* means 'strong or powerful river'. It is worth remembering that such a name does more than describe the physical attributes of a river. It also relates to that river's spiritual power, the name of the deity that dwells within it. This name is reflected in all rivers called Stour – of which there are eight in England, with four in Kent alone. This does not reveal a lack of imagination among local tribes but rather a belief that a single, extremely powerful deity surged through all of them. Often it was felt that the best way to honour him was to name the local river after him.

Teva the strong
The Sanskrit word *teva* similarly means 'strong or powerful'. The Taw, in north Devon, and the Tay, which flows from the Scottish Highlands to the Firth of Tay, share this root. The latter is the largest river in the UK in terms of the amount of water is carries and pours into the sea, so it was entirely appropriate that our ancestors acknowledged that power when they named it.

More River Rivers
Some Sanskrit-based names are purely descriptive and have no sacred element, such as the Ouse. This majestic river's name comes from the Sanskrit root *ved* or *ud*, which simply means 'river'. Likewise, the name Humber may have a descriptive Sanskrit root, and in the past this word was applied to many of Britain's streams.

Celtic names

While many rivers' names reveal this extraordinary link between Britain and India, many others are specifically Celtic British – meaning pre-Roman – from which Welsh is derived. Again, there are some key words to look out for.

The cleansing stream

The British word *clouta* means 'cleansing river' and its associated notions of purification and ritual. Clearly, this denotes a sacred river, and it is found in the Clyde in Scotland, the Clydach in Wales and the Clyst in Devon. In dictionaries, the root of this word is usually given as the Latin *cluo*. However, as we have seen, there are many links between Latin and Sanskrit, so originally this may well have been another Sanskrit name.

Waters from the underworld

The word *iska* means 'water that rushes forth'. The Celts believed that water emerged from and returned to the underworld, so such power was both natural and supernatural to them. *Iska* rivers begin with the letters 'E', 'U' or 'A' and include the Exe in Devon, the Axe in Somerset, the Usk on the Welsh Borders and numerous Esks in Scotland and northern England.

Waters of the holy place

Nymet is a very old name for the various tributaries that flow into the river now known as the Yeo, in Somerset, and it is preserved in the names of various villages along the Yeo's course in north Devon, such as Nymet Rowland and Kings Nympton. It comes from the British word *nemeton*, meaning 'holy place', which also features in the Roman name for Buxton in the Peak District, Aquae Arnemetia ('Waters in the Sacred Wood'), and in Nympsfield, Gloucestershire, which literally means 'Field by a Holy Place'.

Shining saint

In Cornwall, the tiny River Allen runs through the city of Truro. Its name comes from the British word *alaunas*, meaning 'bright or shining'. Again, there is a hint of something numinous here. It might also be a good example of the way in which early Christians incorporated earlier beliefs into their new religion. Some four miles inland from Truro, on the River Allen, lies the small village of St Allen, whose Norman church is dedicated to St Alunus. However, there is no St Allen or St Alunus in any of the major biographies of the saints. Some historians have suggested that Alunus was a Breton bishop who came to the area from Wales, but it is just as likely that the name has far more ancient roots that the locals did not wish to abandon.

Holy Brent

Many rivers and hills (see below) – and even one of the pre-Roman tribes of Britain – were named after the word *brent*, which means 'holy'. Examples include the River Brent in Middlesex – which gave rise to Brentford and Brent Cross – and the River Braint on Anglesey. Before the Romans arrived in the first century AD, the Briganti tribe ruled over most of northern England and it is probable that their name is a version of brent.

Descriptive names

The word *frome* means a 'fair or fast river'. It is found in the names of the River Ffraw on Anglesey as well as several Fromes, such as the rivers that flow through Gloucestershire and Somerset and the town Frome. The Wey, Way and Wye (in Dorset, Hampshire and the Welsh Borders, respectively) have the same origin, although this time the name probably describes a 'wandering river'.

HOLY WELLS AND SPRINGS

Recently, I met a vicar from a medium-sized rural town. He was worried about the lack of inter-faith dialogue in his parish. There were no mosques, temples or synagogues in his town – just traditional Christian churches – but he wanted to open up the discussion so that if and when other religious communities arrived, the townsfolk would not feel intimidated. Knowing the town quite well, I pointed out that it was already multi-faith. The books donated to the local charity shops proved that. There were copies of the Hindu scriptures, such as the *Bhagavad Gita*, Daoist texts, such as the *Dao De Jing*, editions of the Qur'an, and various Buddhist books, many by the Dalai Lama. The people of this town were clearly exploring many spiritual and religious traditions in addition to Christianity. They didn't need lectures on those religions but a specific sacred place where they could meet, share that sense of the sacred and start the discussion. I suggested that the vicar should invite people on a pilgrimage from the parish church to the local holy well, which lies about three hundred metres from his church. The well even has a seventh-century saint associated with it and was a healing well. The vicar had no idea it was there, but he soon warmed to the idea, and the pilgrimage duly took place. It is now a regular feature of the exploration of the sacred in that community, and the well once again provides a sacred site where people of any and no religious inclination can celebrate together.

Britain has a thousand or more holy wells, but for centuries the vast majority of them were ignored and lay overgrown and abandoned. However, interest in them has grown over the past century or so, with a number of books written on the topic. There are also local guides to holy wells in many parts of the UK. All of these are worth looking at, as are old tithe maps and old town maps, especially those that pre-date 1848, as that was when many of these wells started to be buried or covered because of the fear of cholera.

The goddess Danu arises

Some wells were sacred for centuries before Christianity arrived in Britain, and there are clues that their sacredness continued in a seamless fashion once the new religion was adopted by local communities. For example, any well or spring dedicated to St Ann (or Anne or Anna) – the mother of the Virgin Mary – was probably a pre-Christian holy well dedicated to the Sanskrit goddess Danu (who was often known as Annu). The process of converting the British countryside to Christianity took some time, as the many Anglo-Saxon and Norman episcopal edicts banning pre-Christian activities bear witness. Promulgation of these edicts finally started to tail off around the start of the thirteenth century, presumably because they were no longer needed, but that was a good seven or eight centuries after Christianity had first arrived in Britain.

St Ann doesn't even make it into the top thirty of church dedications, coming in at a lowly thirty-second, and there is no theological reason why she should be particularly associated with holy wells, yet she is the third most popular Christian dedication for wells in Britain, with over forty still recorded.[23] So we need to find another reason why so many wells were dedicated to her. By far the most plausible explanation is that communities simply dropped the last letter from the traditional names of their wells, perhaps in response to edicts condemning their continuing worship of Annu.

Of wells, heads and the underworld

We know from Roman reports that British tribes hung the heads of captured enemies over their holy wells and springs, which were believed to be doorways into the underworld, charged with sacred power. The Romans banned this practice, so the British started to carve stone heads instead. A remnant of this tradition survived into early Christianity, because a number of holy wells and springs supposedly arose where the head of a saint hit the ground after he or she was decapitated.

One such story concerns a beautiful young woman called Gwenfrewi – known in English as Winifred – who lived in Flintshire, North Wales, in the seventh century. Her uncle, St Beuno, converted her to Christianity, whereupon she decided to dedicate her life to Christ. However, a young chieftain called Caradog was already in love with her, and repeatedly asked her to marry him. She always refused until finally, in a terrible rage, Caradog pursued her, intent on having his way with her. Gwenfrewi fled towards St Beuno's little chapel, but Caradog caught up with her and cut off her head with his sword. A spring instantly gushed from the spot on the ground where her head had fallen. St Beuno, having heard his niece's terrible cry, rushed out of the chapel, picked up Gwenfrewi's head and placed it tenderly on her neck, miraculously restoring her back to life. It was said she lived for many more years, with just a scar to show for the assault.

The holy well at Holywell, where this story took place, still flows to this day. It is also the only well in Britain to retain the typical medieval array of pilgrims' pool, chapel and pilgrims' walkways, and it is still visited daily by those seeking healing in its waters. It was rebuilt and endowed around 1500 by another strong Welshwoman – Margaret Beaufort – which explains how it managed to survive the Reformation's attacks on such places. For Margaret was the mother of Henry VII, the grandmother of Henry VIII and the great-grandmother of Edward VI. By all accounts, she was not someone to be trifled with, even after her death, and certainly not by her direct descendants. So, while virtually every other holy well in England and Wales was destroyed in the 1530s and 1540s, Holywell was left well alone.

It is significant that the place is known simply as Holywell. It is likely that this was a sacred place long before the seventh century, and its new association with St Gwenfrewi merely allowed it to continue to perform that function in the Christian era. Such conversions of sites

Holywell in North Wales is the only surviving complete medieval holy well with a pool, pilgrim walkways and chapel.

from pagan to Christian worship seem to have been extremely common, but they still marked a radical change. The Celtic tradition was of triumph over dead enemies; the Christian was of suffering and redemption. The church of St Martin in North Stoke, Somerset, contains a unique example of this transformation. The font, uniquely, is rectangular. The theory goes that it was originally a Romano-Celtic sacrificial altar to the spirit of the holy well in a nearby field. Made out of local stone, it once featured a carved head at each corner, in that typical echo of the older Celtic tradition of hanging actual heads over sacred wells. When the local area converted to Christianity in the fourth or fifth century, the altar was turned into a font. Part of this process involved chiselling off one of the corner heads. The three that remain now signify the Trinity, and the font as a whole celebrates the

Christian belief that there is no need for any further blood sacrifices because Christ's death was the supreme sacrifice.

Often the simple name 'holy well' reflects the continuity of the sacred and the recognition of the holiness of such places. One very clear example of a holy well with ancient foundations and pre-Roman remains is Holy Well at Wookey in the Cheddar Gorge, Somerset. Prehistoric burials lay around the well, but not complete bodies – just fourteen skulls.

The coming of the saints

With wells called Lady's Well, the lady in question at the time of the Reformation would have been 'Our Lady', the Virgin Mary. However, such wells might have been originally dedicated to a pre-Christian goddess of the spring; quite likely Danu/Annu. It is also possible that the name was changed from one associated with the Virgin Mary at the Reformation to a more generic name in order to lose its former Catholic association.

Another classic case of conversion from a Celtic deity to a Christian saint is provided by the fascinatingly named St Hawthorn's Well, at the Wrekin in Shropshire. There has never been a St Hawthorn, so this must have been a somewhat simplistic attempt to convert an old pagan well into a socially acceptable Christian one. Anywhere called Ashwell also probably indicates the presence of a pre-Christian holy well. The ash was sacred to the Celts (see below), so if one grew by a well, the local community was doubly blessed.

Throughout the Celtic and Gaelic areas of Britain – Cornwall, Wales, Cumbria and Scotland – wells tend to bear the names of a very local holy people who are unknown almost everywhere else and certainly are not to be found in official church hagiographies of saints. Many of these names were probably local Celtic deities, transformed into 'saints' (whether officially acknowledged or not) with the coming of Christianity. Local libraries are excellent places to research the tales and legends associated with these pseudo-saints.

Here be ancient gods

A few wells were never Christianised. For example, Puck wells, such as those at Aynho (Northamptonshire), Rode (Somerset) and West Knoyle (Wiltshire), reflect the old Celtic belief in mischievous spirits. Others retain their original pagan deity names: for instance, Nicker's Well in Church Holme, Cheshire, and Nykarspole, Lincoln, are both derived from the word *nicere*, meaning 'water spirit'. Thor's Well on Spaldingmoor, East Yorkshire, is obviously named after the Norse god. This well is especially interesting because it seems that it was originally pagan, then was Christianised in the seventh or eighth century, but then became pagan again when the Vikings invaded the area in the ninth century.

Fairy wells – sometimes called pits – similarly indicate pre-Christian origins, although they were also places that were feared by Christians over many centuries. The kind, pretty little fairies of nineteenth- and twentieth-century literature would have astonished our Anglo-Saxon and medieval forebears, who not only believed whole-heartedly in these creatures, but thought of them as tiresome, irritating and even deeply dangerous. One fairy well lies next to the strikingly named Wildcountry Lane near Barrow Gurney, Somerset. Close by is Brideswell, which may originally have been dedicated to the pre-Christian goddess Brigid.

Jacob's Well

It was not only Christians who used wells for sacred purposes in the Middle Ages. An area of Bristol has been known as Jacob's Well for centuries. But it was a mystery how it got that name until the 1980s, when an eleventh-century room was excavated near the well itself. Carved over the doorway was the Hebrew word *zochalim*, meaning 'flowing'. The mystery was solved: this was the *mikveh* or ritual bath of the Jewish community of Norman Bristol, and the well was used to purify women before they entered the synagogue.

The shunning of the wells

You may need considerable patience and a good map or history book to find your local wells, because so many of them were hidden or filled in during the Reformation. This was done precisely because they were associated with saints, and were therefore viewed as papist, sources of superstition and even evil. Nevertheless, some survived with secular names because of their supposed health benefits. For example, St Vincent's Hot Spring in Clifton, Bristol, was rebranded as Hotwells in the seventeenth century and was much praised for its healing properties. Daniel Defoe, in *A Tour through England and Wales*, says of the place:

> The water of this well, possess'd its medicinal quality no doubt from its original, which may be as antient as the Deluge. But what is strangest of all is, that it was never known before; it is now famous for being a specifick in that otherwise incurable disease the diabetes; and yet was never known to be so, 'till within these few years; namely, thirty years or thereabout.[24]

By 'the Deluge', Defoe means Noah's Flood, which at the time was widely assumed to be the origin of everything that was visible in the world. Of course, this assumption would be rudely shattered in the next century, not least by the kind of questions that people such as Defoe were beginning to ask.

Apart from the loss of faith in saints as a result of the Reformation, the other main reasons why wells have disappeared (particularly in built-up areas), are cholera and taps. The pollution of the waters by the factories, mills and mines of the Industrial Revolution, and the massive rise in people living in unsanitary and overcrowded conditions in towns and cities, led to wide-scale cholera outbreaks throughout the 1830s and 1840s. These epidemics spread like wildfire through the overcrowded, polluted slums and thousands of people lost their lives. Once the link to water sources was made, hundreds of wells were sealed up and piped water systems were introduced. If you look at maps of towns and cities before the 1840s, there were wells everywhere. The sanitation laws led to the world of piped water, cleansed and secure, and this led in turn to the installation of taps and safe running water in almost every house. The old need for wells was gone and they were not much missed. Unfortunately, we also lost the sense of wonder and awe that such water sources used to provide.

Today, reopening and testing the water of old sacred wells can be both environmentally and spiritually illuminating. If the waters are polluted, usually by agricultural run-off or industrial effluent, they provide a powerful indicator of the extent to which we are abusing the local environment. Meanwhile, reopening and celebrating a sacred well can act as a powerful focus for each and every faith and belief in a community, because everyone is free to bring their own spiritual understanding to such a natural phenomenon. In a number of places, pilgrimage to and reflection upon an ancient, previously forgotten but now rediscovered holy well have recommenced. People are finally finding the time to honour the sacred gifts of nature that we have neglected for so long.

It doesn't take much to find a sacred, natural geography lying just below the surface of our modern world. Old names have persisted because they speak of something timeless. Christian interpretations reflect both the continuity of that sacredness and the need to find a new way of expressing it. When the Sacred Land Project was launched in 1997, one of its first actions was to reopen the ancient holy well of St Mary in Willesden, London – once one of the most popular pilgrims' wells in Britain. Excavations of the site prior to the

reopening revealed evidence of Iron Age and even earlier use, indicating that this was almost certainly a pre-Christian sacred site, too.
The church now uses the water from the well for baptisms, and
passers-by can sit beside it to meditate, pray or just relax. For the first
time in centuries, the ancient name Willesden – which means 'the hill
with the spring' – is entirely appropriate.

There are other traces of old sacred wells throughout the rest of
London. For instance, the Harrow Well translates as 'heathen well',
while Tottenham has four holy wells: Bishop's, St Dunstan's, St
Eligius's and St Mary's. Meanwhile, the route from Old St Pancras
Church to King's Cross (which has a well) and on to St Chad's Well
was known as Paradise Valley because it was considered so sacred –
and was once so beautiful.

ISLANDS

The names of many of Britain's islands speak strongly of a spiritual
significance, and some of them incorporate the names of very powerful deities. Once again, every so often, there will be a Sanskrit link,
weaving its way across the landscape.

Islands of the dead

The drama of the sun setting in the west is perhaps one reason why
pre-Roman Britons believed that the dead dwelt in the Isles of the
Blessed in the far-distant Western Ocean. These were the Celtic alternative to heaven – places where the blessed lived in complete
contentment. Hence the ancient British tradition of laying their dead
to rest in a ship that was pushed out to sea, or burying them in plots
that looked west.

The most famous Scottish holy island is Iona, from where St

Columba launched his mission to convert the Picts in the sixth century. Iona then became the chosen burial place of Scottish kings for several centuries, thereby continuing the association of the west with the dead, but this time under Christianity. Thereafter, though, a new tradition gradually took hold, as Christian graves started to face east – towards the rising sun and towards where paradise, the Garden of Eden, was believed to be. (This also started to be considered the sacred direction of cities and churches, as we will see in the next chapter.)

The island of the sea god

One deity with a large following throughout Iron Age Britain was the Celtic sea god Manannan Maclir. The origins of his name possibly lie in the Sanskrit word *men,* meaning 'to tower'. Certainly, the Isle of Man – named for Manannan Maclir – looks like a towering island when viewed from the sea. The ancient Celtic name for Anglesey – Ynys Mon – might also have been chosen in honour of this deity, and the same could be true of Manan Gododdin, the ancient name for the lower reaches of the Firth of Forth, north of Edinburgh.

From Caesar to the saints

As we have seen, pre-Roman Britons named places because of both their natural appearance and their sacred role or significance. By contrast, the Romans were much more pragmatic in their naming policy. Sometimes they reworked the old names in Latin. On other occasions, they were entirely factual: for instance, their name for Lincoln – Lindum Colonia – means simply 'Colony of the Lake' (the river widens in the town centre), while Venta Icenorum (now Caister St Edmunds, Norfolk) means 'Town of the Iceni Tribe'. However, even the phlegmatic Romans showed respect to a sacred dimension when they came across hot springs, as is clear from their names for Buxton (Aquae Arnemetiae: 'Waters of the Holy Wood') and Bath (Aquae Sulis: 'Waters of the god Sulis').

When Christianity gained a foothold in Britain in the last century or so of the Roman era, the celebration of sacred islands assumed a new character. Many of them were renamed after saints or were simply called 'Holy Island'. There are three of the latter in Britain to this day – one in northern England, one in Scotland and one in Wales – while scores of islands are named after saints. England's Holy Island, also known as Lindisfarne, was home to St Cuthbert in the seventh century, and it still attracts thousands of pilgrims each year. On the shoreline of his holy island you can even find Cuthbert's – or to use the local, familiar name for the saint, Cuddy's – beads. These are in fact the tiny fragments of crinoids – ancient sea plants whose stems were fossilised millions of years ago and, as they break up, create thin circles of fossil with a hole in the middle. Legend says that Cuthbert would string these together to make prayer beads.

The vast majority of the saints' islands lie off the coasts of Wales, Scotland and Ireland, revealing the fusion of Celtic Christianity with the much older tradition of the mysteries of the west. Some of them still fulfil their original Christian purpose of providing secluded places for prayer and meditation: Caldey Island is home to a community of Cistercian monks; Bardsey is used for very austere retreats (it can be cut off for days at a time by the sea); Iona hosts an ecumenical community; Holy Island, off Arran, is a multi-faith retreat centre run by Tibetan Buddhists; and Lindisfarne has a number of retreat centres alongside the ruins of the ancient abbey. The sacredness of many of these places has been rediscovered and reasserted over the last century or so, and especially since the 1960s.

In Wales, St Margaret's Island lies beside Caldey Island, also known as Pyr's Island – perhaps named after another, more local saint. Off Abersoch, on the Llyn Peninsula, there is St Tudwal's Island, while off the western tip of the same peninsula is the mystical, magical Bardsey Island. Here, according to legend, once lay the remains of ten thousand saints. However, Norman barons visited Bardsey and dug up the graves of many of the saints, including St Deimiol and St Dyfrig, in the hope that these relics would boost their power. They then constructed great cathedrals around them, but all of the relics were either destroyed or lost in the Reformation.

Three of the Isles of Scilly are named after saints – Martin, Mary and Agnes – but these date only from the Middle Ages, so they probably derived from the names of the local churches.

Avalon

As many a festival-goer will report, the land around Glastonbury is still very boggy. However, before this whole area was drained in the early Middle Ages, it was so waterlogged that the high ground in the centre formed a true island. Known as Avalon, legend has it that this was the burial place of King Arthur. In the twelfth century, the monks of Glastonbury Abbey even claimed to have found Arthur's tomb. It has to be said that sceptics raised doubts about the authenticity of this story even then, mainly because the abbot needed money for a quite ambitious rebuilding project and was keen to attract pilgrims.

The ancient Welsh name for Glastonbury was Ynyswitrin, which might have meant either 'Island of Woad' (the plant from which Celtic war-paint was made) or 'Island of Glass'. In Celtic mythology, the underworld was sometimes depicted as made of glass, and islands were seen as doorways to the underworld.

HILLS

Like islands, many hills retain their ancient names and sacred connotations. They feature in every great story around the world – biblical, Norse, Chinese, Japanese, Mayan and so on – and are often seen as exceptionally sacred places. They are the points where heaven and earth touch; places of trial and revelation. Think of Moses on Mount Sinai, Jesus on the Mount of Transfiguration and Muhammad on Jerusalem's Temple Mount. Every Daoist sage had his or her own mountain, too. The remoteness and the lack of intrusion of the human world on rugged hilltops and mountains have only enhanced their perceived spirituality over the millennia.

Some hills are simply named Brent, which, as we saw above, means 'holy'. This name might be applied to whole outcrops, such as Brent Knoll, Dorset, but often it is applied locally to some particularly sacred aspect of a hill. Elsewhere, though, hills have been associated for millennia with specific gods and saints.

The Mother Goddess Mountain – and Manchester

I first saw Mam Tor in Derbyshire on a wet, cold day many years ago, when visiting the wonderful ruined castle at Castleton. Below the castle lies one of the Peak District's treasures – the dramatic cave system that the Victorians named the Peak Caverns. More recently, those caves have reverted to their traditional name – the Devil's Arse – on account of the strange winds and noises that rise from their depths. Not surprisingly, the number of visitors has risen dramatically since the reversion to the old name.

The huge, looming mass of Mam Tor lies to the west of the castle. It is composed primarily of shale rather than solid rock, and is nick-named the 'shivering mountain' because of its instability. This powerful, brooding place also has one of the holiest names of any hill in Britain. For Mam Tor means 'Mountain of the Mother'. Mam can also be translated as 'breast' or 'womb', which clearly carries a similar sacred feminine connotation. (In Ireland, the word 'paps' is used to describe this type of landscape. For instance, in County Kerry there are the Paps of Danu – the Breasts of Danu.)

The word 'mam' occurs in a number of other hill names throughout

The sacred mountain of Mam Tor is now protected by the Daoist and Romantic notion of wilderness as a place of human rest and recovery from the urban world.

the British Isles, and especially in Scotland. Almost all of them were sacred. The Roman settlement of Mamucium took its name from the small hill upon which it was built. Today, it is known as Manchester. Incidentally, the road leading to Mam Hill is Deansgate, which takes its name from the Dene River – another river named after the Sanskrit goddess Danu. It is possible that these two natural features were linked in the belief system of pre-Roman Britons – the breast-shaped hill and the river dedicated to the goddess. Such a thought certainly causes you to look at central Manchester quite differently.

A sky god – or possibly not

Some people believe that the name of the Pennines, which make up the mountainous backbone of northern England, derives from the Celtic sky god Poeninus.[25] However, this name was not recorded until the eighteenth century, and it might just have been taken from the Celtic word for hill – 'pen' – as in Penrith ('Ford by the Hill'). It might even have been invented by antiquarians. Nevertheless, the link between hills and the sky is obvious, and several hills have been named because of it. For example, on the Isle of Skye, there is the Beinn-na-Greine – 'Mountain of the Sun' – which strongly hints at a spiritual and physical link between the hill and the sky.

St Giles' Hill

The sacred dimension of some hills was made explicit by naming them after saints: for example, St Giles' Hill, outside Winchester. This name reveals more than the mere fact that the hill was a holy place, because in the Middle Ages St Giles was invariably associated with lepers and the disabled (see the box on St Giles in Chapter 5). For instance, near the Barbican in London, the church of St Giles' Cripplegate now occupies the site where a hospital once stood. The hill near Winchester once housed a hospital too, for which it raised money through a famous annual fair.

Whenever a hill has been named after St Michael or St Catherine, the chances are that it was a very ancient sacred site, far pre-dating the arrival of Christianity in Britain. We shall explore the stories and associations of these two saints in the next chapter.

Towards the end of the eleventh century, King William II granted Bishop Walkelin the right to hold a three-day fair on and around the feast day of St Giles – 1 September. Walkelin was also given special dispensation to keep any money raised (especially tolls), and used it to fund the local hospital. The length of the fair steadily increased over the next century: Henry I granted five days; King Stephen six; and Henry II twelve. Ultimately, the fair

▶

usually ran for sixteen days, although this could rise to twenty-four days in exceptional years. Despite the noble cause for which it was founded, the fair tended to be an extremely rowdy, bawdy affair, and it was finally suppressed after a near riot.

Hill Hill Hill Hill

A surprising number of hills are known simply as the Hill. That worked fine when all of the people living in the vicinity of the Hill shared the same language, but it became complicated when new groups moved into the area and wanted to give the Hill a name they could understand. Torpenhow Ridge, near Plymouth, is a supreme example of what can happen in this sort of situation, because *tor* is Anglo-Saxon for hill, *pen* is Celtic for hill, *how* is Norse for hill, and *ridge* is Middle English for hill. So this hill's name is Hill Hill Hill Hill! Kinder Scout, the highest peak in the Peak District, gets the first half of its name from the Celtic word for 'high' – *celto* – while *scout* is Old Norse for 'High Hill'. In effect, then, this is the High High Hill. The Chilterns, stretching from Oxfordshire to Hertfordshire, derive their name from *celto*, too, as does Cheltenham, which sits in the shadow of a dramatic high hill. Finally, the Malverns are named after the Celtic for 'Bare Hills' – *moel* meaning bare and *fryn* meaning hill – while the Long Mynd in Shropshire means simply 'Long Mountain' – a very apt description.

Lost names

The Victorians were very keen on changing the names of natural features, either to make them more romantic or simply because they didn't understand the significance of the original names and wanted to use what they thought were better descriptions. For instance, the name Kelston Round Hill now exactly describes the main feature of a circular hill in Somerset. But the old name of this hill was Henstridge (still preserved in the name of the old barn at the bottom of the hill), meaning 'Place of the Stallion'. Given that this hill top is visible for miles, could it have been where a tribal standard flew? Or was it where the chieftain's horse was kept? Exploring an old name like this opens so many more doors than the purely descriptive Victorian names sometimes do. It is interesting to note however that sometimes a name has been attached that brings the past to life – for example, Battle Hill or Hanging Hill (I explore this in Chapter 8, Walking on the Dead).

SACRED FIELDS

In the late 1960s, my godmother took me to a high point on the Quantock Hills on a bright and sunny late autumn day. The light that falls as autumn takes hold is at such an angle that it highlights details in the landscape that are bleached out by the strength of the summer sun. From our vantage point – and with the aid of the autumn light – she took me on an astonishing journey through time, simply by telling me about the fields that lay beneath us.

It was as if I saw the landscape for the first time, not in terms of ruined castles or abbeys, ancient churches and burial mounds, scattered villages and the great estates and houses which were all visible from the hilltop. Instead she showed me the way we had carved the landscape to provide us with food and, in doing so, had told our story even more clearly than in the buildings we had raised. She took me on a journey from the earliest farmers struggling to cut fields from the forests, through the Roman and Anglo-Saxon stories of the land and of God, to the medieval world. From there she told me of the Enclosure Acts and the violence done to the land, people and the sense of the sacred. She showed me how the straight lines of the square fields told a very different tale from that of earlier field systems and how this had laid the ground for the destruction of hundreds of thousands of hedgerows in the 50s and 60s, as the drive for profit grubbed up nature and history. This was in the late 60s so although she was involved in the early organic farming movement, she could not have guessed how it would come to tell its own story, but I know she would have rejoiced at the progress made – but hope for yet more to come.

I have never been able to look at fields in the same way since. I love the way that they can reveal our ancestors' great sacred stories in their lines and shapes. This is beautifully captured by Prue Fitzgerald in her poem 'We Have Forgotten the Names':

> We have forgotten the names
> We ignore the places
> And the face of God
> Lies unrecognised
> In the fallow fields
> Of our desecration
>
> Become the flower
> Of the rock's memory.
> Be heard as the groan
> Of the high mountains of the world
> And in the curve
> Of the straight line,
> Behold your God.[26]

Wandering through the British countryside, you can still see traces of all of the great stories, in spite of the best efforts of agri-businesses. Ancestor worship is literally embodied in the long barrows in which communities laid their founders to rest. Back then, the land and faith were inextricably linked. When that belief system died out at the end of the First Great Cycle, the model of farming continued, but now it served the needs of people who worshipped at stone circles. In turn, when that great cycle collapsed, it seems that the sacred focus shifted to the fields themselves. The people were now reluctant to put their faith in any designated holy spaces, so they invested much of their sacred energy in their own rapidly growing farms (in addition to natural features, such as rivers and springs). However, several centuries of Roman mismanagement resulted in the land becoming exhausted and the third great collapse. Eventually, though, monastic Christianity rebuilt the farming landscape and facilitated the development of the villages of Britain that we know today.

This brings us to a particularly fascinating aspect of the British landscape. In the farmland around ancient villages, you will find corners and sides of fields that are overgrown or wooded – small patches of wilderness. This is because the model for good farming used by the monasteries was based upon a book in the Old Testament of the Bible: Ruth.

Ruth herself is not an Israelite, but she marries an Israelite who has moved to her homeland with his family. When her husband dies, Ruth loyally decides to accompany her mother-in-law on her return to Israel. In a moving scene, the mother-in-law tries to persuade Ruth to create a new life for herself, but Ruth replies:

> Wherever you go, I shall go,
> Wherever you live, I shall live.
> Your people will be my people,
> and your God will be my God.[27]

Once in Israel, the two women initially live in poverty. Then, one day, Ruth goes into the fields around their village to collect corn left around the edges by the reapers. She is able to do this because the wealthy landowner, Boaz, has obeyed Israelite law, as laid down in Leviticus 19:9–10:

And when ye reap the harvest of you land, thou shall not wholly reap the corners of thy field, neither shalt thou garner the gleanings of thy harvest. And thou shalt not glean thy vineyard, neither shalt thou gather every grape of thy vineyard; thou shalt leave them for the poor and stranger.

Boaz notices Ruth gleaning the corners, falls in love with her, and they marry.

For those who heard this love story it was an example, divinely ordained, of how to look after land with compassion. Through this story the idea of leaving areas of your fields not just for the poor but also for other creatures to live within, became part of farming practice in Europe and, through monasticism, part of our tradition in Britain. Further afield, this tradition was codified into Islamic law, which forbids both destruction of animals' habitats and denying someone in need access to a water source, fruit trees or crops. The Prophet Muhammad even said that planting a tree is an act of charity because it allows birds to shelter in it and other creatures to feed off it.

One of the main forms that this story took in the landscape was through small fields, and the survival of small fields around the world is one of the objectives of the Alliance of Religions and Conservation, and the Sacred Land project, because these fields express not just a profound sense of the sacred in relation to the land, but also the importance of small local communities.

This tradition led to the development of small-field systems in Britain's farms in the early Middle Ages. These could be one of two types: strip lynchets; or ridge and furrow fields. Lynchets run along the contours of hillsides and are easily spotted because they look like waves frozen on the landscape. The upper part of a lynchet rises to meet the one above and drops down with a curve to meet the rising side of the one below. This pattern is formed by centuries of ploughing along the side of the hill. By contrast, ridge and furrow fields tend to be on level ground. They can be identified by the distinctive 'S' shape at the end of each strip, caused by the turning of the plough over centuries. Modern farming has destroyed the vast majority of these fields, but traces of them are still visible where the land is now used mostly for grazing. For instance, around Cheswick, just south of Berwick on Tweed, and to the east of Doddington, Northumberland, you can still see the patterns of these ancient fields.

Both of these field types were eventually superseded by the open field system. In the eighth and ninth centuries, the invention of a more powerful but less easily turned plough led to lynchets and ridge and furrow fields being turned into much longer 'furlong' fields. These were so named because they were judged to be the length of a furrow that a farmer could plough in one day – eventually formalised at 220 yards. Most of these have disappeared now, too; but some can still be found, often lined by old hedgerows, as in the fields surrounding Butterton in Staffordshire, where they radiate from the village in all

© Topfoto

The vast fields and intensive farming methods demanded by modern agriculture has meant the loss of ancient field systems, hedges, woods and lanes. This has not just destroyed centuries of history in the landscape but also vital wildlife habitats.

directions. Only one village still farms its land in this traditional way: Laxton, in Nottinghamshire. Uniquely, these fields are not worked as part of some tourist heritage trail. Rather, they form part of the real agricultural life of the place, just as they have for a millennium.

In addition to the guidelines provided by the Book of Ruth, the village way of life in the Middle Ages was founded on a deep-rooted belief that God cared for each and every individual. As the Gospel of Matthew (10:30) puts it, 'every hair on your head has been numbered'. Theologically speaking, every villager was part of a huge family that included not just the rest of humanity but all of nature. This allowed even the most humble, feudally obligated peasant to feel part of a greater story, as is revealed in the medieval poem *Piers Plowman*. Here, the honesty and integrity of a simple ploughman are set against the corruption of the ruling classes and especially the Church.

William Langland, a frequently poverty-stricken cleric, is credited with writing *Piers Plowman* at some point in the late fourteenth century. The poem is structured around the ritual year of the Church, starting with the Nativity, going through Epiphany and Lent to Easter, then on through Pentecost to Advent. This is paralleled by the sacred history of the Bible, from the patriarchs and the prophets to the story of Christ. Through these grand narratives, *Piers Plowman* reveals how ordinary people viewed and made sense of the world in the 1300s.

In this poem, and in other texts written around the same time, the ploughman serves as an allegory for Christ – true, steadfast and honourable, in touch with the earth and nature, not corrupted by power, politics, wealth or the Church. In short, he is part of the greater narrative of love and integrity.

This traditional vision was shattered from the late seventeenth century onwards. The integral relationship between the land, those who worked in the fields and God passed into history, to be replaced by utilitarianism (see Chapter 3). This was exemplified in the new practice of landowners enclosing common land to form vast new fields of extraordinary regularity. In England and Wales, this land grab was known as 'the Enclosure', after the Acts of Parliament that sanctioned it. Something similar happened in Highland Scotland with 'the Clearances'. Many farm workers and their families were made redundant and lost their access to the land. They were no longer able to eke out even a basic level of survival, and so were forced to emigrate – usually to the burgeoning cities of Britain but sometimes much further afield, such as America. The results of this process still form the basis of modern farming in Britain. The fields are regular – often square or rectangular – and are edged by hawthorn hedges, which were planted because they grew quickly and soon provided cattle- and deer-proof barriers around the agricultural land.

In Scotland, the Clearances were so called because they involved clearing away hundreds of farmsteads, hamlets and even entire villages and turning the land into pasture for the sheep flocks of a few powerful families. The ruins of farmhouses, village streets and churches can still sometimes be spotted in these enormous estates and moorland landscapes. Famous examples are the remains of Glencalvie in the Highlands and Strathnaver in Sutherland. Such places no longer appear on most road maps of Britain; only detailed OS maps show where they once stood.

The personal God of the medieval period gave way to the more intellectual, abstruse God of the utilitarians and Enlightenment thinkers. Those who carved the landscape into neat squares in order to make it more profitable did so because their God was the 'Great Architect' who had set the world in motion but was no longer involved in its day-to-day running. Humanity functioned best within the rules and laws established by this God – such as gravity – by being as mathematical and systematic as possible. Furthermore, the rest of nature was now viewed as no more than a resource to be exploited.

For instance, in the mid-seventeenth century, Henry More praised God for creating cattle and sheep in such a way that their meat remained fresh 'till we shall have need to eat them'.[28] It was this change in attitude towards nature that allowed common land to be annexed so brutally and villagers to be cleared from their homes in the name of greater efficiency. Neither animals nor the lower orders mattered in a world without a personal God and with no sense of the whole of humanity being part of nature.

To illustrate this, consider the shift away from seeing livestock as co-witnesses to the birth or Christ, which is evident in any traditional nativity scene, to the human-centric, utilitarian approach exemplified by eighteenth and nineteenth century artists.

Sadly, despite the lobbying efforts of such organisations as Compassion in World Farming, which have led to animals being defined as sentient beings in EU law, this view of the natural world persists to this day. We 'factory-farm' animals, especially chickens, and of course inherent in that dreadful phrase itself is a whole host of utilitarian beliefs. In fact, we have gone even further down the utilitarian line. Farmers have cleared thousands of miles of hedgerows in order to create vast fields, devoid of anywhere for most wildlife to find shelter or food. In the process, topsoil has been lost and the land no longer has the ability to regenerate itself because of an over-reliance on chemical fertilisers. Consequently, we have polluted most of our streams and rivers with run-off chemicals.

However, in the mid-twentieth century, a group of primarily Quaker and Anglican farmers started to fight back with a vision of a more holistic way of farming. They called their new system 'organic' because it followed nature, working with it rather than against it. Gradually, this notion of forging a relationship with nature, rather than exploiting it or even battling against it, started to have an impact. The development of organic farming over the past forty years marks a return to a greater narrative in which we, God and nature all work together. Now, when our fields tell their stories, we might be able to hear them.

SACRED TREES

In addition to natural features of the landscape, certain plants – and especially trees – have been a focus of sacred attention for millennia. In the Christian era, this has reflected a sense that nature itself is a second book of God which complements His written book – the Bible.

The yew

The oldest living things in Britain are sacred trees: three yews that are believed to be over five thousand years old.[29] The most ancient of the three, in Fortingall churchyard, Perth and Kinross, might even be seven thousand years old. All of the important history of Britain, from Neolithic peoples to the present day, has occurred during the lifetime of this tree. It may have begun its life around the same time that nearby stone circles were erected, or it may already have been three thousand years old when those monuments were conceived. Several millennia later, the sacredness of the place was acknowledged by the first Christians in the area, who built a church beside the yew. That same sense of sacredness also gave rise to an extraordinary story which claimed that Pontius Pilate was born here. Of course, the legend almost certainly has no basis in fact. But it is significant because it links this ancient, sacred site to the most significant events in the Christian story. In this way, the legend ensured that the tree and all it represented were not bypassed or made redundant by the coming of Christianity. It is powerful evidence of the symbolic significance of the yew in both pre-Christian and Christian Britain.

Many churches with ancient yew trees have been built close to standing stones or stone circles. Sometimes the stones are even within the bounds of the churchyard itself. For example, at Kennington, in Kent, a 2000-year-old yew stands opposite the church on an ancient burial mound; in Knowlton, Dorset, the church was erected within the banks of a henge and near to 3000-year-old yew trees; and at Llanerfyl, in Powys, there is a fifth- or sixth-century AD pre-Christian inscribed burial stone beside the church as well as a 1600-year-old yew.

The common yew (*Taxus baccata*) is indigenous to the British Isles, and the earliest fossil record of one here (a species known as *Taxus jurassica*) dates from 140 million years ago. It is also indigenous to Scandinavia, where it is almost certainly the cosmic tree Yggdrasil – the tree of knowledge and life, and the pillar of the universe. The Druids' sacred groves were probably formed of yews, too. When a yew grows, it can create a ring of off-shoots with a clear space in the centre. It is likely that these natural rings were used by the Druids as ritual centres. The traditional Christmas yule log is also fashioned from a yew tree. And it is said that the Magna Carta was signed under a giant yew tree on Runnymede in 1215. That tree still stands today.

Clearly, then, the yew has been considered sacred by Christians, Celts and even earlier people. But why? The answer probably lies in its ability to survive – it is a symbol of eternity. The yew can stop growing when conditions are unsuitable; and then, decades or even centuries later, it can spring back to life as if nothing had happened. Many yews have been chopped down unnecessarily because people have incorrectly assumed they are dead. But in churchyards little changes over time, so yews have tended to survive better within their confines.

Yew branches were laid to rest alongside the dead in barrows, which seems to indicate that these trees were sacred to Neolithic peoples, as does their frequent presence at or near major Neolithic sites. The persistence of the yew through centuries of change must have had a major psychological impact on Neolithic and Bronze Age societies. Scholars have commented on ancient yew trees almost since written records began in this country, and it is fair to assume that the oral tradition of pre-literate Britain did the same.

Oak and ash trees

The oak and the ash both have sacred connotations, but neither lives more than seven hundred years, so few individual trees can lay claim to any sacred status. However, one or two are worthy of note. Carmarthen's museum now houses what remains of Merlin's Oak (see Chapter 6). This tree – along with many others – was probably planted in 1660 to celebrate King Charles II's coronation. In 1651, when escaping from the Parliamentarian forces after his defeat in the Battle of Worcester, Charles took refuge in a vast oak whose branches concealed him from his enemies. For many years after the Restoration, 29 May was celebrated as Oak-Apple Day, and oak leaves were worn to commemorate the king's 'miraculous' escape. To many, it seemed as if the oak had cared for Charles and had performed a sacred rite in preserving him.

The oak was linked to the sky god, often known as Penneos Jupiter in Britain, combining a Celtic god with a Roman one. As oaks usually stand alone, they provide a perfect target for lightning, which adds to their drama and probably explains their link with the sky god. Mistletoe was considered especially blessed because it was believed to grow on oak trees that had been struck by lightning. The oak thus became the wand of the sky god, and its twisted shape is reflected in the shape of a Druid's staff.

The ash was also thought to possess great power. As we saw earlier, many holy wells are named after ash trees, and it seems that the presence of the tree was very important to the Celts who first decreed that these places were sacred. The oldest well at Glastonbury is called Ashwell; at Ashover, in Derbyshire, the holy well was originally covered by an ash tree; Ashstead Well, in Surrey, was originally known simply as Ash Well; and at Myddle, in Shropshire, there is Astwell.

There were surely many more 'ash wells' before the arrival of Christianity and the renaming of sacred wells after saints.

DISCOVERING THE SACRED BOOK OF NATURE

As we begin to understand that without respect for the natural features of our world, we are in danger of abusing or even destroying them, it is time to recover what our ancestors knew only too well. The land you walk upon, the miracle of fresh water and the glories of nature are all sacred gifts; they are the other Book or Revelation of the Creator and the meaning of creation itself. They should be respected, treasured and protected, because they protect us in return.

GAZETTEER

Sacred rivers

- Allen, Cornwall: from the British word *alaunas*, meaning 'bright' or 'shining'
- Avon: from the Anglo-Saxon word *afon*, meaning 'river'
- Braint, Anglesey; Brent, Middlesex: from the British word *brent*, meaning 'bright' or 'shining'
- Clyde, Scotland; Clydach, Wales; Clyst, Devon: from the British pre-Roman word *clouta*, meaning 'cleansing river'
- Dane, Peak District: named after the river deity Danu
- Exe, Devon; Axe, Somerset: from the word *iska*, meaning 'water that rushes forth'
- Ffraw, Anglesey; Frome, Somerset: from the word *frome*, meaning 'fair, or fast, river'
- Humber, Lincolnshire: may have a Sanskrit root
- Nymet Rowland and Kings Nympton, north Devon; Nympsfield, Gloucestershire: from the word *nymet*, a very old name for the various tributaries that flow into the River Yeo in Somerset
- Ouse, North Yorkshire: from the Sanskrit root *ved* or *ud*, which simply means 'river'
- Severn, south-west England: from the Latin name *Sabrina*
- Stour, Kent: one of many rivers with this name in Britain, from the Sanskrit word *sthavard*, meaning 'strong, or powerful, river'
- Thames; Tamar, Cornwall; Tavy, Devon; Tame, Staffordshire; Teme, Herefordshire: from the Sanskrit word *tamasa*, meaning 'dark river'
- Taw, north Devon; Tay, Scotland: from the Sanskrit word *teva*, meaning 'strong' or 'powerful'
- Way, Hampshire; Wey, Dorset; Wye, Welsh Borders: root is uncertain, but probably means 'wandering river'

Holy wells

All the following are places where holy wells or their remains can be seen.

Wales
- Holywell, North Wales (CH8): the only well in Britain to retain its full medieval array of pilgrims' pool, chapel and pilgrims' walkways (see page 103)

Northern England
- Nicker's Well, Church Holme, Cheshire (CW1)
- St Hawthorn's Well, the Wrekin, Shropshire (SY5)

Southern England
- Harrow Well, Harrow, London (HA7)
- Holy Well, Wookey, Cheddar Gorge, Somerset (BS27)
- Holy Well of St Mary, Willesden, London (NW10)
- Holy Well, King's Cross, London (N1)

- Jacob's Well, Brandon Hill, Bristol (BS35)
- St Martin's (church), North Stoke, Somerset (BA1)
- St Vincent's Hot Spring, Clifton, Bristol (BS8)
- West Knoyle, Wiltshire (BA12)
- Fairy Well, Wildcountry Lane, near Barrow Gurney, Somerset (BS48)

Holy islands

Scotland
- Holy Island, Arran (KA27): owned by the Tibetan Buddhist community at Samyeling, this is a now an interfaith retreat centre
- Isle of Iona, Scotland (PA76): the monastery of St Columba and the burial place of many of the Scottish (Pictish) kings, now the centre of an international retreat and social engagement Christian movement, the Iona Community

Wales
- Anglesey (Ynys Mon) (LL77): major Druid centre destroyed by the Romans c.60 AD
- Bardsey Island, Pwllheli, Gwynedd (LL53): isle of the 20,000 saints
- Caldey Island, Tenby (SA70): ancient monastic retreat now the home of a Catholic religious order
- St Margaret's Island, Tenby (SA70)
- St Tudwal's Island, Llyn Peninsula (LL53)

Northern England
- Holy Island (Lindisfarne), Berwick-upon-Tweed, Northumbria (TD15): the island of St Cuthbert and a major centre for pilgrimage

Southern England
- Avalon (now Glastonbury), Somerset (BA6): most mythologised landscape in Britain
- Isles of Martin, Mary and Agnes, Scilly Isles (TR21)

Isle of Man
- Isle of Man, Irish Sea: named after a Celtic god

Sacred hills

Scotland
- Beinn-na-Greine, Isle of Skye, Scotland (IV47): name means 'Mountain of the Sun'

Northern England
- Kinder Scout, Derbyshire (S33): from the Celtic word *kinder*, meaning 'high', and the Old Norse word *scout*, meaning 'high hill'
- Long Mynd, Shropshire (SY6): translates as 'Long Mountain'
- Mam Hill, Deansgate, Manchester (M3): the 'Man' in Manchester is actually the Celtic word mam for breast and the Deansgate takes its name from the sacred stream Dene
- Mam Tor, Derbyshire (S33): means 'Mountain of the Mother'

Southern England
- Brent Knoll, Somerset (TA9)
- Chilterns, Oxfordshire/Herefordshire: name derives from the Celtic word *celto*, meaning 'high'
- Kelston Round Hill, Bath (BA1): Victorian rename of older Henstridge Hill, meaning Place of the Stallion

- St Giles' Hill, Winchester (SO23): this name is usually associated with hospitals for lepers and the disabled
- Torpenhow Ridge, Plymouth, Devon (PL1): translates as 'hill hill hill hill'

Sacred fields

The following have sites where ancient field systems can still be seen.

Scotland
- Site of Glencalvie, Scottish Highlands (IV19): a 'clearance' village destroyed in the early nineteenth century for sheep farming
- Site of Strathnaver, Sutherland, Scotland (KW11): a 'clearance' village site

Northern England
- Butterton, Staffordshire (ST13): good examples of furlong fields from the medieval period
- Cheswick, Ancroft, Northumberland (TD15): many examples of ridge and furrow fields from the Anglo-Saxon to medieval period
- Doddington, Northumberland (NE71): good examples of ridge and furrow visible from the hill down on to the farmland
- Laxton, Nottinghamshire (NG22): last village which farms using furlong fields

Southern England
- Quantocks, Somerset (BA2):

many different field systems visible on and around the Quantocks, especially looking south

Yew trees

Scotland
- Fortingall churchyard, Perth and Kinross (PH15): oldest living tree in Britain, thought to be between 4000 and 7500 years old

Wales
- Llanerfyl, Powys (SY21): ancient Christian site with contemporary yew tree from c.500 AD

Southern England
- Kennington, Kent (TN25): over 2000 years old and sited opposite the church and on an ancient burial mound
- Knowlton, Dorset (BH21): 3000-year-old yews in a charged and ancient sacred landscape
- Runnymede, Egham, Surrey (TW20): the Magna Carta is said to have been signed under this yew tree in 1215

Sacred oak and ash trees

Wales
- Merlin's Oak, Carmarthen, Dyfed (SA31): fragment in museum of myth-laden tree

Southern England
- Ashwell, Glastonbury (BA6): one of the sacred wells of Glastonbury

PART TWO

BUILDING SACRED BRITAIN

Having explored some of the great movements and disasters of the past, we now turn our attention to uncovering evidence of them on the ground. Part One was a journey into the beliefs and stories that have shaped the landscape of Britain. In Part Two, I want to show you how to spot them in the grand buildings – burial mounds, stone circles, churches and castles – and in the small details – the shape of a field, the bend in a road or the missing detail on a Georgian façade.

All around us lie the clues not just to the past, but to understanding the sacred that has created that has created that past and where we are today. In the following chapter we uncover what those clues are, how to understand them and what they mean. By beginning to piece together the clues of what forces, what stories, what disasters have brought us to where we are today, we might just be better equipped to comprehend our current state of affairs. We are in the end days of the latest great story – and if you have skipped Part One then you need to just go back and find out what that story is. The future will depend upon the story or stories we decide to live in and at this moment we have a number of possible alternatives. By travelling through Part Two we can arrive at a much clearer picture of where we are heading and why. Through the details we can understand the bigger picture and through the bigger picture, begin to find our own place within the story.

Human beings are storytellers. That is how we make sense of the world and our place within it. In these chapters we can see how this was done in the past and how, even to this day, the stories that have been told and have lived over the last six to seven thousand years still shape us – for better or for worse.

5

How to read the story of a church

Step into this porch, port
for the ship of faith
between the worn corbel faces of a king and his forgotten queen
feeling the sea-swell under you
in the stillness of stone
in the cool out of the sun.[30]

Growing up in vicarages, I was always fascinated by the sacred layout of churches. In particular, I was intrigued by the fact that virtually every ancient church faced east. If you found yourself lost in any old town, you could always use its church as a compass point.

However, when I asked adults about this, I usually received a very odd reply. Most people said that, just as Muslims face Mecca for their prayers, Christians like to face Jerusalem, where Christ was crucified. This left me totally confused because I knew that Jerusalem was not east of Britain; it is most definitely south-east. So, either every church architect in the land had no access to a compass, or they were all saying something else entirely when they drew their blueprints. Even if you subscribe to the view that medieval builders were unsure where Jerusalem was, it seems certain that they would not have located it due east of the British Isles. A quick look at a medieval map – such as the late thirteenth-century *Mappa Mundi* in Hereford Cathedral – puts Jerusalem at the centre of the world, while Britain is far to the north-east, approximately where Oslo is in reality.

Then, in my early thirties, I went to Jordan and discovered that all of the Christian churches in that country face east, too – even though Jerusalem is almost due west of Jordan. What was going on?

I finally found the answer when discussing this issue with some Orthodox priests, who told me that all of their churches faced not Jerusalem but the rising sun and that this was also believed to be the direction of Eden itself. They said they were built in this way in recognition of the coming of the light each morning, a sentiment that echoes the opening chapter of Genesis, where God brings the world into being and then creates day to follow night. This is a frank acknowledgement of the sun as the source of all life on earth, which in most faiths' theologies is itself a divine gift.

So why, as a boy, was I told something different? The answer probably lies in the fact that there is a deep embarrassment in both the Established Church and British society as a whole about our spiritual traditions and heritage. It is much easier to pretend that a human-built holy city lies to the east, which is why we pray in that direction, rather than enter into discussion about 'pagan' ideas and symbolism, veneration of the sun and mythological lands such as Eden.

But we need to have that discussion because British people have been praying in the direction of the rising sun for hundreds of years in the name of Christianity. This is even explicit in certain church traditions. For example, vigils have long been held in churches throughout Easter Saturday night in order to see the sun rising through the great east window at dawn. The idea is that such services aid remembrance of Christ rising from the tomb. Somehow, though, this has become divorced from the wider recognition that Christianity effectively venerates the sun, albeit symbolically.

Discovering this link between Christianity and the veneration of the rising sun set me on a path of exploration. I learned that the layout of a church is mystical, revealing depths of symbolism and meaning that our ancestors knew instinctively but that we, in our post-Enlightenment rejection of such mysteries, only half remember – if we remember them at all. The direction of the rising sun is only one aspect of the mystical symbolism of the average British parish church. I want to take you on a journey to, around and within such a church. First, we will look at a typical Anglican church – although, if it were built before 1530, it would once have been a Catholic church, too. Then, at the end of the chapter, we shall examine Nonconformist and Methodist chapels and meeting houses, most of which were built between the seventeenth and the nineteenth centuries.

© Akg-imagaes/Bildarchiv Monheim

St Laurence Church in Bradford-on-Avon is the only surviving complete Anglo-Saxon church. It preserves the unique Anglo-Saxon internal layout, including going down to the sanctuary rather than up.

THE IMPORTANCE OF DEDICATION

The dedication will often tell you a great deal about who built a church and why. Remember, though, that many churches have changed their names over the years. For instance, since the Reformation, some churches have dropped their original saints' names, especially local ones (see the section below on local saints). Instead, they opted for less controversial and Papist-sounding dedications – such as Christ Church – to emphasise their belief on the uniqueness of Christ. St John the Baptist was another popular reformers' dedication, because his simple, austere lifestyle appealed to them. Moreover, John called people to repent, something Puritans were very keen to do. Many churches built since the eighteenth century have been built with little understanding or knowledge of the older Christian geomantic tradition.

Below is a list of some of the saints who frequently appear in church dedications.

The major saints

- All Saints and All Souls/All Hallows are collectively the second most common dedications of churches in Britain. They were very popular in the Middle Ages, because it was thought that the wrath of the Day of Judgement could be avoided through the invocation of all the saints' names. As a bonus, they might also answer your prayers for health and wealth in this life. Churches with these names are often found in town centres or to the east – the direction of the Garden of Eden and, thus it was assumed, paradise as well.

- St Andrew. A church in the north of England might have been dedicated to St Andrew because relics of the saint were said to have rested there in the late Anglo-Saxon period, en route to St

Andrews in Scotland (see box). Andrew was also considered the model disciple, so devout benefactors often insisted on naming the churches they had funded in his honour.

The oldest surviving church site in Newcastle is dedicated to St Andrew, which initially seems strange, as he has no obvious connection with the city. However, legend has it that the bones of the apostle rested on this spot – perhaps for no more than twenty-four hours – before continuing their journey to Scotland. The church was then erected to celebrate that moment in time. It is likely that this happened during the eighth century.

St Andrew was a popular regional saint in the north-east of England, and his relics were a treasure of inestimable worth. They were originally housed at Hexham Abbey, but were taken north to consolidate the alliance between the Kingdom of Northumbria (which at this stage reached as far north as Edinburgh) and the Pictish Kingdom of Southern Scotland. (Incidentally, the Northumbrian hold over Edinburgh at this time is reflected by the fact that the city's oldest church is still dedicated to St Cuthbert, who was effectively the patron saint of Northumbria.)

It is believed that the relics were transported along old Roman roads from Hexham to Newcastle, leaving a series of churches dedicated to the apostle along the way: Corbridge, Heddon-on-the-Wall and Newcastle itself all have extremely ancient churches dedicated to the saint. The bones then presumably completed their journey to St Andrews by sea. Interestingly, in and around the Scottish town, only the cathedral abbey itself is dedicated to the apostle – there are no similarly named churches in the surrounding countryside. However, the presence of the relics had a profound impact on the layout of the town. The three main streets all lead to and from the cathedral: pilgrims approached on South Street, left via North Street, and bought provisions on the aptly named Market Street.

- St Anne, the mother of the Virgin Mary, was often associated with holy wells (see Chapter 4), and any nearby church would be dedicated to her, too.

- St Bartholomew is often associated with healing: hence the famous hospital in London – usually known as St Barts – founded in 1123 and still going strong.

- St Brigit/Bridget. Churches with this dedication tend to be very old and often occupy sites that were previously dedicated to the Celtic goddess Brigit. Most of them are located close to water, on account of Brigit's association with sacred rivers and streams. For example, the church of St Bride (a variation of Bridget) is on Fleet Street, named after the River Fleet, one of the major rivers of old London. There seems to have been a Christian church here for at least fourteen hundred years, and it was built over a sacred Roman site dating to the second century AD.

- St Catherine was supposedly martyred during the Roman persecution of Christians in Alexandria, Egypt: hence her full title, St Catherine of Alexandria. However, the details of her life are so fantastic that even the most devout Catholic scholars of the saints admit that she is probably an invention. Nevertheless, we still know her because of the Catherine wheel, now a mainstay of Bonfire Night, so called because of the story of her failed execution. A Roman Emperor is supposed to have ordered Catherine to be put to death on a spiked wheel, but when her body touched it, it exploded and fell apart. Thereafter, she was invariably represented in art alongside a large wheel. This, in turn, led to her becoming inextricably linked with a pre-Christian belief system – that of the Celts. In Celtic symbolism, the sun was depicted in its full radiant glory in the shape of a wheel with spikes radiating out from the centre. So, once Christianity supplanted the Celtic religion, it made sense for Catherine and her wheel to assume the role once occupied by the sun deity. Furthermore, the Celtic god had always been closely associated with hills and mountains – unsurprisingly, as the sun sets behind them and reappears above them – so Catherine came to be regarded as the saint of high places, too. A tiny chapel on the summit of St Catherine's Hill, above Abbotsbury in Dorset, is dedicated to her, as is St Catherine's Point and Downs on the Isle of Wight. There is another St Catherine's Hill to the north of Bath, and there was once a St Catherine's chapel on the hillside above Carmarthen (see Chapter 6).

S. Catherine.
From Stained Glass, West Wickham Church, Kent.

© Author

Churches and chapels dedicated to St Catherine are often on hills. This is probably due to her symbol of a wheel, a symbol also associated with Celtic hill gods.

- St Christopher, the patron saint of travellers, is especially associated with fords and pilgrim routes. Bells dedicated to him were believed to confer safety and good health to the traveller. Seven of these ancient bells still exist, with one in the church at Shapwick, Dorset, on an ancient pilgrimage route from the coast to Glastonbury.

- St Clement is associated with sailors and the sea, so churches dedicated to him are often found in ports. He was also a favourite saint of the Danes: hence St Clement's Dane in London and St Clement's in what was once the Danish quarter of Cambridge. His association with the sea is somewhat macabre, given how he died. As one of the first popes, Clement was exiled to what is now the Crimea by the Emperor Trajan. He was eventually martyred by having a huge anchor tied around his neck and being thrown into the Black Sea.

- St Cuthbert is probably the most popular saint in the north, and especially the north-east, of England. He is also strongly represented in Lowland Scotland. His travels (and the travels of his relics after the Vikings attacked the holy island of Lindisfarne) have resulted in many St Cuthbert's churches throughout these regions. Meanwhile, Kirkcudbright, a town in Dumfries and Galloway, translates as 'Church of Cuthbert'.

- St David is linked by legend with such ancient sites as Crowland, Suffolk, and Glastonbury, Somerset. However, he is most associated with Wales, where he is the patron saint, and many churches in the principality now bear his name. At Llanddewi Brefi, near Tregaron, Ceredigion, the land is said to have risen up to provide a platform from which David could preach. Unsurprisingly, the village's parish church is dedicated to him.

- St Dunstan's churches usually have a monastic connection, as he was a great tenth-century reformer of the monasteries and an abbot of Glastonbury. He was also a dynamic Archbishop of

Canterbury, and his work in that role is sometimes honoured by church dedications in places where he had a major impact.

- St George tends to be a late dedication as he only became England's patron saint in the fourteenth century and only rose to prominence in the sixteenth century. Witness Henry V's rallying cry: 'Cry God for Harry, England and St George.'[31] He was especially popular in the eighteenth century as a symbol of the union between England and Scotland, as several dedications in Edinburgh indicate.

- St Giles is the patron saint of lepers, the sick and the lame. He is therefore almost always associated with hospitals or leprosaria, which, by law, had to be located outside city walls.

© Author

St Giles was hit by an arrow in his hand as he defended a hunted deer. This led to him being associated with those who suffered skin diseases, as his wound never healed properly.

St Giles lived as a hermit in a deep forest where he befriended the wild creatures. One day, a hunter rode into the forest and startled a hind, who ran to Giles for safety. The hunter, not realising that the saint was there, fired an arrow in the direction of his prey. Giles put out his arm to protect the terrified animal, and the arrow sank deep into his hand. He suffered with the wound for the rest of his life: hence his role as patron saint of the wounded (and those suffering from skin afflictions). Consequently, many hospitals, and especially leprosaria, have been named after him, and many miraculous cures have been credited to his intervention.

A St Giles church will often be found on the edge of a town or even in the countryside – the only place where lepers were allowed to live. This is why one of the London churches dedicated to the saint is known as St Giles in the Fields; at one time, it literally was in the fields. Sometimes villages grew up around these hospitals and churches, such as St Giles in the Wood, Cornwall, and St Giles on the Heath, Essex – both remote places.

One exception to this rule is St Giles Cathedral, Edinburgh, which sits in the heart of the Old Town. The reason for its unusual name is rather touching. The Queen of Scotland in the late eleventh century was Margaret, who was eventually proclaimed a saint because of her charity and generosity to anyone in need. Her two sons decided to found a church in her memory, but they wanted it to do more than merely cater for the spiritual needs of Edinburgh's citizens. Consequently, they decreed that the parishioners' fees for baptisms, wedding, funerals and so on should be used to fund a hospital in the north-east of England run by the Lazarites, a religious order much admired by their mother.

- St Helen was believed to have found the True Cross in Jerusalem in the early fourth century. Consequently, churches dedicated to her usually face (much larger) churches or cathedrals that claim to hold a relic of the True Cross. The latter were sometimes renamed Holy Rood after their acquisition of the precious relic (from the Anglo-Saxon word *rood*, meaning 'cross') – as in Holyrood, Edinburgh. In Wales, Helen is also associated with roads and with the protection of travellers.

Sarn Helen (Saint Helen), once the main route between north and South Wales, is one of the most famous stretches of Roman road in Britain. It is approximately 160 miles in length and runs from Caernarfon to either Carmarthen or Brecon. (Considerable degradation means that there is much debate over its original route.) Some parts have been developed into modern highways, such as the A4085 from Caernarfon to Beddgelert, whereas other sections are now just minor roads or footpaths, or have disappeared completely.

Helen was the mother of the first Christian Roman Emperor, Constantine, who ruled from 312 to 337 and founded Constantinople. He and his mother are venerated together in the Orthodox Church: he for having made Christianity a legal religion in the Roman Empire, ending centuries of persecution; she for having discovered the True Cross on which Christ was crucified. Legend says she was born in Caernarfon to a Roman soldier and his wife, and she is known in Welsh mythology as Elen Luyddog, meaning Helen of the Hosts. She is credited with persuading her husband, the Western Roman Emperor Magnus Maximus (known as Macsen Wledig in Welsh), to build a network of roads throughout Wales so that soldiers could defend the land against invaders and travellers would be safe from danger. Sarn Helen served a different purpose, though: it was supposedly built on Helen's orders to facilitate her journey to Rome.

- St James' relics lie at the most important pilgrimage site in Europe outside of Rome: Santiago de Compostella in Spain. Churches dedicated to James tended to be starting points for pilgrims on the long journey to this shrine. For example, St James Barton, in Bristol, was built at the end of the main harbour from which the pilgrims set out to sea. Bristol was Britain's main pilgrimage port in the Middle Ages, which is why two famous sherries – Bristol Cream and Bristol Milk – were named after the city. It was pilgrims out and sherry back for the ships of the city. James is also regarded as a warrior saint, so some military churches have been dedicated to him.

- St John the Baptist is usually associated with water. Churches dedicated to him often sit beside the point where a water course enters (or once entered) a town or city. There might even be an associated baptismal site, close to a river or stream. John was also the patron saint of the Knights Templar, and a stunning thirteenth-century painting of his head is preserved at the old Templar church of Templecombe, Dorset.

- St John the Evangelist/Divine is believed to have written the Book of Revelation, the last book in the Bible. This tells the story of the end of the world and the emergence of the New Jerusalem, which will descend from heaven at the end of time. Anglo-Saxon and medieval planners and architects felt they could build towns to reflect John's vision, so it came to dictate the design of many British towns and cities. Occasionally, churches dedicated to John the Divine were built just outside the town, perhaps to represent him looking towards his vision. St John's, Chester, is one such church, although today it is dedicated to John the Baptist (the two Johns have often been confused in the past). He is also a favoured saint for new churches, especially those with an evangelical tradition, such as St John's, Carlisle, which was built in the Victorian period, and when a new church building replaces an old one.

- St Lawrence is another saint who is associated with healing and hospitals. As with those dedicated to St Giles, St Lawrence's chapels and hospitals were usually built outside town or city walls. The fifteenth-century chapel of St Lawrence at Lansdown, north of Bath, was one such example (it is now a private home). It was probably originally attached to a leprosarium, which the law stipulated had to be located at least a mile and a half from any major city or town. Other churches dedicated to St Lawrence might have been attached to monastic hospitals or refuges for the old and infirm.

Lawrence, one of the most popular saints of the medieval period, was one of seven deacons responsible for looking after the poor in Rome. However, in the mid-third century, he was hauled before the Emperor, who was convinced that he knew where the Church's wealth was hidden. Lawrence told the Emperor he would deliver the Church's treasure, but asked for three days' grace. The greedy Emperor agreed and let Lawrence go free. Over the next three days, Lawrence sold everything the Church owned, distributed some of the proceeds to the poor, bought medicines for the sick and handed out crutches to the lame. Then he asked all of the beneficiaries to join him at the Emperor's palace. When the Emperor saw the crowd, he was horrified and demanded to know what they were doing there. Lawrence replied, 'These are the treasures of the Church.' He was then tortured to death.

- St Margaret of Antioch is associated with childbirth and with providing protection against powerful natural forces, such as fire and lightning. Most of the stories relating to her are entirely fictitious. For instance, it was said that she tamed a dragon, attached a collar to it, and then led it around like a pet. She is therefore often pictured with a dragon in religious paintings.

Despite – or perhaps because of – the fantastic stories that were concocted about her life, Margaret was immensely popular in the Middle Ages, and many churches, especially those founded by women, were dedicated to her. One of the most famous is the parish church of the Houses of Parliament in Westminster.

- St Martin's churches were often founded at a very early date, sometimes even in Roman times. This is certainly true of St Martin's, Canterbury, and possibly also of St Martin's, North Stoke, Somerset, which was built above a Roman villa and on the foundations and probably with some of the stones of the Roman temple. Furthermore, of the eight holy wells dedicated to St Martin, six occupy former Roman sites – Canterbury, Exeter, Haresfield (Gloucestershire), Leicester, Stony Middleton (Derbyshire) and Winchester.[32] It was also a favourite dedication for churches in castles, such as the now gone St Martin's chapel in Bristol Castle. Elsewhere, it was often associated with a healing ministry, in which case the church would be located outside the city walls, as in St Martin's in the Field, London.

Chapels in castles often have names chosen to challenge the military way of thinking. For example, the Tower of London's chapel is dedicated to St Peter in Chains – a reminder that castles often serve as prisons and that the great saint was once bound in chains in just such a place. Likewise, many castle chapels were dedicated to St Martin, who served as a soldier in the Roman Army but who left the army when he converted to Christianity, believing that it was impossible to be a Christian – a follower of the prince of peace – and a soldier. In this way, the Church tried to remind the kings and nobles who built castles that a true Christian should eschew violence and warfare.

- St Mary, also known as the Virgin Mary, was the mother of Jesus Christ. Today, more British churches are dedicated to her than to anyone else – over 2300 bear her name. In the Middle Ages, it was felt that she would always listen to the cries of the poor and helpless, and to those of sinners in general. Hence most major churches have a 'Lady Chapel' dedicated to Mary, which is usually located behind the high altar. Those who felt unworthy to stand directly before Christ because of their sins or humility would bypass the high altar and enter the chapel to ask Mary for help instead. She is often depicted above the west doors of cathedrals – welcoming all believers, no matter who they are or what they have done. Market-place churches are often dedicated to her too, because of her perceived fairness.

- St Mary Magdalene is probably the most famous sinner in the gospels. She is identified as being the woman whom Christ prevented being stoned to death and was thus a popular dedication for someone repenting an action or abuse. In Provence, great festivals are held in her honour and homesick Frenchmen may well have opted for her as their saint of choice.

- St Michael's churches are usually associated with a hill and/or the north. St Michael is the guardian angel who fought against Satan and threw him out of heaven, so he stands as a bulwark – the protector of Christians against evil forces. Hence, he is often associated with high hills to the north of a town or city, to protect it from evil forces descending from the north. Prime examples are St Michael's Mount and St Michael's, Penkevil, both in Cornwall, and St Michael's Tor, above Glastonbury. Many other hills are topped by a St Michael's church – above Bristol, for example, or on the very steep, narrow hill above Burrowbridge, Somerset. By watching and protecting communities from on high, St Michael replaced several Celtic hill gods and deities, who had performed the same function in pre-Christian Britain.

Alnwick, Northumberland, has been home to the Percy family for centuries, and their vast castle still dominates the town. The Council of the North met here in the Middle Ages to coordinate the defence of England against marauding Scots. Alnwick was therefore the most northerly town that was always English. (Berwick-on-Tweed is further north, but it continually moved in and out of Scottish and English control.) The oldest part of the town is a square (actually more of a pentagon), formed by St Michael's church to the west, the castle to the east of Bailiffgate, and Narrowgate and Pottergate on two of the three other sides. Over time, buildings spread south down the hill from Pottergate, and it is there that the heart of the town, with its fine market place, is located today. To the south of the market is a magnificent fountain, dedicated to St Michael and showing the archangel with great wings and the sword of justice in his hand, and St Michael's Square.

This does not seem right. If the town were laid out according to the usual medieval theological conventions, everything associated with St Michael should be to the north, to protect the community from evil forces (see the box below). So why is he so prominent in the south of Alnwick? The answer is that the *whole town* is dedicated to him. As England's most northerly town, and the operational centre of its northern defences, it made theological and symbolic sense to dedicate all of Alnwick to the archangel who defeats invading forces from the north. This dedication of a whole town to a single saint is unique in England.

In the Old Testament, the Babylonians and Assyrians always attacked the Israelites from the north. Hence it was considered the direction of evil. The key northerly city of the Kingdom of Israel was Megiddo, which defended the northern pass into Israelite

▶

territory and was thus attacked and conquered repeatedly. Records
show that it was first besieged in 1478 BC by the Egyptians, and
it was finally destroyed by the Babylonians in 586 BC.

So many conflicts occurred in and around Megiddo that it
became synonymous with vast struggles between warring empires.
Consequently, around the second century BC, when Jewish
prophets were looking for a symbolic location for the Battle to
End the World, they chose Megiddo, or Har Megiddo, in reference
to the hill that overlooked the town. When translated into Greek,
this place became Armageddon.

- St Nicholas is associated with sailors as well as being the
  patron saint of children (as Santa Claus). His churches – which
  are often the principal places of worship in port towns and
  cities – are frequently found on quaysides. Medieval sailors
  would routinely say, 'May St Nicholas hold the tiller,' before
  setting off on a voyage. Newcastle-on-Tyne's huge cathedral
  is dedicated to him, while London has St Nicholas Cole Abbey,
  just above Victoria Street and the old line of the river bank.
  Sailors attended both of these churches for blessing before
  heading out to sea. Meanwhile, St Nicholas's role as protector
  of children comes from a story of his kindness and compassion.
  A father with three daughters fell on hard times and had no
  money for their wedding dowries, so he told them they would
  have to become prostitutes to earn their keep. Hearing of this,
  on three successive nights Nicholas threw a bag of gold
  through the girls' bedroom window, thus giving them the
  means to escape. It is a powerful story of a saint saving young
  women from abuse.

- St Paul, although often linked with St Peter, is far less popular.
  He is often associated with missionary work, which is probably

why the great cathedral in London is dedicated to him. For it was here that St Augustine established his first mission church outside Canterbury in 604.

- St Peter holds the keys to heaven and has the right to admit – or turn away – souls.[33] He is therefore closely associated with death. In the Middle Ages, it was believed that heaven lay to the east – the direction of the Garden of Eden, according to the Bible. This is indicated on many medieval and even some sixteenth- and seventeenth-century maps. Therefore, St Peter's churches are often found to the east of town centres: for example, in Shepton Mallet, Somerset. Other churches might be dedicated to him if they have some sort of link to Rome (because Peter was the first pope and therefore the founder of the Church of Rome) or if they are located within a castle (on account of his imprisonment in a dungeon).

- St Sepulchre refers to the Holy Sepulchre in Jerusalem (the site of Jesus' crucifixion), rather than a person, and any church dedicated to it tends to be linked to the Crusades. The church of St Sepulchre in London, founded by the Knights Templar is dedicated to this place. This name may also indicate a very old – sometimes even pre-Christian – burial site.

- St Stephen was the first Christian martyr, stoned to death outside the city walls of Jerusalem. His churches are therefore usually found outside city walls, such as the tenth-century church in St Albans, Hertfordshire, which was built on the site of a Roman cemetery and on a pilgrimage route from London.

- St Thomas's churches might be dedicated to either the apostle Thomas or Thomas Becket, the murdered Archbishop of Canterbury. However, in the sixteenth century, many churches that had originally honoured the most famous English saint subtly changed their dedications from Becket to the apostle in

St Thomas was the disciple who said he would not believe in the Resurrection of Jesus until he could touch the wounds himself, hence his nickname of Doubting Thomas.

order to avoid the displeasure of the king. At the time, of course, Henry VIII was in the process of asserting his power over that of the Church, so it was wise to abandon any connection with an archbishop who had famously challenged one of the king's predecessors. Any remaining St Thomas (Becket) churches tend to be associated with pilgrimage to Canterbury, such as the one in the now-deserted village of Fairfield, Kent.

Local saints

Many Welsh and Cornish churches are dedicated to saints who are known only in the local area. My father, an Anglican priest, was once asked to preach at the festival of one such Cornish saint. However, search as he might for any information on this saint, he could find nothing. So his sermon merely commended the saint as a model of Christian purity, and speculated on the long life of faithful witness he must have given to be so commemorated. After the service, the churchwarden thanked my father and then casually mentioned that the saint was martyred at the age of seven ... and was a girl.

Most local saints are not quite so obscure. For instance, a carving or painting somewhere within the church will often tell the story of why they are revered, or there will at least be a pamphlet in the local library.

As we have seen, some regional saints now enjoy much wider recognition – such as St David (primarily associated with Wales) and St Cuthbert (usually linked with the north-east of England). Two other well-known north-east saints are Aiden and Bede (a saint in much of Britain, but not recognised by Rome), while four Anglo-Saxons – Boniface, Dunstan, Aldhelm and Alphege – are held in high regard in the south-west and beyond. Boniface was born in Crediton, Devon, but later went to Germany to convert the tribes who were invading Britain at the time. Today, he is revered in such places as Mainz. St Chad, who founded Lichfield Cathedral, is a popular regional saint throughout the Midlands, while the eighth-century Guthlac is the local saint for the Fenland areas around the East Midlands and the edge of East Anglia.

Many place names capture the community's dedication to a local saint, such as Whitchurch Canonicorum in Dorset, which honours St Whit. In Wales, many village and town names feature the name of the local saint after the prefix Llan, which means 'Church of' or 'Settlement of'. Examples include Dewi (David), Stephen, Fihangel (Michael) and Fair (Mary). It is possible to trace the route of the life and ministry of a particular saint through the churches or villages that are dedicated to him or her. This is quite straightforward for David in Wales. Meanwhile, in south-west England and Wales, several places are named after Petroc, including Padstow (originally Padristowe, a Cornish version of his name), St Petrox (Pembrokeshire) and Petrockstowe (Devon).

Sometimes church dedications reveal a distinct Scandinavian connection – usually in areas where Vikings settled in order to trade with the Anglo-Saxons. One such is St Olave's, near the Tower of London. St Olaf was an eleventh-century King of Norway who died in battle and is honoured to this day in his home country. The church of St Clement Danes, in the same part of London, indicates that the Norwegians' Scandinavian neighbours settled around there, too. Meanwhile, churches dedicated to St Dennis or St Deny (such as the one in York) usually indicate the presence of homesick Normans, because St Deny is the patron saint of Paris. The village of Coln St Dennis, Gloucestershire, is also named in his honour.

WHERE IS THE CHURCH?

As we have seen, certain churches tend to be located in specific places. For instance, those dedicated to St Michael and St Catherine are usually found on hills. But there are other, more general, patterns to the positioning of churches, especially in urban areas. For example, if a church occupies a commanding position in a town, it was probably one of the first buildings to be built in the area. By contrast, if it is subordinate to a castle, a hill fort, a major crossroads or a market place, it was probably built after these landmarks and is therefore unlikely to occupy the site of the town's first Christian church. The original church might have disappeared hundreds of years ago, but it might still be commemorated in street names or even house names.

If the church is right next door to an old pub, the latter might originally have been the church's alehouse. This is often confirmed by the pub's name: the Bells, the (Papal) Bull and the Seven Stars (a symbol of St Mary as Queen of the Seas) all indicate links with a church. Meanwhile, any pub with a blatant royal reference – such as the King's Head or the Oak Tree – might once have had a religious name that was changed in either the Reformation or the Restoration in order to display loyalty to the monarchy. Other pub owners may have changed the names of their establishments to avoid accusations that they favoured Catholicism, so the Cross Hands might once have been known as the Cross Keys – symbol of St Peter and Rome. (See Chapter 6 for more on the significance of pubs' names.)

THE SECRETS OF THE ENGLISH PARISH CHURCH

Outside the church

Many British churches are built in the shape of a cross, with the main body of the building representing the vertical and the transepts (or small chapels) on either side representing the cross beam. Of course, this is deliberate, as we shall see later, when looking at church interiors.

Outside, the most striking feature of many churches is the tower or spire, which has practical functions as well as the symbolic role of pointing to heaven. The tower enables people to see the church from a considerable distance, and it might house bells, which summon the faithful and let them know the time. This role was later enhanced by the addition of clocks, which became popular from the seventeenth century onwards, when advances in technology made them affordable for even modest parish churches.

The considerable size and weight of church bells mean that they have to be housed in very substantial towers, so these often form the oldest parts of churches. Stafford parish church and Uffington church in the Vale of the White Horse, Oxfordshire, both have particularly impressive (and rare) octagonal towers. They were probably designed in this way to symbolise the liturgical cycle, which is divided into eight sections.

In addition to their daily and weekly functions, church bells are rung to mark the death of a parishioner – traditionally with one knell for every year of the deceased's life – and to warn of attack or threat. For example, when the Spanish Armada was spotted off the coast of England in 1588, church bells rang from Cornwall to London to warn of the impending invasion.

The technical problem of dispersing rainwater from church roofs led to the development of extraordinary medieval waterspouts, which stonemasons carved into increasingly grotesque and extremely humorous figures. These gargoyles (from *gargouille*, Old French for 'throat') often depict monsters or misshapen faces. They served the symbolic purpose of illustrating that all the powerful, evil forces of the world had been defeated by the authority of the Church.

Sometimes a sundial can be found scratched into the south side of a church building. If it has just a few lines radiating from the central hole, it will once have been used by monks and nuns to indicate the times of their prayers. There are a few Anglo-Saxon scratch sundials in Britain, but most are medieval.

On the same (southern) side of most churches you will usually find the porch. This was considered an auspicious side of the building because it lay opposite the devil's northern side (although not as auspicious as the eastern side, as we shall see later). Many old porches have two stone benches down either side, with the distance between them just shorter than the length of an average coffin. At a funeral, the coffin would be gently set down here for a few minutes, with one end on each bench, prior to entering the church. This was done because the porch symbolised a port of departure – the start of the deceased's final journey to heaven. ('Port' and 'porch' share the Latin same root – *portus*.) In fact, the whole church building was usually designed to represent a ship – the ship of faith that would carry the

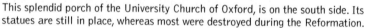

This splendid porch of the University Church of Oxford, is on the south side. Its statues are still in place, whereas most were destroyed during the Reformation.

faithful through the storms of life and ultimately bring them safely to harbour in heaven.

Occasionally, the porch will contain a stoup – a stone bowl set into the wall. In the Middle Ages, this would be filled with holy water so that those entering the church could make the sign of the cross and bless themselves. Others have magnificent carvings above the main door showing dramatic scenes of the struggle of good against evil or the triumph of the saints to indicate that worshippers will soon be safe inside, and protected from evil. Malmesbury Abbey, in Wiltshire, has an outstanding array of saints ranked along each side of the inner porch.

Inside the church

The font

Once inside the church building, the first feature you are likely to see is the font, where infants have been baptised for centuries. According to ancient tradition, the devil is cast out of children during baptisms and he must be allowed to escape. Of course, he would want to go north, to 'his' side, so many churches obligingly provided a door on the north side of the building, opposite the font. However, as this belief faded away during the eighteenth and nineteenth centuries, many of these doors were sealed or removed entirely. For instance, at the church of St Mary Magdalene, Langridge, Somerset, only the threshold stone remains. In other churches, the original hood of the door frame might be buried behind the new stonework.

Some churches – such as St Andrew's, Newcastle, and Ufford, Suffolk – boast huge, elaborately carved wooden covers over their fonts. In 1236, it became compulsory for fonts to have a lockable cover. This was to stop people stealing the holy water that had been blessed, usually on Easter Sunday, and remained in the font through-out the rest of the year. Many people thought that this 'magic' water could cure illnesses, while a few may have stolen it for use it in occult rites. Today, priests bless the water on the day of the baptism and then let it drain away after the ceremony. But the old fear that the water might be misused remains, which is why the drain hole in most fonts leads straight down to the church's foundations.

Centuries of vicars

Many churches display a list of their vicars or priests in a prominent position. These often date right back to the early thirteenth century, when the Great Lateran Council of 1215 decreed that the Church should keep proper records of its clergy and parishes. Sometimes these lists reveal major upheavals in British history that tore apart both the clerical and the temporal community.

For example, as we know, radical changes took place between 1534 and 1547: every English and Welsh parish church acquired a copy of the Bible in English; services were held in English rather than Latin; all monasteries were closed and their lands were seized, including their parish churches; shrines were demolished; and pilgrimage was banned. Some members of the clergy found these changes unconscionable and left the new 'Church of England'. Others were driven out of their parishes for their alleged continued devotion to Catholicism. So, if a church list shows a priest leaving his parish in these years, the chances are that he did not fit in with the new order.

Then, in 1553, just as most parish churches had re-established some sort of equilibrium, Queen Mary came to the throne and reintroduced Catholicism. Over the next five years, many hard-line Protestant clergy left not just their parishes but the country. They often headed to Switzerland, and into the congregation of John Calvin in Geneva or Heinrich Bullinger in Zurich. Their places in Britain's parish churches were taken by a new generation of Catholic clergy. However, Mary died in 1558, which meant that the Anglican Elizabeth I came to the throne. Just two years later, she introduced a new set of rules, which led to another mass exodus from the clergy and a new influx of Protestants.

Thereafter, peace reigned for almost a hundred years, until the Civil War began. In 1649, Charles I was beheaded and the Church of England was dissolved. England became a Presbyterian and Puritan country (similar to Scotland at the time) and yet again many priests left their parishes, unable to bear the execution of their 'Supreme Governor' or to meet the extreme demands of Puritanism. For example, the Dean of Wells Cathedral fled overseas with King Charles II and spent fifteen years in exile. In 1660, upon his triumphant return with Charles, he donated a magnificent brass lectern to the cathedral. It still stands in pride of place there to this day.

In 1662, Charles demanded that all clergy must sign the Act of Uniformity, which obliged them to conform to the rules and regulations of the newly reinstated Anglican Church. Thousands of Puritan clergy refused to do this and were subsequently ejected from the Church of England.[34] Many of them became the clergy of new churches that were often set up in direct opposition to local parish churches. Collectively, these various groups became known as Nonconformists (see below).

It is possible to trace much of this turbulent clerical history simply by looking at your local parish church's list of clergy.

Wall paintings and windows

Few parish churches still have wall paintings, but where they exist, they often follow a pattern. First, there will usually be a large portrait of St Christopher opposite the main door, obviously placed here so that the traveller can give thanks for his or her safe arrival. A wonderful example is in the beautiful Norman church of Ashby St Ledger, Northamptonshire, where many of the original medieval paintings are still intact.

Some churches retain what is known as a 'doom painting', which hangs above the arch between the nave and the chancel. This always shows Christ in Glory, coming to judge the world, and sometimes souls being tortured and others being carried to heaven by angels. Other doom paintings use the imagery of the Day of Judgement found in the Gospel of Matthew (25:31–46). Here, Jesus separates the sheep (those who are saved) from the goats (those who are condemned to hell). A fine example is at Dauntsey, Wiltshire.

Sometimes scenes from the Old Testament are depicted on a church's northern wall, while scenes from the New Testament appear on the more favoured southern side. (The Old Testament was considered to be less important than the New.)

Stained glass was a major feature of many medieval churches, but most of it was destroyed during the Reformation and especially the Civil War, when Puritans expressed their hatred of Catholics by smashing anything that had been created by them. Consequently, while some cathedrals, such as Canterbury, have retained their magnificent medieval stained glass, most parish churches have only a few fragments left. One exception is the church of St Lawrence, Ludlow, Shropshire, which boasts a splendid set of windows that tells the story of the saint.[35]

Stained-glass windows usually depicted saints and/or major scenes from the Bible, such as the Nativity. A fine example of the latter is still to be found in All Saints' church, York. The east window of Carlisle Cathedral has a fine doom picture, while the magnificent windows of Fairford church, Gloucestershire, show Christ's resurrection.

The nave

The central part of the church is the nave. This word shares its root with 'navy' (both are from the Latin *navis*, meaning 'ship'), so we are once again reminded that we are in a symbolic ship of faith, carrying us through life's troubles. Looking down the nave to the chancel, where the altar is housed, you might notice that the chancel seems slightly off centre – not a straight continuation of the line of the nave. There are two possible – and equally intriguing – reasons for this slight misalignment.

Many old churches are not orientated due east but rather to the precise point on the eastern horizon where the sun rises on the feast day of their patron saint. It was through the patron saint that the 'gospel light' was believed to shine into the community, so linking him or her with the sunrise makes excellent theological sense. A fine example of this tradition is the parish church of Corsham, Wiltshire. This church is dedicated to St Bartholomew, whose feast day falls on 24 August, sufficiently far from the autumn equinox for the two points of sunrise to be very distinct, and thus perhaps to explain the somewhat skewed orientation of the chancel.

The other possible explanation for the lopsidedness of many chancels is that the architect wanted to represent Christ upon the cross. As we have seen, churches are usually built in the shape of a cross, and the chancel is roughly where Christ's head would be on that cross. However, in paintings of the crucifixion, Christ is almost always depicted with his head to one side, so it would have made sense for the church builders to set the chancel slightly off centre. This

The classic view from the nave to the chancel, sanctuary and altar. Note the Protestant addition of the lectern in the middle and the pulpit on the left.

would explain why churches whose saints' days fall very near the equinox – such St Michael's in Hathersage, Derbyshire (St Michael's feast day is 29 September) – still have off-centre chancels.

Down into hell or up to Golgotha

The nave is usually the lowest part of the church. Looking down the centre aisle, you will see that the chancel is set higher, and the sanctuary – housing the altar, which today usually sits behind a rail – is higher still. The reason for this is that every medieval church (and many more recent Anglican and Catholic churches) represents the sacred topography of Jerusalem, with the chancel as Golgotha, the hill on which Christ was crucified. So every time the parishioners walk through the church to the altar, they are re-enacting the final mortal journey of Christ, climbing up the hill towards Golgotha. However, churches were not always designed in this way.

Only one church in Britain retains its original Anglo-Saxon layout: St Laurence, in Bradford-on-Avon, Wiltshire (see page 135), which was built around AD 1000. This little church was lost for centuries when a rival was erected in the town in celebration of its growing wealth – the result of the burgeoning wool trade. The original church became surrounded by houses that were built into its external walls; for a while, it was even turned into a house itself. But then, in the nineteenth century, it was rediscovered and restored, and today it is a precious gem of a building.

Crucially, it was never 'modernised' in the medieval period, in contrast to many other Anglo-Saxon churches, such as the equally beautiful but altered church of Escomb, County Durham, and the two churches in Deerhurst, Gloucestershire. So it gives a unique insight into how the Anglo-Saxons worshipped. The first thing you notice is that the approach to the altar is very narrow indeed (as it is also at Escomb): it is more like a doorway than the arch of a typical medieval church. Then there is an even greater surprise: the sanctuary and the altar are positioned below, rather than above, the nave. The symbolism must have been obvious to the parishioners every time they approached the altar to take Holy Communion: rather than journeying upwards, towards the cross, they were descending into the tomb to be with Christ after the crucifixion. This explains why the entrance is so narrow: it symbolises the door to the tomb, and therefore the door to the afterlife.

Anglo-Saxon Christianity was a warrior theology. In their day-to-day lives, Anglo-Saxons were members of the extended family of their lord and they pledged to follow him wherever he led. They feasted with him, fought with him and suffered with him. So when Anglo-Saxon Christians took Holy Communion, it was natural for them to believe that they were dining with their (spiritual) lord. Rather than falling to their knees at the foot of the cross, they descended into the tomb and joined Christ in a triumphant feast to celebrate his victory over the forces of evil.

Amazingly, then, the little church of St Laurence and the unusual positioning of its altar reveal an entire theology, a whole story of belief.

Entering the holy of holies

In every medieval church, below the doom painting, across the arch separating the nave from the chancel, would stand a rood screen. *Rood* is the Old English word for 'cross' or 'tree', and the screen – carved out of wood or stone – depicted Christ upon the cross, with the Virgin Mary standing to his right and his most beloved disciple, John, to his left. These figures were often life size. Many English churches still have the ledge on which the screen once stood, although the screen itself is usually long gone.

The rood screen depicted the most dramatic moment in the Christian story, the point at which heaven and earth met in the death of the Son of God, who came from heaven and died on a tree. This moment is magnificently captured in the seventh-century Anglo-Saxon poem 'The Dream of the Rood', which tells the story of Christ's crucifixion from the point of view of the cross itself. This poem once again reveals the warrior element in Anglo-Saxon Christianity, with Christ cast as the lord who leads the faithful into battle with, and victory over, death:

> *Men bore me on their shoulders and set me on a hill.*
> *Many enemies held me fast there.*
> *I saw the Lord of All coming swiftly and with such courage to*
>   *climb upon me ...*

Then the young warrior,
God Almighty Himself,
stripped and stood firm and without flinching.
Bravely before the multitude
He climbed upon the cross to save the world.
I shivered when the hero clung to me,
but I dared not bend to the ground, nor fall to the earth.
I had to stand firm.
I was a rod raised up,
I bore on high the mighty King,
The Lord of Heaven . . .

On that hill I saw and endured much.
I saw the God of Hosts stretched on the rack.
I saw darkness covering the lifeless body of the Ruler with clouds.
Against His shining radiance shadows swept across the land,
strange powers moved under the clouds.
All creation wept,
weeping and moaning for the death of the King.
For Christ was on the cross.[36]

In the sacred geography of early Christian churches, walking from the nave to the chancel and then the altar was not just a journey to Golgotha (or to Christ's tomb, in Anglo-Saxon churches) but a voyage from earth to the edge of heaven. Every time the faithful stepped forward to take Holy Communion, they *almost* passed from this world into the next. This concept is made even more explicit in Orthodox churches: the sanctuary is separated from the nave by a wooden screen called the iconostasis, on which icons are hung or painted, and only the priests are allowed to pass through its doors to the sanctuary.

Similarly, in Britain's medieval churches, the sanctuary was the special domain of the priests (although parishioners were allowed to enter it occasionally) and the rood screen signified its supreme holiness. In medieval Catholic theology, the priest was seen as a channel for divine power, grace and curses. Whenever a bishop ordained a new priest, it was believed that the power of God had entered the clergyman and that he now had the power and authority to act on Christ's behalf. So he could offer forgiveness for your sins or he could condemn you to hell. He could literally turn bread and wine into the body and blood of Christ (transubstantiation), a magical ceremony that he performed in the sacred space beyond the rood screen, beside the altar. He stood aside from the rest of the community – hence his celibacy – and was to be honoured, and possibly even feared. As a result, any illicit behaviour by priests – sex with parishioners, greed,

© Author

This nave to chancel view shows the traditional place of the rood screen. The screen closes off the priests' section – the chancel – from the nave.

corruption and so on – always deeply shocked their congregations. Nevertheless, such behaviour was so commonplace that priests were routinely ridiculed and satirised, as in Chaucer's *Canterbury Tales* and *Piers Plowman*.

Some Anglican churches – especially cathedrals – rebuilt rood screens in the nineteenth century, separating the nave from the choir and the sanctuary with a carved stone or wood partition, although they rarely feature the statues that once adorned rood screens. However, the vast majority of parish churches lost their screens during the Reformation and never reintroduced them.[37] Today, in most Anglican churches, there is an uninterrupted line of sight from the back of the church right up the nave to the altar.

Protestant reformers tore down the rood screens because they rejected the idea that any part of the church should be considered more sacred than any other. The priest was no longer a magician – in fact, he was no more holy than the parishioners – so he no longer needed a special place in which to perform his tricks. Furthermore, Protestants believed that statuary went against the commandment that forbids the worship of idols and images, so they felt fully justified in smashing them to pieces.

The Word of God

While the reformers removed several of the most prominent features of the typical medieval church, they also introduced a particularly significant one: the pulpit (from *pulpitum*, Latin for 'stage').[38] Very few medieval pulpits existed and have survived.

Before the Reformation, the Bible was available only in Latin, and the local parish church's copy would not be on public display. Reading and understanding the Word of God were considered the preserve of the clergy. Ordinary people had to make do with scenes from the holy book that were painted on the church's walls or represented in its stained-glass windows. Furthermore, throughout the medieval period, parish priests celebrated Holy Communion only on major feast days, such as Christmas, Easter, Whitsun and Trinity

Sunday, so the altar and the sanctuary went unused for months at a time. Even when these services did take place, they were conducted solely in Latin and preaching was minimal. This started to change towards the end of the fifteenth century, when the Catholic Church realised that it needed to cater for an increasingly educated and questioning laity. However, preaching and reading from the Bible in English were virtually forbidden until the Reformation. Thereafter, the priest would rest the Bible on a lectern and preach the Good News directly to the parishioners from the pulpit – with no screen separating him from them. In effect, the clergy had left the sacred space of the sanctuary and had entered the people's space of the nave.

Church services no longer revolved around the bread and the wine. Instead, they focused on the Word. The sacred act of Holy Communion was now secondary to hearing (and increasingly reading) both the Bible and the Book of Common Prayer. The decline in the significance of Holy Communion was emphasised by the fact that it was no longer reserved for special occasions. Early Methodists took Communion two or three times a week, and Anglican churches eventually celebrated it only three times a year until the twentieth century, when the idea of weekly communion returned.

Altar of sacrifice or table for dinner?

The word 'chancel' comes from the Latin *cancelli*, meaning a 'lattice screen'. So the chancel was originally the part of the church beyond the rood screen. The altar was always located in this area, too.

As we saw above, during the Reformation, the rood screen was usually torn down and the notion that the chancel was a particularly sacred part of the church was rejected. Often this was taken a step further and the altar was also destroyed, to be replaced by a simple table.[39] This substitution indicated a profound theological shift. The Catholic view is that the altar is where Christ was sacrificed. The stone altar reflects the sacrificial altars of the Old Testament, such as the one Abraham built when he thought God wanted him to sacrifice his son

Isaac. Stone altars were part of the paraphernalia of pagan temples in Rome, where blood sacrifices were carried out to appease the gods. In Christian theology, Christ's death was a blood sacrifice, which removed the need for any further such sacrifices – hence the stone altar, to remember and honour this.

Most reformers did not view the altar in this way. To them, it was merely the place where Catholic priests had pretended to turn bread and wine into the actual body and blood of Christ. This rejection of the magical powers of the clergy was a major component of the Reformation. However, the reformers still wanted to remind themselves of Christ's sacrifice for them, so they started to treat the consumption of the bread and wine as a re-enactment of the Last Supper. In other words, they continued to celebrate Holy Communion, but now the bread and wine were acknowledged to be no more than bread and wine. As a result, it made perfect sense to replace a symbolic sacrificial altar with a symbolic dining-room table – or often an actual dining-room table.

With the special sacred status of the chancel and altar abolished, the parishioners were free to wander wherever they wished inside churches. But this liberation led some of them to start behaving disrespectfully, and in the 1620s the Church felt compelled to react. It ordered parish churches to erect rails around the altar (or what was left of it) so that parishioners' dogs could not approach the communion table. Congregations soon took to leaning on these as they took Holy Communion, but that was merely a useful by-product of their introduction, not the reason for it.

There are still traces of side altars in many medieval churches. Here, chantry priests were paid to say prayers for the souls of local wealthy families or for local guilds. Each guild had its own patron saint, and they would celebrate Mass at their guild altar, where business was also conducted. These particularly well-funded parts of the church tended to boast an abundance of paintings, stained glass and statues. The side altars in any Catholic cathedral today are similarly ornate.

The sepulchre

In most parish churches there is nothing to the left of the altar. But a few feature a niche cut into the north wall, ranging in length from a couple of feet to almost as long as a human body. Known as Easter Sepulchres, these niches tend be a few feet off the ground and they are often beautifully carved. Simple examples can be seen at Pilton, Somerset, and Ringmer, East Sussex, while the most elaborate and ornate is at Hawton, Nottinghamshire.

Before the Reformation, most parish churches had an Easter Sepulchre. On Good Friday, a statue of Jesus, wrapped in cloth, was laid in the recess. This re-enactment of Christ's burial yet again reveals that every church was seen as a symbolic representation of Jerusalem. On Easter Sunday, the congregation would enter the church to see that the statue had disappeared, leaving only the cloth behind, just as Jesus disappeared from the tomb on the third day.[40]

Unsurprisingly, this ceremony – which gave such a prominent role to a statue – was swiftly abandoned by the reformers; but that still left most churches with a conspicuous (and unused) niche to the left of the altar. Some of these were simply filled in, but some soon had a new function: they served as display cabinets for some very impressive sculptures. The carved figures may well be kneeling in prayer and facing the altar, but they tend to evoke a sense of authority and power rather than piety and reverence. That is because they usually commemorate and represent the local gentry. After the Reformation, these powerful families effectively had full control over their local parishes. Sometimes they even assumed responsibility for appointing the clergy. They had made fortunes out of the sale of monastic lands and buildings, and they wanted to announce that they were in charge. This was their church now.

The parish church, so many elements of which had once symbolised parts of Jerusalem, had become truly parochial. It was now part of the Church *of* England, not the Church *in* England.

Holy washing

To the right of the altar, near the southern wall, there may well be a carved stone basin – the piscine (from the Latin 'fishpond' or 'reservoir'). Just like the font, it drains directly to the church's foundations. This is because it was where the priest washed the communion cup and plate (chalice and paten), so he had to be certain that any crumbs or drops of wine could not be misused. Of course, in Catholicism, these are literally the body and blood of Christ after consecration, so they are very powerful as well as sacred. If there are two piscinae, one would be used to clean the chalice and paten, while the priest would wash his hands in the other, taking care to remove even the slightest crumb. The church of Little Wittenham, Berkshire, has *four* piscinae. The main one, by the high altar, features fine carvings of two angels and a tiny cross-legged knight.

Consecration crosses

Whenever a bishop dedicated a new church, he would mark the sign of the cross on each wall. Sometimes this would be done just once on each wall, but on other occasions twelve crosses – one for each of the apostles – would be marked out. The bishop usually made the marks with oil, and the crosses were then carved into the stonework. Few of these crosses have survived, but there is a fine collection of painted ones at All Saints', Carleton Rode, Norfolk, and external ones at St Mary's, Sellindge, Kent.

The church as sanctuary

Each and every parish church was viewed as a fortress against evil, and many elements in their design were included specifically to reinforce that sense of security: provision of a north door, which allowed the devil to escape; the lockable font cover, which prevented misuse of holy water; the piscine, which prevented similar abuse of Christ's body and blood; the consecration crosses, which protected the building from the moment it was consecrated; the carved gargoyles on the outer walls, which indicated that Christ now control evil spirits; and the layout of the church itself, in the shape of a cross. All of these features encouraged the parishioners to feel safe within the confines of the church.

Some churches (not all) also offered protection to anyone who had been unjustly accused of a crime. The person claiming sanctuary first had to touch a specific object within the church – such as the 'sanctuary-knocker' on the west door of Durham Cathedral or the 'sanctuary stool' at Hexham – and thereafter they could not be apprehended. However, this ancient right did not last long after the Reformation: Henry VIII limited it, and it was abolished altogether in 1623.

REJECTING THE SACRED AND EMBRACING THE HOLY

One of the major causes of the English Civil War was the question of who should run the Church of England. Should it be the priests and the bishops of the reformed – but still very Catholic in orientation – Established Church? Or should it be the radicals – the Puritan Presbyterians – who wanted to do away with the bishops and everything else that smacked of Roman Catholicism? The Puritans won the war, and rapidly put their plans into practice.

By the time Charles II returned to England in 1660, the Church of England had been banned for over a decade. Bishops' palaces and many cathedrals were being used as stables or warehouses in a deliberate bid to downgrade them, and Puritan ministers had replaced priests in the country's parish churches. All of those churches were now being run under the Presbyterian system of local democracy, which closely mirrored the organisational model of the Scottish Presbyterian Church, which had been established in the late sixteenth century.

As we have seen, all of this changed when Charles reinstated the

Church of England and insisted that every member of the clergy must sign the Act of Uniformity. Deprived of their churches when they refused to sign, thousands of ministers – now known as Nonconformists – set about building new ones. For the first time in the Christian history of Britain, the monopoly of the parish church was broken.

There were several branches of Nonconformism: Congregationalists, so called because the congregations chose the minister; Presbyterians, who claimed their system most closely followed the model outlined in the New Testament, where church leaders are called Presbyters, mean-ing 'elders' in Greek; Baptists, who baptised only adults, not children, because they believed the person being baptised had to have full understanding of what they were doing; Unitarians, who rejected the Trinity and viewed God as a single being; Quakers (Society of Friends), who rejected all ideas of priests or ministers completely and therefore worshipped in silence, although in their early days they were said to tremble during their services – hence their nickname.

The Church of England expressed grave concern about the rapid rise of all of these groups. In response, just three years after the Act of Uniformity, in 1665, Parliament passed the Five Mile Act. This prohibited any Nonconformist minister from preaching or establish-ing a church building within five miles of the parish church or town where he had last ministered. This is why many of the earliest Quaker, Presbyterian, Independent and Congregational churches and chapels are in the countryside. For example, a group of Puritans renovated a derelict medieval chapel in Charlesworth, Derbyshire, and renamed it the Independent Chapel. The authorities had no choice but to allow them to continue worshipping there as the chapel lay roughly five miles from any parish church, and a thriving Nonconformist community soon developed. In the mid-nineteenth century, the Church of England built a rival church in the village, but to this day there are more practising Nonconformists (Independents and Baptists) than Anglicans.

Ironically, other great strongholds of Nonconformity lie in areas where Catholicism was never really superseded by the Anglican Church after the Reformation: for example, Cornwall, Lancashire, Norfolk and Essex. The people of these places may not have liked the trappings of Catholicism, but they had no affection for the royal religion, either. Consequently, they were ready to embrace something radically different.

In 1689, William of Orange, having driven the Catholic King James II out of Britain, was declared joint monarch alongside his wife, James's daughter Mary. Shortly thereafter, Parliament passed an Act of Tolerance that finally allowed most Nonconformists[41] to establish their own organisational systems and build churches wherever they liked, within reason. However, powerful local clergy and gentry still often made life difficult for the Nonconformists, and there were even anti-Nonconformist riots in 1715 and the 1790s. Meanwhile, Catholicism remained banned in Britain until 1828.

Hidden chapels

Although the Nonconformists were now officially free to build their churches within towns and cities, they were not keen to draw attention to themselves. So for many years they concealed their chapels and churches. As we saw in Chapter 3, many medieval towns were made up of burbages – those uniform plots of land that faced a high street at the front and backed on to a rear lane. Many early Nonconformist chapels were built on the private land to the rear of these burbages, with their main entrance facing the back lane. There is a classic example of this type of bottom-of-the-garden chapel in Berwick-on-Tweed. It can be reached only by going through an alley under a house off Church Street and then passing a small row of houses. This brings you to the end of the alley on which the little church stands, well hidden from potentially antagonistic neighbours. Berwick used to have at least three more of these back-alley chapels: one at the rear of a burbage that faces Golden Square; and two on the alley at the back of the High Street. One of the latter – the town's High Presbyterian chapel – has gone now, but the other remains. The back alley on which it stands was originally known as Shaw Street, but its name was changed in the early nineteenth century to Chapel Street – a good indication that, by then, Nonconformists no longer felt the need to hide.

In Marshfield, Gloucestershire, a lovely back-garden chapel was founded in 1680 and then rebuilt in its current elegant Georgian style in 1752. Other fine examples are the Baptist chapel in Tewkesbury, also in Gloucestershire, and the Quaker chapel in Banbury, Oxfordshire. Two chapels in Essex – one in Manningtree and the other in Maldon – are still quite difficult to find, reflecting the real fear of persecution that caused them to be built where they are.

This fear is sometimes manifest in the design of the chapel itself. For example, a chapel that can be reached down an alley that runs beneath a house off St Nicholas Street, Ipswich, features a main door with a spy-hole. During a service, a member of the congregation would keep watch through this little hole and warn of any attack.

Plain and simple

The addition of a spy-hole was not the only divergence from the traditional church layout. In fact, these groups even rejected the word 'church' itself, preferring to call their places of worship 'meeting houses' (indeed, Quakers still call them this). Nevertheless, just as Catholics and Anglicans had done before them, Nonconformists took great care to express their theology in the design of their chapels.

Old Nonconformist chapels are invariably quite plain. Outside, there are none of the Gothic curves, spires, towers or arches that can often be seen on even a modest parish church. There are also no empty niches, as these buildings never displayed statues of the saints, unlike many (formerly Catholic) medieval parish churches. In fact, there is almost no decoration at all. Most early chapels look like

This little corrugated iron chapel perfectly illustrates the plain functional design favoured by Nonconformists – it is built for the simple purpose of preaching.

simple town houses. Finally, purpose-built Unitarian chapels differ from both Anglican churches and other Nonconformist chapels in that they do not have windows in sets of three, because this configuration symbolises the Trinity, a concept that was rejected by the Unitarians.

Inside, there is no doubt about the building's function. Essentially, it is a large preaching hall. Both the altar and any sense of sanctuary are absent. Instead, the entire focus of the building is on spreading the Word of God. An unusually grand chapel might have a huge wooden construction at its centre, with a large solid table at the base on which rest various books (although *not* the Bible). This table is used for the Holy Communion service. Above the table is a reading desk, on which rest the Bible, with two large chairs on either side for the minister and their assistant. Finally, rising high above the desk is the pulpit, often with a sounding board like a huge wooden halo hanging above it. Some of these vast edifices to the Word can be more than five metres high. The aforementioned chapel in Ipswich has a magnificent reading desk and pulpit dating from 1700, and another fine example is in the New Room, in The Horsefair, Bristol. The latter is now a Methodist chapel, but it was built in 1739, long before Methodism became a distinct denomination, so it has a traditional Nonconformist design.

As far as internal adornment goes, that is usually it. Most Nonconformist chapels have almost no other decoration, and certainly no statues or paintings, although many did install stained-glass windows in the nineteenth century. The starkness of the chapel interior was a deliberate rebuff to what Nonconformists viewed as the idolatry of the Catholic and Anglican churches. It should be remembered that the people who built the first chapels – or their fathers and grandfathers – had gone to great lengths to destroy all of the statues, stained glass, wall paintings, crosses and other decorations in Britain's parish churches. So they were never likely to make their own buildings artistically beautiful. However, many of them were skilled woodworkers, so there is often a simple elegance to their reading desks and pulpits. For instance, these features in the Ipswich chapel resemble Shaker-style furniture.

The United Society of Believers in Christ's Second Appearing – commonly known as the Shakers – shared many characteristics with the Quakers. They arose in Bolton, Lancashire, in the middle of the eighteenth century and followed the teachings of two charismatic women: Jane Wardley and Ann Lee. Their services were extremely ecstatic in nature – hence their nickname. In the 1770s, Lee and eight of her followers emigrated to America, where they eventually established several communities. However, as they were strictly celibate, these communities could grow only with new

▶

converts, and their numbers started to dwindle in the middle of the nineteenth century. By the 1950s, the last few Shaker villages were being wound up. Ironically, it was around this time that the simple beauty of their furniture and buildings started to have a major influence on a new generation of American and especially Scandinavian designers.

Many Nonconformists were successful, hard-working businessmen and industrialists, so their churches' wealth grew enormously in the nineteenth century, partly because they spent so little money building and decorating their chapels. Eventually, with so much cash in their coffers, some congregations could not resist taking on the Established Church architecturally. They generally built medieval-style churches – preferring early English style over Gothic, probably because it was considered less papist. However, these buildings tend to be no more than poor imitations of the real thing. They give the impression that the builders' hearts were not really in it – which, by and large, they weren't. Other nineteenth-century meeting houses sometimes resemble Greek or Roman temples, with classical porticoes and symmetrical window layouts. Usually more successful than the medieval-style chapels, these buildings were inspired by the Empire theology that was shaping England's towns and cities at the time (see Chapter 6).

THE CHURCH OF SCOTLAND

The Church of Scotland became officially Presbyterian in 1560, and it has remained so, despite several attempts by the crown to make it Episcopalian (from the Greek *episcopos*, meaning 'bishop'). The purge of statues, paintings and other 'papist' paraphernalia was almost total in sixteenth-century Scotland, and while stained glass made a come-back in the nineteenth century,[42] Scottish churches remain generally plain and simple to this day, even when the building is ancient.

As in English Nonconformist chapels, the pulpit is the dominant internal feature of most Scottish churches, taking precedence over everything else. Once again, these are effectively preaching halls. The church at Ruthwell, Dumfries and Galloway, has a magnificent pulpit and reading desk, but these are outshone by the extraordinary, six-metre-high 'Ruthwell Cross', which dates from the eighth century and features images of Christ, the saints and the Runic text of 'The Dream of the Rood'. Of course, this fabulous monument could scarcely be less in keeping with the austere simplicity of the Presbyterians, and indeed the cross was smashed into several large pieces (which were subsequently used as seating) in 1662. Thankfully, in 1818, the new minister recognised the significance of the cross and restored it, giving this Church of Scotland church a unique mixture of simplicity and extravagance.

Both the English Nonconformist churches and the Church of Scotland and its various offshoots – such as the United Secessions Church – were democratic long before Britain's parliamentary system could make such a claim. They set a model for community participation in local governance, and ministers were fully answerable to their congregations. Many of the democratic principles that we take for granted were first put into practice in these churches. They were strong supporters of the French and American revolutions, and were central in the founding of many trade unions – although the Methodists played an even greater role here. In 1828, the law was changed to allow Nonconformists to stand for public office, and hundreds of them immediately took the opportunity to seek election to local councils. Around the same time, and over the next century, thousands of other Nonconformists left Britain –

▶

either emigrating or devoting their lives to missionary work. The ideas these pioneers carried with them have helped to shape notions of democracy around the world, and there are still Nonconformist communities everywhere from Patagonia to the South Pacific.

THE PEOPLE OF GOD

Methodism (the name comes from the methodological way in which Methodists study the Bible) arose when an Anglican clergyman, John Wesley, sought to reignite evangelical enthusiasm in the rather rigid and dull Church of England of the eighteenth century. He preached the Gospel directly to the lowest levels of early industrial society, such as the coalminers of Kingswood, near Bristol, who had been left largely to their own devices by the local secular and religious authorities. To Wesley, it seemed that the Church of England – and, indeed, most of the Nonconformists – had abandoned these people. He wanted to reform the Established Church from within, but by the end of the eighteenth century the church authorities had had more than enough of his criticism and forced him and his fellow Methodists to leave. They did so reluctantly, but they were soon attracting new members to their congregations in unprecedented numbers.

It may well be that the Methodists, who brought hope and faith to so many previously neglected working-class communities, helped to avert a French-style revolution in eighteenth-century Britain. Rather than being stirred up to attack the establishment, Methodist congregations were encouraged to improve themselves through hard work and a commitment to God, and they followed this simple instruction in their tens of thousands. From the coalmines of Wales and the mills of Lancashire, ordinary working people were caught up in the

fervour of faith. Moreover, because studying the Bible was so important to the Methodists, the members of their congregations received
some of the best education in the land. For instance, in eighteenth-
century Wales, the level of literacy rose from 10 to 75 per cent in
the space of a generation, almost entirely due to the efforts of the
Methodists. Later, their locally organised, laypeople's groups formed
the bedrock of the trade union movement; and it is doubtful that
there would ever have been a Labour Party without Methodism.

Early Methodist chapels and churches reflected the movement's
working-class, industrial roots. They often resembled terraced houses
or small industrial workshops, and they were almost always no bigger
than either. In Wales, they frequently stood like small barns or isolated
houses on main roads, drawing people from the surrounding area.
These chapels were very rudimentary and cheaply built, which led
to many of them being demolished, primarily because they were
difficult to maintain. Once Methodism became more established,
its ambitions rose accordingly. Huge buildings were erected, often
replacing the original humble chapels. One example is the former
Methodist Campus in Old Glossop, Derbyshire (now in private use),
which boasted an enormous Sunday school, institute and manse, in
addition to a vast chapel. It was built almost directly opposite the old
parish church and was such a dominant architectural feature that the
street on which it stood was renamed Wesley Street.

As can be seen in Glossop, Methodists had no qualms about siting
their chapels in close proximity to Church of England churches, as
was dramatically demonstrated when the Methodist Central Hall was
built immediately opposite Westminster Abbey in 1912. This vast,
domed building cost over a million pounds – equivalent to around
two hundred million pounds today. It was large enough to accommodate the first General Assembly of the United Nations, and could
not have been a more stark contrast to the original, simple Methodist
chapels.

As we have seen, Methodism developed out of Anglicanism; in a
sense, it became the working-class branch of the Church of England,

even though it was entirely independent of the Established Church. Consequently, Methodist chapels always have an altar table, albeit alongside or just below a pulpit. However, in their simplicity of design and lack of decoration, the buildings themselves resemble Nonconformist chapels rather than parish churches. From the outside, only the stained-glass windows, usually installed in the mid-nineteenth century, hint at the denomination's Anglican roots. These now give Methodist chapels considerably more colour than their Nonconformist rivals.

Another distinction between Nonconformist and Methodist chapels lies in their names. One impact of the Reformation was that no Nonconformist churches were named after saints. Whenever a new Nonconformist building was erected, it would be known simply as 'the chapel'. This might have a preface such as the 'independent' chapel or it might just have been a denominational name – the 'Presbyterian' chapel. Early Methodism split into a bewildering array of subsets and they used these to distinguish between the various chapels, thus for example the 'primitive' Methodist chapel or the 'Calvinist' Methodist chapel. However, showing their roots in Anglicanism, with its sense of key holy people or places, the Methodists had the idea of naming their chapels, and even some villages, after people and places that appear in the Bible, especially the Old Testament.

During the First World War, David Lloyd George, who grew up in the Methodist stronghold of North Wales,[43] said that the battle sites in the Palestine Campaign were much more familiar to him than the names of French and Belgian towns and villages. During his childhood, he had lived in or visited Bethel, Bethlehem, Pisgah and Bethany – all places that feature in the Bible. Other biblical names that started appearing on maps in the nineteenth century were Ebenezer (which in Hebrew means 'Stone of Help' – a good name for a building), Elim and Boaz (both of which mean 'Strong') and Zephaniah (meaning 'The Lord is my Secret'). All of these names tell the story of diligent, disadvantaged, working-class communities who identified

© English Heritage Photo Library

Looking more like a terraced house than a traditional church, Goodshaw Chapel in Lancashire (c. 1742 to 1809) is an atmospheric example of Nonconformist style.

with the Israelites – God's 'chosen people' – who themselves suffered so much persecution and hardship. They reveal a sense of resistance, strength and community that sadly has now often been lost.

Universal and local

Every church or chapel embodies both the universal and the local – either because its designers tried to recreate Jerusalem within the building itself (the typical parish church) or because the universal Word of God found a home in the local chapel (Nonconformists and Methodists). These buildings helped to cement a sense of community, and one sign of the loss of that community spirit has been the closure and conversion to other uses of so many of Britain's churches and chapels. In part, this was inevitable, because some towns had far too many places of worship. Mass conversion movements, which swept through Britain repeatedly from the late eighteenth century onwards, almost always resulted in dozens of new religious buildings, which then gradually fell into disuse as the initial enthusiasm ebbed away. However, most towns and cities still have places where people can gather together. The same cannot be said for remote villages and hamlets in Wales, Cornwall and the Scottish isles, where the chapels are now often in private hands. These people no longer have anywhere to meet as a community.

I recall travelling through Manchester with an Ethiopian Orthodox Christian friend who kept asking why was that church closed or converted. Eventually, after we passed a dozen such places he sighed and asked, 'But where do your people go for their rituals and ceremonies?'

As we think about the future and the stories we want to be part of, we would do well to reflect on the need for communal places for rituals and ceremonies and the need for places of reflection and space simply to be.

GAZETTEER

Parish churches, abbeys and cathedrals

Please refer to pages 136–54 for the significance of the names of churches.

Scotland
- St Giles Cathedral, Edinburgh (EH1): main ancient church of Edinburgh and very unusual in being called St Giles and in the middle of a town

Wales
- St Davids, Llanddewi-Brefi, Ceredigion (SY25): site of famous miracle associated with St Dewi (David)

Northern England
- Anglo-Saxon church, Escomb, County Durham (DL14): exquisite little church with tomb doorway entrance to the sanctuary
- Norman church of Ashby St Ledger, Northamptonshire (CV23): excellent medieval wall paintings
- St Andrew's, Newcastle-on-Tyne (NE1): so-named after a relic of St Andrew spent a night here in the early medieval period
- St John's, Carlisle (CA1): indicates influence of Biblical story
- St John's, Chester (CH1): indicates influence of Biblical story
- St Michael, Hathersage, Derbyshire (S32): 'Christ on the cross' shape of nave and chancel; also to north of the village as protector

- St Nicholas Cathedral, Newcastle-on-Tyne (NE1): a sailors' church

Southern England
- Anglo-Saxon churches, Deerhurst, Gloucestershire (GL19): royal Anglo-Saxon churches with outstanding carvings
- Malmesbury Abbey, Wiltshire (SN16): one of the most magnificent and well-preserved porches in Britain
- Parish church of Corsham, Wiltshire (SN13): a 'Christ on the cross' layout of the nave and chancel
- Round Church, Cambridge (CB5): Knights Templar church designed to imitate the Dome of the Rock in Jerusalem
- St Bride's, London (EC4Y): ancient church site over pre-Christian site with possible link to the goddess Brigid
- St Christopher's, Shapwick, Dorset (DT11): classic village church in an ancient site
- St Clement's Dane, London (WC2R): indicates a Viking/Danish presence here in the eleventh century
- St Clement's, Cambridge (CB2): indicates a Viking/Norse presence here in the eleventh century
- St Giles in the Field, London (WC2H): this is where St Giles churches were usually (i.e. 'in the fields'), as they were linked to lepers and thus outside the main human habitation centres

- St James Barton, Bristol (BS1): indicates a pilgrimage church to the shrine of St James in Santiago de Compostella, Spain
- St Lawrence Chapel, Bath (BA2): outside Bath as it was a hospital for lepers
- St Laurence, Bradford-on-Avon, Wiltshire (BA15): most significant Anglo-Saxon church in Britain and indicates the very different beliefs of the Anglo-Saxon Church from that of the medieval Catholic Church
- St Martin's, Canterbury (CT5): Roman church remains
- St Martin's, North Stoke, Somerset (BA1): Roman church remains and converted pre-Christian sacrificial altar as font
- St Martin's in the Field, London (WC2): a leper church hence outside the city walls
- St Mary, Sellindge, Kent (TN25): original consecration crosses on the walls
- St Mary Magdalene, Langridge, Somerset (BA1): remains of north door for the devil to escape
- St Nicholas Cole Abbey, London: originally a sailors' church
- St Paul's Cathedral, London: the greatest work of Sir Christopher Wren but still incorporating old traditions of leaving something unfinished
- St Peter's, Shepton Mallet, Somerset (BA4): typical example of St Peter church to east of town centre because Peter holds the keys to heaven and east is the direction of Paradise
- St Sepulchre's, London (EC1A): built on Roman burial site

- Wells Cathedral, Somerset (BA5): magnificent West Front with story of salvation

Church exteriors

Wales
- Derwen, Denbighshire (LL15): has a fifteenth-century preaching cross

Northern England
- Eyam, Derbyshire (S32): has a superb Celtic preaching cross
- Lincoln Cathedral, Lincolnshire (LN2): fine carvings of the Day of Judgement on the west wall
- Stafford parish church (ST16): has an octagonal tower

Southern England
- Malmesbury Abbey, Wiltshire (SN16): the south porch features scenes from the Old and New Testaments
- St Mary's, Sellindge, Kent (TN25): has rare external consecration crosses
- Uffington church, Vale of the White Horse, Oxfordshire (SN7): has an octagonal tower

Church interiors

Northern England
- Hawton, Nottinghamshire (NG23): has a fine Easter Sepulchre
- St Andrew's, Newcastle-on-Tyne (NE1): fine font cover
- St Lawrence, Ludlow, Shropshire (SY8): excellent medieval stained glass windows

Southern England

- All Saints', Carleton Rode, Norfolk (NR16): has rare consecration crosses
- Canterbury Cathedral, Kent (CT1)
- Cold Ashton, Gloucestershire (GL54): an unusual early pulpit in an Anglican church
- Dauntsey, Wiltshire (SN15): fine fourteenth-century Doom Board above the Rood screen, still in its original plus and thus very rare
- Little Wittenham, Berkshire (OX14): has one of the best collections of piscinae in the country
- Pilton, Somerset (BA4): has a fine example of a surviving Easter Sepulchre
- Ringmer, East Sussex (BN8): also has a Easter Sepulchre
- St Laurence, Bradford-on-Avon, Wiltshire (BA15): unique layout of Anglo-Saxon church
- Stratford Tony, Wiltshire (SP5): contains a rare medieval stone altar
- Ufford, Suffolk (IP13): has the most magnificent medieval font cover

Southern England

- Banbury, Oxfordshire (OX16): Quaker Meeting House still down a side alley
- Horsefair, Bristol (BS1): 1740's Methodist chapel still clearly at the end of a alley and garden off the main street
- Ipswich, Norfolk (IP1): the Unitarian Church is one of the finest examples of Nonconformist architecture
- Marshfield, Gloucestershire (SN14): magnificent former chapel at back of burbage
- Tewkesbury, Gloucestershire (GL20): examples of early chapels (e.g. Baptist) down alleys to be away from attack

Church of Scotland church

- Ruthwell, Dumfries and Galloway (DG1): contains the Ruthwell Cross of the seventh century with Rune version of Dream of the Rood

Nonconformist chapels

The following are all examples of fine chapels but also of the placing of these in hidden or secluded areas of the town or city for fear of persecution (see pages 173–4).

Northern England

- Berwick-on-Tweed (TD15): many examples of alleys with chapels at the end

Methodist chapels

- Methodist 'Campus', Old Glossop, Derbyshire (SK13): with former chapel, Sunday Schools and other Methodist buildings
- Methodist Central Hall, Westminster, London (SW1H): built to attempt to rival Westminster Abbey and the Anglican Church

6

Creating heaven on earth

This is our story
where we all have a place
in how we live and choose
and move through each day.[44]

THE ART OF DECODING

I was once taken round an art gallery by an expert on symbolism in medieval art. It was an eye-opening experience. There were worlds and layers within each painting that I had never glimpsed or even imagined. For example, we looked at a painting of the Virgin Mary holding the infant Jesus. At first, I saw little else but that. I vaguely knew that there was some significance in the blue colour of Mary's robes, but I couldn't remember precisely what it was. Then my friend started to explain this and numerous other details of the picture.

She asked how Mary was sitting: was she regal or submissive? The answer was obvious: 'Regal,' I replied. My friend told me that you could tell when a picture had been painted purely on the basis of this single fact. Mary was depicted in a submissive pose only from the fifteenth century onwards, when Renaissance artists started to emphasise her youthful beauty. By contrast, the regal pose almost always dates from the eleventh to the fourteenth century. In those years, Mary was shown as an older, wiser woman – almost a mother goddess in her power and majesty. The way in which the infant Jesus is represented in a painting reinforces this. If he stares in devotion at his mother – or looks straight at the viewer from the centre of the canvas – then the picture was probably painted in the earlier period.

Once I had learned how to date a picture, my friend moved on to what each element within it symbolised. For instance, she pointed out the difference between Mary's and Christ's haloes: Christ's is divided into three sections, symbolising the Trinity. Other features needed more deciphering. Sometimes a picture would feature flowers, and my friend told me that these were never chosen at random: lilies stood for purity and therefore emphasised Mary's virginity; roses represented the blood and pain of Christ's Passion. Similarly, if there were birds in the painting, each species had a specific meaning.

The colour blue was the most expensive colour in the medieval paint box, as it was made from lapis lazuli and came all the way from Afghanistan. It was therefore reserved for the mother of Christ alone.

My friend explained all of this to me as we studied seven or eight pictures, spending fifteen minutes or so in front of each one. After a couple of hours, I had to go and have a lie down. I was exhausted because I had just been taught a whole new discipline: how to decode all of the hidden stories and symbols, messages and inferences in medieval art. Yet, in the Middle Ages, any peasant – let alone any theologian – would have been able to do this effortlessly, almost automatically. It is a skill we have lost.

And so it is with our landscape. We find it easy to spot the obviously sacred: the church, the mosque, the stone circle, even the burial mound (with a little practice). But we have lost the ability to read the wider picture within which the church, for example, sits. We need to view that church in the landscape as my expert friend views the Virgin Mary in a painting – as a centrepiece that can be fully understood only by considering the elements that surround it. In this chapter, I shall explore how our towns, cities and even villages were created in much the same way as a medieval artist created a painting. The church may have been the sacred, central point, but a much greater story lies all around it. We just have to learn how to decode it.

If you ask the right questions, any town or city in Britain will reveal at least one, and possibly two or three, of the great stories of our history. They are the first to suffer during a great apocalypse, because they are the most difficult to maintain when the ecology collapses. When the Roman Empire disintegrated due to over-farming, abuse of the soil, desertification and general mismanagement, it was impossible to feed the towns and cities. Their inhabitants either perished or returned to the countryside. For example, London was all but abandoned between the fifth and the seventh centuries; and even when the Anglo-Saxons settled in the area they built on the edge of, rather than within, the old city. We know this because Aldwych means 'Old Market' in Anglo-Saxon, and this was how the new arrivals described the original settlement. Other towns and cities disappeared altogether, never to recover. The third-largest city of Roman Britain was Viroconium, in what is now rural Shropshire. At its peak, it was probably home to some fifteen thousand people. The small village of Wroxeter occupies just one small part of a corner of the original site today.

The Anglo-Saxon and Viking invasions, the Black Death and even the Reformation all had significant impacts on Britain's urban environment. Walsingham, in Norfolk, was a huge medieval pilgrimage centre, but after the Reformation it shrank to no more than a little village. Also in Norfolk, Thetford once boasted twenty churches, eight monasteries, twenty-five principal streets, five market places, six hospitals and numerous other chapels and religious sites. It was an Anglo-Saxon metropolis, but it started to decline as soon as the Normans moved the region's cathedral to Norwich. Over the next few centuries, Thetford's religious and trading power ebbed away, a fall from grace that was hastened by the arrival of the Black Death, and in the end it was left as a shadow of its former self.

Towns and cities have to reinvent themselves in order to survive; and each time they do, they start to write a new story. Birmingham was a small market town until the Industrial Revolution allowed it to become the engine room of the British Empire and the factory of the world. This new story created much of the city we know today. Liverpool has lived through at least three stories, and it is now trying to reinvent itself yet again. Meanwhile, Manchester and Glasgow have risen from the dust of the collapse of the industrial story to become cultural and service centres.

A TALE OF TWO CITIES

At the dawn of each great cycle, the survivors of the recent collapse need to find a way to channel their energy, funds and faith into reconstruction and redevelopment. Over the last two thousand years, two great models – the classical and the biblical – have helped them achieve this.

The classical model

The earlier model – which reappeared in the eighteenth century and is still with us today – is the Greek city plan. This was adopted by the Romans, who brought it to Britain in the middle of the first century AD. It is epitomised by order and regularity – hence the straight streets, formal squares and symmetry of the classical Roman town or city. Such features can still be discerned in the layouts of Exeter, Gloucester and Chester, despite the terrible damage wreaked by town planners over the last century.

Inherent in the planning of these urban areas was the belief that humanity and the divine shared responsibility for making the world ordered and efficient. It was felt that every town could and should reflect the greater, stable pattern of the universe. We could create hundreds of miniature versions of this ordered universe, and thus, in a sense, become little gods in our own right.

Georgian architects and planners fully embraced this sacred vision and made it their own, which resulted in Bath, Edinburgh's New Town, Tenby, Clifton in Bristol, the area between Regent's Park and Pall Mall in London, Cheltenham and Tunbridge Wells, among others. To some extent, all of these places came into being because a generation of architects collectively rejected the alternative, biblical model (see below). It is interesting to note that many of them even refused to include churches in their plans. In part, this was because churches, which have traditionally been orientated from due east to due west, would have disrupted the graceful sweep of the architects' beautiful circuses and crescents. But far more important was the fact that the designers felt their inclusion was unnecessary. Why bother incorporating the sacred in the mundane when the mundane itself is designed to be sacred? Generally, the only churches to be found in these sacred urban areas are Nonconformist chapels, and even these usually resemble Greek temples. For example, right beside the Royal Pavilion in Brighton there is a Unitarian church, built in 1819 and modelled upon the Temple of Theseus in Athens.

One of the finest examples of the classical model is Edinburgh's New Town, which arose because of the collision of politics, demographics and the rediscovery of the classical model in the middle of the eighteenth century.

On a cold, wet day in 1746, English and German troops loyal to the Hanoverian King of Britain, George II, destroyed the Scottish army of the 'Young Pretender', Charles Edward Stuart, in a place known as Culloden to the victorious English and as Blar Chuil Lodair to the crushed Scots. Bonnie Prince Charlie fled, never to return, and the Scottish clans' hopes of seceding from the Union were dashed for centuries. In effect, Scotland became an occupied country. Even its name was changed, as loyal Scots started to refer to North Britain – an early example of political correctness in modern British history.

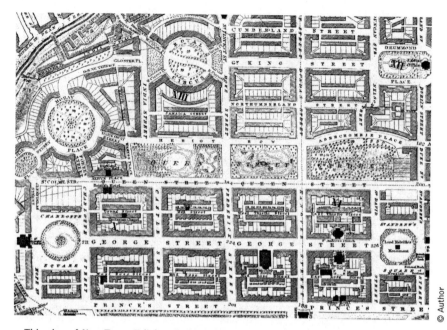

This plan of New Town, Edinburgh shows both the Georgian fascination with symmetry and order, inherited from the Greeks and Romans, and the new theological narrative of British identity after the defeat of Bonnie Prince Charlie.

All of this left Edinburgh in a very difficult position. The city author-ities knew that they had to display unstinting loyalty to the House of Hanover, to England and to the very idea of being British. Yet, they presided over the ancient capital of the Kingdom of Scotland, a city with a rich and proud history that its citizens were not minded to forget. As if that were not enough, Edinburgh was also in desperate need of more accommodation and modernisation. The Old Town was overcrowded and unsanitary, problems that were exacerbated when the Hanoverian troops enlarged their barracks in the city.

By the 1760s, the authorities acknowledged that they had to create a whole new town. They launched a competition and chose the plan of a young architect, James Craig. After a couple of years and a few amendments to Craig's original plan, building work began.

The New Town's principal features are two large squares, one at the eastern end – St Andrew's Square – and one at the western end –

originally called St George's Square (now known as Charlotte Square, in honour of Princess Charlotte, the only daughter of George IV, who died in childbirth in 1817).[45] Written into its very design, this was a patriotic declaration of the unity of Britain's great patron saints. The intention was to reinforce this on a spectacular scale by the creation of two vast churches – one dedicated to St Andrew on the eastern side of his square and one dedicated to St George on the western side of his. However, while the magnificent St George's was duly built exactly where it appeared on Craig's plans,[46] St Andrew's was not. There is a St Andrew's church in the New Town, but it is rather more modest and sits on George Street (named after the Hanoverian kings rather than the saint), which runs between one square and the other. This happened because the prime plot that was originally assigned to St Andrew's was grabbed by Sir Lawrence Dundas, one of the richest and most power-ful men in the city, who wanted to build a very fine house for himself. His home is now the headquarters of the Royal Bank of Scotland, so it could be said that in the great cosmic battle between Mammon and God, Mammon has ultimately triumphed ... in Edinburgh at least.

The theme of two unified nations is repeated elsewhere in the New Town. For instance, Thistle Street (named after the Scottish national emblem) runs to the north of Rose Street (honouring the English national emblem), with George Street running between the two – presumably to emphasise the even-handedness of the monarch. Hanover Street and Frederick Street (named after one of the Hanoverian princes) continue this lauding of the royal family, as do the prominent Queen Street and Princes Street.

None of this symbolism was particularly subtle, but it was effective. The layout of the New Town was a physical representation of a grand narrative that allowed the rising classes of Edinburgh literally to walk through their past and present while they planned their future, guarded spiritually by two patron saints and framed by loyalty to the ruling House of Hanover and to the Georgian era itself. Meanwhile, the inclusion of St Andrew and the thistle meant they could continue to hold up their heads as proud Scots.

The biblical model

The Bible is rather ambivalent about the whole idea of cities. Whereas the Greeks and Romans viewed urban living as the pinnacle of human society, supported by the (far inferior) countryside, the Bible is much more equivocal. There is considerable tension between the rural and the urban, the pastoral and the planned, in the Bible – and it is far from certain which system is favoured by God. On the one hand, there is an arc of development – from the Garden of Eden in Genesis to the City of God in Revelation. On the other, according to Genesis (4:17), the very first town was built by the murderer Cain – hardly a glowing endorsement of urbanism. This well captures the suspicion that all pastoral and nomadic people had – and often still have – of town-dwellers.

Nevertheless, the Bible had an unsurpassed influence on the shape of towns and cities in medieval Britain – and indeed throughout the Christian world, from Ireland to Moscow. Fortunately for medieval town planners, the Book of Revelation (21:11–27) describes the perfect city – the New Jerusalem or the City of God – in wondrous detail. This vision of perfection allayed – at least in part – people's uneasiness about cities. They still viewed them as inherently dangerous places, yet all medieval Christians believed that their ultimate destination was a heavenly city, not some sort of heavenly countryside, and this drove town planners to try to replicate the City of God in the midst of the mess and chaos of the typical medieval town.

Biblical towns and cities are easy to recognise. While a classical town is regular, symmetrical and ordered, a biblical town is much more concerned with creating symbols in the landscape. So there may well be a cross right in the town centre, the result of the intersection of four main roads converging from the north, south, east and west. In turn, this set of roads leading to the crossroads may be encircled by another road to symbolise the unity of God. Elsewhere, three streets may converge to form a triangle, to echo the Trinity. As we saw in Chapter 5, biblical towns also pay heed to auspicious directions, so the major religious site usually lies to the east of the centre, as in the cathedral cities of Norwich, Lincoln, Winchester, Glasgow and St Andrews; and any church to the north will usually be dedicated to a protector saint.

The sacred is manifest in all of these shapes, directions and locations. Of course, the most obvious place to find this is in the town's parish church itself, and this will usually have been reinforced by locating the building on a specific sacred site – clues to which may still be possible to work our (see the list of saints in Chapter 5). Next, try to find the market cross (or, as it is known in Scotland, the mercat cross), because that will have been the sacred centre of the town, where the market was held. Good examples are in Forfar (Angus), Chapel-en-le-Frith (Derbyshire), Llanidloes (Powys), Sandbach (Cheshire) and Shepton Mallet (Somerset). The layout here may well form a distinct crossroads of the four main streets, even if the rest of the town is more higgledy-piggledy. Chichester, Winchester and Rhayader, Powys, all have very clear crossroads right the centre of town.[47] If there is more than one church, try to work out why buildings in certain locations are dedicated to particular saints. Find out where churches or chapels used to be. Many will have been swept away in the Reformation, and others will now be used for other purposes. Ancient gates into the town (now probably long gone) will once have had chapels above them or churches beside them. Their names will tell you a great deal about the fears and hopes of the people who built the town walls. Holy wells, pilgrimage routes that run through or terminate in the town and cemeteries are other features that contribute to the sacred landscape of the biblical town.

THE ANCESTORS AND THE SACRED MARKET PLACE

The typical biblical town or city has two key forces working side by side, but often struggling against each other: commerce and religion.

These are represented by the market place and the sacred space – the parish church. These two places reflect the basic beliefs and great stories of the past six to seven thousand years.

To some extent, the church is a form of ancestor shrine. The dead lie within and around the confines of the building, with those buried inside being especially honoured. Some parts of the church – chantry chapels – might have been built simply so that priests could say prayers for the parishioners' forebears. If an archaeologist with no knowledge of religious practice were to examine an average parish church, he would probably conclude that it was no more or less than an ancestor tomb – a more recent form of long barrow, in other words.

In prehistory, as the long barrows indicate, communities felt the need to remain close to their forebears and honour them. That need disappeared with the collapse of the First Great Cycle, but it re-emerged with the rise of Christianity. In the earlier period, people revered their dead ancestors in the hope that they would provide protection against evil forces. Now, we revere our forebears in the hope that *we* – and especially the saints and Christ – can help *them*. This is a major theological shift, but in both cases the ancestors occupy a central position in the sacred picture.

As we saw in Chapter 3, the stone circles of the Second Great Cycle probably functioned as sacred market places. In a pre-literate culture, it was essential to have spaces where deals could be struck and honoured. By the Middle Ages, of course, traders were able to record their deals on paper, which gave them some insurance against defaulters. But extra insurance, especially if it were provided by a higher authority, was always welcome, so the vast majority of deals were still conducted in a sacred location: the town's market place. Almost every such market place had a cross in its centre, leaving no one in any doubt about its sacred dimension. These crosses were fundamental to the sacred duty of business.

While the market cross indicated the central point in the biblical town, a statue or some other marker often performed the same function in the classical town. In both cases, this familiar architectural feature stood in the middle of an open space that hosted festivities, drama, music and news announcements as well as commerce. People felt safe to gather in these spaces, just as their ancestors had felt safe inside stone circles, because everyone acknowledged their sacredness and neutrality. In Greek town planning, such a place was called the omphalos, after the sacred stone that stood in the centre. Every town, most villages and many cities still have their original omphalos, the heart of the original settlement, even if the cross or stone has long gone. On the outskirts of old towns, or on the main roads leading to them, you might find waymarkers saying something like '10 Miles to the Market Cross of ...' or '4 Miles to the Market Place'. The way-markers to London all give distances to Hyde Park Corner – for centuries the place where public announcements were made in the capital, as is celebrated today in the form of Speakers' Corner.

© Les Gibbon/Alamy

This lovely old mercat cross is in the historic village square in Culross in Scotland.

Mercat crosses can still be found in many Scottish towns and cities. Public announcements are still made at Edinburgh's, on the High Street, while the one in Glasgow gives its name to the Glasgow Cross area. These are still impressive monuments – small buildings rather than simple crosses. By contrast, just a stump remains of the cross that once stood in the centre Fettercairn in Aberdeenshire.

Of course, it was no accident that the centre of each and every medieval town was marked by a cross, rather than some other symbol. In feudal society, religious power was the only significant counterpoint to the power of the local lord and his soldiers. This is reflected in the character of Friar Tuck, from the medieval legend of Robin Hood. By joining Robin's band, Tuck embodied the widespread belief that Christianity was on the side of the poor, rather than the rich. There was another aspect to Tuck, though: he was a wandering monk, and as such was free from many of the constraints of the Established Church. Market crosses were often used as preaching stumps by such friars, and these men were generally far more critical of wealth and greed than the Church itself. One of the greatest mass rebellions in English history, the Peasants' Revolt of 1381, was led by one of these itinerant preachers, John Bull.

In Devizes, Wiltshire, the original market cross was destroyed. Consequently, in the early nineteenth century, a new monument was erected in the town's market square. It is a very fine neo-Gothic monument, but it does not remotely resemble a cross, and it has a somewhat strange sacred role. Inscribed on the monument in neat Victorian lettering is the story of a local woman – Ruth Pierce. On Thursday, 25 January 1753, Pierce and three other women bought a sack of wheat in the market, with each woman paying her agreed share. However, it seems that Pierce did not contribute the full amount and, on being challenged, uttered the fateful words: 'May I drop dead if I am not telling

▶

the truth.' She was so angry that she repeated the phrase and then promptly fell to the ground and died, with the money she had held back still clasped in her hand. The coroner declared that she had been 'struck down dead by the vengeance of God'.

Many market crosses were demolished as symbols of superstition and papism during the Reformation. The reformers felt that people who wanted to gather together should do so not in the market place but in the local church, as that was the *truly* sacred part of town. Banbury cross, famous in the children's songs, was demolished by Puritans in 1600 and a plaque was recently unveiled on the spot where the cross once stood. But the market squares remain, and they retain at least some of their ancient sacredness. This is because trade and financial agreements – activities that are conducted in market places to this day – have been treated as sacred since at least the time of the stone circles. And this extends far beyond Britain and Christianity: in Islam, for instance, whenever a deal is agreed, God is invoked as a witness.

In London, the pivotal role played by crosses is obvious from a quick glance at a map of the Underground. King's Cross is a relatively recent name for an area that was once known as Battle Bridge, to commemorate the final great battle between the British Queen Boudicca and the Romans in the middle of the first century AD. Its current name comes from an enormous monument erected on the site in 1835 to honour King George IV. It was sixty feet tall and topped by a double-life-size statue of the portly king. Thankfully, this ghastly monument lasted only ten years before being demolished, but the name it inspired has proved more enduring.

Charing Cross's story is much more inspiring. When Eleanor of Castile, wife of King Edward I, died in 1290 in Lincolnshire, the king was heartbroken. First, he had her body brought to Westminster – a journey of twelve days. Then he ordered crosses to be erected at each place where her body had stopped overnight. Three of these still survive – at Geddington, Lincolnshire, Northampton and Waltham Cross (so called because of the cross to Eleanor). The final cross – at Charing Cross – was destroyed by Puritans in the seventeenth century, but it was rebuilt in 1865, and this impressive Victorian monument still stands outside the rail station to this day. This unique procession of crosses from Lincoln to London represents a fusion of piety, mourning and the sacred tradition of the market cross.

The cross has returned to the centre of many towns and cities in the form of the war memorial. The natural place to erect such a monument after the First World War was in the town omphalos. In planning terms, this signified a recognition that neither a church nor a civic building could do justice to the enormity of the loss. For instance, in Derbyshire, the war memorial in Glossop's Norfolk Square commemorates more than three hundred men who died in the trenches – tragedy on a scale that ripped apart the community.

In most villages and small towns, if you want to find the church, look for the market ... or vice versa. Trade and faith were the foundations of Anglo-Saxon and medieval town development, often combined with defence – town walls – and burbages (see Chapter 3). The Church was deeply involved in this urban expansion: for example, the Bishop of Winchester designed Farnham, in Surrey, while the Bishop of Lichfield laid out medieval Lichfield on top of an Anglo-Saxon settlement.

Sometimes, though, the planners would not develop the original settlement but rather build near by. This is what happened in Hay-on-Wye. The church of St Mary's was built beside the original motte and bailey castle of Hay – which was abandoned in the twelfth century in favour of the site in the town centre where the more recent, but still ramshackle, castle of Hay sits today. The town was laid out to surround this second castle site, with the exception of the south side, where the town wall and the castle meet. The area below the castle gate was the site of the main markets – for cheese, butter and cattle. A small chapel was built just below these market places, but the main church of St Mary's remained a third of a mile away, down the appropriately named Church Street. The new town was designed to create a secure working environment where the locals could do business, safe from attack from marauding Welsh and the troops of rival Norman lords who were eager to grab a piece of the commercial action. Church attendance was a secondary consideration. Nothing spells this out more clearly than the fact that Hay's main church was left outside the new town walls.

Almost the exact opposite of this took place in Salisbury – where the cathedral and the city relocated from Old Sarum to the meadows below in order to escape the overbearing presence and bad behaviour of the soldiers in the castle (see Chapter 7).

As these two examples show, the locations of the parish church, market, castle, manor house can reveal a good deal about the rival forces that were in play within a town as it developed. The key to most old towns – although not Hay – is that the sacred was inserted in their layouts in order to redeem them, because the builders were still far from certain that urban living was in any sense holy. Some whole towns were laid out according to this concept, using the names and powers of the saints to create an entirely sacred environment and even building sacred symbols – such as the circle and the cross – into the street design. The finest example of this in Britain is the city of Bristol, which was built according to the rules of Christian geomancy – literally, 'earth magic'.

THE CHRISTIAN GEOMANCY OF BRISTOL

Created in the ninth century on a virgin piece of land, Bristol was laid out in the form of an almost perfect Celtic cross. (In case you're wondering why the land was 'virgin', it had once been a marsh but dried out when the west coast of Britain rose by about a foot as a result of the landmass still recovering from the weight of ice during the last ice age.) The smaller of its two rivers, the Frome, was diverted to create a curving moat around the western town wall, while the eastern wall followed a similar curve, aside from a slight dent where a steep cliff made it impossible to be completely circular. In Celtic Christian symbolism, as we have seen, the circle represents the unity and love of God. The town's four main streets ran from north to south and east to west, forming the familiar cross in the centre of the circle.

Once this sacred symbolism had been established, the people of Bristol set about protecting themselves theologically by dedicating churches to appropriate saints, thereby literally building their power into the fabric of the town. For protection against evil spirits and forces, they built St Michael the Archangel on the Mount Without (to give the church its full title) – on a hill to the north of the city wall. As a port, Bristol also needed churches that could cater for the needs of sailors. So, beside the bridge over the River Avon that gave Bristol its original name (Brigstow, meaning 'Place of the Bridge'), they built a church dedicated to St Nicholas, patron saint of sailors, over the main port gate.[48] The church of St John the Baptist was erected to stand guard over the main water conduit into the city. And the church of St Peter (the town's funeral church, according to early documents) is positioned just outside the eastern city wall – pointing towards paradise.

Everybody knows about Bristol's role in the eighteenth-century slave trade, but there was an early precursor to this shameful episode in the city's history. In the tenth and eleventh centuries, Bristolians traded slaves captured in the Midlands to Ireland until the preaching of a great local bishop – St Wulfstan of Worcester – eventually persuaded them to abandon the practice. To celebrate this victory of good over evil, the church of St Leonard – the patron saint of prisoners and slaves – was built over the city gate leading to the new harbour that was created in the thirteenth century.

A fascinating theological story is told in church names in the very centre of town. There were originally three churches here, but only two survive today, and one of them underwent a name change as a result of Protestant theology and reformists' antipathy to Catholic imagery. The church now known as Christ Church was originally called Holy

Trinity – the concept of 'Father, Son and Holy Spirit' that lies at the heart of Christian theology. Diagonally opposite is All Saints and All Souls, its name commemorating all of the faithful who now reside in heaven and can be approached by any lost soul wishing to be saved. This was a core belief of medieval Christianity: invocation of the saints and their intercessions could save even the worst sinner.

The third town-centre church was named after St Ewen. However, there is no St Ewen in any official book of saints, so who was he? In nearby Wales, many churches are dedicated to someone who is known only in that particular geographical location – usually the first person to preach the Gospel there or a particularly holy resident. These are not universally acknowledged saints, but they are treated as such by the local community. With Bristol being so close to Wales, the townsfolk may well have adopted the same practice and dedicated one of their earliest churches to its first priest. Perhaps his name was Ewen.

Near by are the remains of the church of St Mary le Port, which was bombed in 1940. This church, dedicated to the mother of Christ, is built at a strange angle. Instead of running west to east like all the other churches, it is orientated towards the three churches in the centre, from which it is separated by about 100 metres. It seems to indicate that Mary is standing looking up at her son and the Holy Trinity in a position of adoration.

Finally, the church built just outside the city wall is dedicated to St Stephen, the first Christian martyr, who was stoned to death just outside the walls of Jerusalem.

FROM ROMAN TO CHRISTIAN: THE STREETS OF CANTERBURY

In contrast to the systematic Christian layout of Bristol, many towns and cities grow organically, leading to many layers of meaning and sacredness. For example, Canterbury was originally a Roman city, laid out in a grid pattern. However, this settlement fell into ruin in the fifth century AD and so had only marginally influence on the shape of the Anglo-Saxon/medieval city that arose around the mighty cathedral. With some manipulation, the original main streets were made to resemble a basic cross running from north to south and east to west. And the cathedral has always been in the right place – in the eastern part of the city, facing paradise.

The city walls had their chapels and the city itself many churches, each of which had a story to tell. Thus, Canterbury's St Michael's church, unusually, stood above the *east* gate – not to the north – because the townsfolk were so used to invading armies landing on the coast and attacking from the east. St Alphege's church sits right next to the cathedral, because he was a martyred Archbishop of Canterbury. St Helen's church, in the city centre, held a relic of the True Cross (said to have been found by Helen), while the Holy Cross church on the western city gate also signalled the presence of that priceless relic in the city. All Saints' church, also in the city centre, served as a reminder that everyone could be saved, while St Edmund's was built in honour of the most important Anglo-Saxon martyred King of England. St Sepulchre's church is on the site of the major Roman cemetery and appropriately honours Christ's tomb in Jerusalem, while St Mildred's was where the venerated relics of this eighth-century local saint were housed. The latter rivalled the cathedral itself in importance for many centuries.

The façades of burbage houses can still be seen on St George's Street, while both St Mary's Street and St John's Lane still have complete burbages, with their thin strips of land running back from the street.

THE MYTHS AND STREETS OF CARMARTHEN

Great stories are fundamental to both the creation and the growth of towns. It seems that they can prosper only if their citizens invest in a story, or more often a series of stories. This is perfectly illustrated in the strange tales of the town of Carmarthen in Wales. Pre-Christian, Christian and even post-Christian notions of the sacred can be found in Carmarthen's churches and layout, and they tell a variety of stories.

The town originally had a simple, symbolic medieval biblical layout, traces of which are still visible. To the north of the town is St Catherine's Street, named after the long-gone chapel of St Catherine, which used to stand on the hill here. As we saw earlier, St Catherine is often associated with hills because of her link with Celtic sun deity, so the presence of her name may indicate the Christianising of a pre-Christian sacred hilltop site. The town's main parish church is St Peter's, which, typically, stands to the east of the town. As St Peter holds the keys to heaven, churches dedicated to him routinely stand en route to paradise, which in Christian geomancy lies to the east.

There used to be a priory and a friary in the town, as we are reminded by Friars Park and Priory Street. Similarly, St Mary's church used to stand in front of the castle, but today she is commemorated only in a street name. This was right in the heart of the town's market area, and St Mary is a common dedication in such a setting because of her compassion and watchful eye. In this market place, Bishop Ferrer, the Protestant Bishop of St Davids, was burned to death during the persecutions lauched by the Catholic Queen Mary in the 1550s. The site has been held in special regard and visited by Protestants for centuries since. A Protestant memorial has replaced the original Catholic cross.

All of this is very familiar, and echoes similar naming patterns in numerous other British medieval towns. However, Carmarthen has another layer of geomancy, much of it very recent, but some of it buried deep in medieval history and folklore. For, according to the notoriously unreliable twelfth-century writer Geoffrey of Monmouth, it was here that Merlin was born. It seems unlikely that there was any such association until Geoffrey wrote his bestseller *The History of the Kings of Britain*, but it has since become a major theme of the town's geography. This is the reason why there is a local hill called Bryn

Myrddin (Merlin's Hill), not to mention a new shopping centre called Merlin's Walk, with suitably named walkways within it. The most famous physical aspect of the Merlin myth was Merlin's Oak, about which the wizard was said to have uttered the prophecy:

> *When Merlin's tree shall tumble down,*
> *Then shall fall Carmarthen Town.*

However, the town is still standing, even though the tree died in the late nineteenth century. The last remnants of it are now housed in the local museum. Moreover, as we saw in Chapter 4, the oak might not even have begun life until 1660, as it was probably one of thousands to be planted in celebration of the Restoration of King Charles II.

Even more frustrating for the fans who hope to walk in Merlin's footsteps, it now seems that even his name – Myrddin in Welsh – is simply a corruption of the original Roman name for the town: Moridunum. Traces of that settlement can still be found on the edge of Carmarthen, especially in the somewhat bedraggled Roman amphitheatre, which is precariously preserved between the busy, noisy Priory Street and a modern housing estate.

STORIES EVERYWHERE

Every town or city is shaped by particular topographical features as well as the vagaries of its history – wars, fires, rebuilding, the Blitz and the near-universal disaster of post-war town planning. However, precisely because of these calamities, it is possible not only to read the story of a town but to peer beneath the current street layout and buildings. This allows us to explore people's determination to represent the sacred in their built environment – a quest that shaped Britain's towns and cities until the beginning of the nineteenth century.

Even thereafter, the notion of incorporating the sacred was not abandoned completely, as can be seen in the common Victorian practice of erecting magnificent churches in some of the worst slums (see Chapter 7). However, the Victorians simply could not grasp the concept that had been so readily appreciated by the Georgians: that the sacred could and should be interweaved with the mundane in their town planning. Cities and towns were no longer viewed as places where a sacred drama was being played out. Instead, the Victorians started to romanticise the countryside. Urban areas were basically given up as lost causes.

READING THE VILLAGE

Villages share many of the features that were explored above when looking at towns and cities, but they also have their own particular clues and reminders of the past and the sacred. In Chapter 4, we saw how field systems reflect changing beliefs about the significance of humanity in a greater story – the shift from the biblically based vision of humanity as important but not the sole reason for creation to the utilitarian view that gives primacy to our needs (and even our desires) and ignores that greater story altogether.

On one level, villages can be quite difficult to read. They lack a town's diversity of streets, buildings, churches and places of great importance; and there is not the same wealth of place and street names. Consequently, we have to learn how to read the landscape – to see the history and the sacred in the folds of the fields and the size and shape of the hedges. We need to look at the open spaces just as much as the streets. We need to appreciate what is missing as well as what is present.

From my office window in Kelston Park, just outside Bath, I can see a tight bend in the A431, right in the middle of Kelston village. This sharp, steep turn up the hill seems to make no sense, because shortly thereafter the road resumes its logical, direct route to Bath. So why is it there? My theory is that the road might once have bypassed a cemetery at this point. Roman Christian burials have been found in the farm land close to this bend, so it is entirely possible that the A431 holds a memory of what was sacred land.

Often a bend forms part of an old boundary. Anglo-Saxon fields, in particular, were marked by deep ditches that were dug to show where one landowner's rights ended and another's began. Thus, many country lanes bend for no apparent reason, yet they are following the routes of old ditches, which then became pathways between the fields, to avoid walking on the farmer's crops.

Other bends in a road might indicate that something once stood in the way or that a change was made for a special reason. A classic example is the road connecting the Northumbrian villages of Milfield and Fenton. The road wiggles out of Milfield before straightening up for about a quarter of a mile, just after a stream, then turns sharp right and runs in a fairly straight line for another third of a mile. It then becomes the familiar meandering country lane. Archaeological research has recently revealed why it follows this seemingly eccentric course: this was the site of the Anglo-Saxon palace of Meldrum, and the road follows its boundary ditch.

At first sight, the roads around Stanton Lacy, Shropshire, seem similarly chaotic. One runs almost due east into the village from the B4365, before bending to go around the ancient churchyard. But then, just beyond the church, it comes to an abrupt halt at a north–south crossroads. The two roads that form this T junction then both run for only about two hundred yards (one due north, the other due south) before turning at right angles to head east for half a mile or so. At that point, they both intersect with the same upper road, about half a mile apart. The whole layout looks like an old-fashioned farming fork with two prongs. It must indicate an old park or farm-land estate, as there is no other reason for the roads to be laid out in this way. Logically, the first road should simply have continued on past the church.

WHAT IS MISSING?

There are plenty of old barns in the countryside; and hundreds of medieval tithe barns, which housed the Church's share of the harvest. But you will look in vain for ancient cattle sheds, because there were none. Cattle shared the farmhouse, often living below the main living quarters of the family and therefore acting as an early form of underfloor heating. They were treated as part of the family, so their eventual exclusion from the home was a very significant moment. It marked a new stage in humanity's desire to separate itself from the rest of nature. Of course, there were sound hygienic reasons for not allowing cows across the threshold any more, but this still signalled a growing gap between 'us' and 'them'.

Whereas the modern necessity of cattle sheds marks one aspect of our developing – or deteriorating – sacred relationship with nature, the disappearance of fishponds marks another. Every monastery used

Built to house the church's share of the harvest, tithe barns are a reminder that the church was once at the heart of medieval farming communities.

to have them, but now almost all of them have disappeared. The only clues to their former existence are found in place names – such as Fishpond Bottom, in Dorset – and odd depressions in the landscape – as at Witham, Somerset. These deeply practical and rather lovely ponds vanished for the simple reason that the Catholic practice of eating fish on a Friday decreased dramatically after the dissolution of the monasteries in the mid-sixteenth century. A religious tradition had led to their creation and the collapse of that tradition spelled their doom.

WHAT IS THERE?

The average village has just one parish church, and it frequently has a very general or common dedication, such as St Mary's or St John's. However, if the dedication is more unusual it may well reveal an interesting mystical or historical past, so it is probably worth exploring. Many villages also have a Nonconformist and/or Methodist chapel, although these may have been converted into private homes or warehouses in recent years. Nevertheless, they can still reveal plenty about the people who built them, with the foundation stone (usually set into the front wall) and the chapel's name (if any) being particularly important clues.

The church catered for the big religious festivals of the ecclesiastical calendar: Christmas, Easter, Whitsun, the patronal festival of the saint, and so on. It also provided the venue for baptisms, wedding and funerals. It often had an adjacent alehouse, run by the parish, where beer was brewed for these major celebrations. Many of these later became the village pub, but some retain their original connections with the church, as at Chew Magna in Somerset.

However, sometimes villagers wanted to hold celebrations that were not church-related, so they needed another communal space. This was provided by the village green. Generally, the green was – and indeed still is – common land, not under the jurisdiction of any family or authority. The May pole was erected here, and parties and special events were celebrated around it: for instance, the defeat of the Spanish Armada in 1588 and the Diamond Jubilee of Queen Victoria in 1897. Today, the green is often prized as a quiet space in the heart of the village. However, in previous centuries, it was much more busy: animals were free to graze there, rowdy annual fairs were held on it, and most evenings the villager's youngsters would congregate on it to drink, flirt and possibly get up to mischief.

The names of a village's farms and buildings can reveal a great deal about the past. Grange Farm is a very common name and indicates that such a farm belonged to a monastery before the Reformation. The great monasteries were huge agri-businesses: they owned vast tracts of land that generated enormous wealth. It was said in the Middle Ages that if the Abbot of Glastonbury were to marry the Abbess of Shaftesbury, they would own half the land of England!

If a farm, cottage, field or even school is named 'Glebe' (from a Middle English word meaning 'earth'), this indicates that it once belonged to the local priest. He kept any income that it generated, which supplemented the payments he received in tithes from all of the other farms in his parish. He could either farm the glebe land himself or rent it out to others. In the twentieth century, all glebe land came under the administration of the central church authorities (in both Scotland and England), but the income is still used to run local parishes and services.

Other modern names can reveal even deeper layers of a sacred landscape. For example, Bristol's main railway station is called Temple Meads. This comes from the meadows (meads) that were once owned by the Knights Templar, who had a church near here until they were suppressed in 1307. The name remains even though the meadows have long since been covered in railway tracks, factories, warehouses and, most recently, a business district.

We know that the Knights Templar owned the fields around the station because old tithe maps record the owner of every field in

Britain, as well as any woodland. If the map pre-dates the Enclosure Acts, you can use it to trace ancient field systems and will discover a wealth of other details, too, such as the sites of old wells and buildings, and the routes of lanes.

THE POWER OF NAMES

Very few villages, towns or cities are named by accident. There are nearly always several layers of meaning in their names; we just need to learn how to uncover them. The place to start, of course, is with the literal meaning of a place name. So, for example, Edinburgh means 'Fort on the Rock Face'; Alnwick (in Northumberland) means 'Market Place on the Holy River'; and Hackney means 'Hacca's Island'. Edinburgh very much lives up to its name, as the town developed around a castle that is perched on the top of a volcanic hill, but the root (or rather roots) of the name itself reveal considerably more about its origins, because half of the name comes Scottish Gaelic (*edinis*, meaning 'rock face'), while the other half is Anglo-Saxon (*burgh*, meaning 'fort'). This simple etymological exercise therefore uncovers the strategic importance of the site in the shifting fortunes of two competing cultures – the Scots and the English – who fought over this craggy outcrop for centuries. 'Alnwick' is another example of two languages contributing to a single place name. Aln – meaning 'Holy' or 'Mighty One' – the name of the river that runs to the north of the town, is pre-Roman in origin, while *wick* is the Anglo-Saxon word for a market settlement. 'Hackney' simply combines the name of a Danish chief – Haca – with the Anglo-Saxon word for 'island' – *eg*, later corrupted to *ey*.

The process of unravelling names in this way reveals the pragmatic reasons why places were settled in the first place – clearly, Edinburgh's role was defensive while Alnwick's was commercial – but it can also tell us something about the sacred significance of a site. For instance, would Alnwick have been built where it was if it had not been beside a holy river?

Once we have analysed the literal meaning of a place name itself, we need to move on to the names of two institutions in the town or village that have usually remained unchanged for centuries: those of the parish church and the local pub (or pubs). As we saw in Chapter 5, church dedications can tell us a great deal about our ancestors' beliefs and their respect for cosmic forces, while pub names can often take us on a fascinating journey into the stories of the past. (See Chapter 5 for full details on how to interpret church dedications, and below for tips on how to decode the names of pubs.)

Finally, we need to look carefully at street names, because these often have hidden meanings that have been lost or forgotten over the centuries.

Once you learn how to decode these three elements – the name of the place itself; the names of that place's principal communal buildings (the church and the pub); and the names of its streets – you should be able to read the sacred and historic meaning in any settlement, from a village to a major city.

Place names

In Chapter 4, we saw that natural features have retained the oldest names in the country. By contrast, the name of a settlement tends to reflect the last group to invade the area.

The Archbishop of York still signs his documents 'Ebor' – a version of the Roman name 'Eboracum', which itself was derived from a pre-Roman word meaning 'yew' – a tree that has been considered sacred for millennia. When the Anglo-Saxons arrived, they corrupted the Roman name into 'Eoforwick' (with the suffix *wick* indicating that it was now an important market). Next, when the Vikings invaded in the ninth century, they corrupted this into 'Iorvik', which was shortened to 'Iork'. Finally, the Normans simply changed the first letter, to make 'York'.

In 1664, Charles II unilaterally declared that the whole of the New Netherlands coastline of America, which included modern-day New York, was now British territory. Then he gifted it to his brother, James, the Duke of York. The principal town, New Amsterdam, was renamed New York, thus guaranteeing the historic English name (with pre-Roman, Roman, Anglo-Saxon, Viking and Norman roots) more global fame than could ever have been imagined.

Some place names give a clue to a specific sacred dimension or link with religion. For instance, places called Barrow will be located on or near pre-historic burial sites, while those named after saints will reflect those saints' particular strengths or attributes (see Chapters 4 and 5 for examples). But many are simple, workaday names that reveal when they were founded (or re-established), by whom, and possibly some distinguishing topographical feature (such as a particularly large river or an impressive mountain).

Baldock, in Hertfordshire, might have a religious link or, equally, it might have been named after a prominent local landmark, depending on which theory you believe. It was founded in the 1140s by the Knights Templar – the military religious order that was a major player in the Crusades. The Templars' principal aim was to protect Jerusalem, but they were also keen to conquer other 'heathen' cities, such as Baghdad. The medieval French term for Baghdad was Baldak, so some people believe that the little town in Hertfordshire reflected the Templars' ambitions with respect to that city. Others argue that Baldock was simply named after a dead (or *bald* in medieval English) oak tree that stood on the site.

Begin at the end
The suffix of a place name is the best place to start when trying to unravel its meaning.

- Farms and small settlements are indicated by *ham, cot, stoke* (often a monastic settlement), *worth, muir, mor* and *wick. Thorpe, holme* and *by* have the same meaning, but additionally reveal that Vikings settled in these places.

- The Viking word for 'house' was *oft.*

- A manor, estate or larger settlement is often indicated by *ton, tun* or *stone.*

- Water references include *brig* (bridge), *ath* (ford) and, of course, *well. Bourne* means 'river' or 'stream' – so Fulbourne, in Cambridgeshire, is proclaiming that its stream flows throughout the year.

- Fortified settlements are revealed by *burgh, bury* and *borough.*

- Fields and clearings in forests are indicated by *all* and *ley* (clearings), *lann* (wood) and *field. Thwaite* was the Viking word for 'meadow'.

- Physical features are revealed by *don* (hill), *gow* (hollow) and *combe* (valley).

- Roman sites feature the suffixes *caister, chester, caster, caer* and *car* – from the Latin *castra*, meaning 'military camp' or 'fort'.

Learn more from the beginning
The prefix adds an extra layer of meaning to most place names. It is here that you will often find a sacred connection.

- *Llan* is Welsh for 'settlement' or 'church' and it is almost always coupled with the name of that place's original saint (even if that person is not universally recognised as such): for example, Llangollen means 'Church of St Collen' and Llanelli means 'Church of St Elli'.

- Throughout Cornwall and in parts of Scotland and Wales, *tre*, *trew* or *tri* means 'farm' or 'village'. This is then followed either by the name of the original farmer, as in Tregaron, Dyfed, or by a descriptive element, as in Trefriw ('Farm on the Hill') and Tresco ('Farm by the Elder Tree'), both in Cornwall.

- Many place names begin with one of the four cardinal points of the compass. This is especially true of settlements that were founded in close proximity to an existing – and therefore very old (usually Roman) – town that was already a prominent feature of the landscape when the Anglo-Saxons arrived. For example, Westminster was founded to the west of London's church, while Southwark was built to the south of what remained of the Romans' defensive wall.[49] Around Carlisle – meaning the 'Fort of the Legions' to commemorate the town's role as the Romans' northern military base – there are Newby West and Newby East. Similarly, North Stoke and South Stoke, in Somerset, were so named because of their relative positions to the town of Bath, as were the villages of Weston, Kelston (originally Kelwestern) and Batheastern. As all of these examples indicate, a really significant settlement almost demanded that surrounding towns and villages acknowledge its pre-eminence in their names. Occasionally, though, two places will be equally matched, and therefore define themselves in relation to each other. So East Anglia, which was settled by Anglo-Saxons in the fifth and sixth centuries, is divided into Norfolk (the northern people) and Suffolk (the southern people).

- Religious prefixes – such as church, kirk, chapel, saint, abbot, prior, monk, nun, priest, holy and bishop's – are explicit indicators of who originally owned the land. The trick then is to locate the monastery, church or convent that was their centre of power.

- Similarly, a name beginning King's or Prince's reveals that this place probably once belonged to the monarchy. Consequently, it may well contain anything from a hunting lodge to a long-forgotten palace.

- In the past, it was assumed that many prefixes indicated no more than the name of the person who established the settlement. So, for example, Colebourne, in Gloucestershire, meant 'Col's Stream' and Ivington, in Herefordshire, meant 'Ifa's Farm'. However, recent research has suggested that such interpretations can be oversimplistic. Local libraries may help you find meanings that are a bit more exciting than 'This Chap's Farm'.

How the Vikings made their mark

The Vikings – especially the Danes – had a massive influence on the place names of Britain, as is still apparent to this day. As we saw in Chapter 3, their first raid occurred in AD 793, when they sacked the holy island of Lindisfarne in Northumbria. Similar raids continued over the next seven decades – and they were terrifying for the local Anglo-Saxons, Welsh, Irish and Scottish who bore their brunt – but they pale into insignificance in comparison with what the Vikings did next. For, in 865, a huge Viking army arrived in East Anglia with the intention of settling rather than plundering. This permanent invasion eventually changed the political, religious, cultural and linguistic map of Britain in a most profound way. However, it could have had an even greater impact. Were it not for the resistance of the Anglo-Saxon King Alfred of Wessex – a ruler who was convinced that God had called him to create a new Christian country – the whole of England would probably have ended up under Viking rule, as did much of Lowland Scotland. As it was, Alfred halted the invaders' advance, created a strong Anglo-Saxon kingdom in the southern half of England,

and even helped to convert the Vikings to Christianity, thereby saving the Church in England.

Nevertheless, much of eastern and north-west England, and virtually the whole of East Anglia – the area known as Danelaw – was ruled by either Danes or Norwegians from the end of the ninth century until the early eleventh. It is from this period that we derive the Scandinavian names of so many towns, villages and streets. As we have seen, *thorpe* and *holme* both indicate a Viking settlement, while *gate* means 'street' and *kirk* 'church'. In a foretaste of the Norman Conquest, place names with the prefix 'Norman' – such as Normanby, North Yorkshire – reveal that the Norsemen (Vikings) settled there several centuries before their French cousins arrived. Other places with Viking roots are Braceby (Lincolnshire), Whitby (North Yorkshire), Lowestoft (Suffolk), Scunthorpe (Lincolnshire) and Thornthwaite (North Yorkshire). Tracing the roots of these and many other Scandinavian names will tell you a great deal about what happened in this dramatic and often dangerous period of Britain's history.

Banbury, in Oxfordshire, has a fascinating history which is revealed in the name of one particular district. The name of the town itself means 'Banna's Fort', after the Saxon who built his fortified settlement here in the sixth century AD. (The original Saxon spelling was Banesbyrig.) A few centuries later, the Danes arrived in the area and settled to the east of the River Cherwell and Banbury, in Grimsbury (now a suburb of the main town). Grim is one of several alternative names for the Norse god Odin, so there was probably a temple to him on this site. But the *bury* suffix indicates that the Anglo-Saxons eventually asserted their authority over the newcomers and dictated the name of the place.

So the name of one small suburb in a provincial market town reveals a great deal about England's sacred past. The pagan

▶

Vikings settled on the far side of the river from the Christian Anglo-Saxons and erected a shrine to their supreme god. No doubt this was initially viewed with some distaste from the western bank of the Cherwell, but before long the Vikings converted to the local religion and presumably demolished the shrine. Nevertheless, the god's name lives on in the place that was originally dedicated to him.

PUB NAMES

Village pub names now tend to be far more interesting than those in towns or cities, not least because the former have usually avoided the crass and pointless rebrandings suffered by the latter in recent years. Sadly, the story told by a pub's name is often lost when that name is changed.

In the past, though, if a pub's name were changed, this may have indicated a very significant episode in a community's sacred history. For example, the Bull is still a very common pub name, especially near markets, where it probably refers to the animals that were once (and maybe still are) traded there. However, it could also refer to the pope. If the local pub was owned by a monastery or was a pilgrims' hostel, then it had probably gained permission to sell alcohol from the Vatican in the form of a papal bull. Come the Reformation, many pub owners deemed it prudent to drop this association with the Catholic Church. Moreover, this gave them the perfect opportunity to signal their support for the Tudors, so they either changed the picture from a Papal crown, indicating the Papal bull, to that of an actual bull or renamed their establishment the Rose and Crown or the King's Head.

Another old pub name with a religious connection is the Saracen's Head. These pubs often sit right beside a church, such as the one built

© akg-images/PictureContact

A popular pub name, the Saracens Head is often associated with a nearby ancient church. This reflects either a link to the crusades or with providing funds to rescue Europeans captured by Muslim slave traders.

on to the church of St Michael in Bath. As we have seen, this proximity suggests that these were once church alehouses, but the name adds another dimension to their story. For the parishioners who drank in these pubs might well have joined one of the Crusades that were launched between the eleventh and fourteenth centuries. Alternatively, if the pub were named in the fifteenth or sixteenth century, the adjoining church might have used it to raise funds to redeem Christian prisoners and slaves captured by the Saracens (the generic term used in the Middle Ages for all Muslims). Two entire Catholic religious orders were devoted to redeeming such prisoners, and one of them they might well have been the original owner of the church and its alehouse. Muslim corsairs raided the coast of Britain right up until the early eighteenth century, seizing villagers whom they sold as slaves. Nottingham has another fascinating link to the Crusades in the form of the Old Trip to Jerusalem pub, which claims to date from 1189 – two years after the launch of the Third Crusade.

The George and Dragon became a hugely popular pub name when George was made patron saint of England in the fourteenth century. Other variants were especially common on pilgrimage routes, such as the George and Pilgrim in Glastonbury, which dates back to the early fifteenth century, and the George Inn in Norton St Philip, Somerset, which was named in the early 1300s and is one of the most authentic medieval inns in Britain.

Many large villages and towns on major pilgrimage routes feature labyrinths of small closes and alleys that run off the main through road and still recall the names of (usually long-gone) pubs. Berwick-on-Tweed is a classic example of this, especially in the names of some of the tiny alleys and courtyards off West Street and Golden Square. But London has even more: the main departure point for pilgrims and other travellers to the continent was across the river in Southwark, where to this day you will find King's Head Yard, White Hart Yard, George Inn Yard, Tabard Inn Yard, Mermaid Court and Angel Place – all of which were named after pubs.

Many market towns have a White Hart pub, too. The sign usually shows a deer wearing a crown collar. The white hart was the emblem of Richard II, and it was during his reign, in the late fourteenth century, that each pub was first required by law to display a sign with its name upon it. Many of the pubs that became the White Hart around this time presumably chose the name to display loyalty to the king. However, Richard II was overthrown and replaced by his cousin Henry IV in 1399. Many landlords swiftly painted over their original signs and chose a less contentious name and emblem instead – the Red Lion – which was the badge of Henry IV's illustrious father, John of Gaunt. A few years later, when Henry V succeeded his father, many pubs dutifully adopted the new king's emblem – the White Swan.

Politics, religion and pilgrimage are thus the foundations of many of Britain's pub names, which reveal just as much about our villages and towns as do the dedications of our parish churches.

STREET AND DISTRICT NAMES

The history of a place will often be laid out in its street names. As we have seen throughout this book, some of these are explicitly sacred, with streets often named after saints, churches, chapels or temples. Others reflect the places where generations of people have gone about their everyday lives – the places where they have lived, worked, shopped, learned and enjoyed themselves. Castle Street, Market Street, Station Road and Port Street all tell you plenty about what once happened in these places, even if their function has long-since changed. Victoria Street almost certainly indicates that this part of town was built in the nineteenth century, while a far more accurate date can be assigned to a road if it bears the name of a famous battle, such as Waterloo (1815), Alma (1854), Lucknow (1857) or Mafeking (1900). The likelihood is that these streets were all built no more than a few years after the great victories that they commemorate. Similarly, an Edwardian Coronation Street will usually date to 1902 or 1911 – the years in which Edward VII and George V, respectively, were crowned.

Street names can help you trace long-lost city walls, lead you to abandoned wells, tell you where a ford used to cross the local river and reveal no end of historical details that do not appear in any book. A street with the prefix *cheap* – as in Cheapside, London – is not a comment on house prices but comes from an Anglo-Saxon word for 'market'.[50]

London is a marvellous place to explore lost histories through street names. For example, take Fenchurch Street. The prefix probably comes from the Latin for 'hay' (*faenum*) and refers to the hay market that used to be held near here. The suffix likely refers to the long-gone church of St Gabriel, which once stood right in the centre of the road. Houndsditch follows the route of the old city moat, but this eventually became a rubbish tip, which was used especially to dispose of the corpses of dogs. Old Jewry Street housed the capital's

Jewish community before their expulsion in 1290, which also explains why the nearby church of St Lawrence is officially known as St Lawrence Jewry. It was built specifically to convert the local Jews to Christianity before that mission was abandoned and they were forced to leave.

The street names of Mansfield, in Nottinghamshire, reveal an equally interesting history. The town's original layout can be traced through those roads that feature the word 'gate' – Norse for 'street' – which also tell us that the Vikings played a significant role in Mansfield (in fact, they overran the whole area in the ninth century). So, West Gate heads west while Stockwell Gate (literally meaning 'Street Leading to the Wooden Bridge Over the Stream') heads south and eventually crosses the River Maun (which gives Mansfield its name). Meanwhile, Church Street was originally known by the wholly Norse word Kirkgate.

But Mansfield's street layout reveals more than this Scandinavian connection. Centuries after the Vikings, the Nonconformists made their presence felt in the town. Thus, we have Quaker Way, a modern road that passes the site of the original Quaker and then Unitarian meeting house. There is a Quaker Lane, too, and a Baptist Hill. Meanwhile, the imposing Methodist church on Bridge Street serves as a solid reminder of the power of working-class religion and its increasingly blatant opposition to the Established Church. It quite clearly lauds it over the much smaller and simpler parish church just up the road. All of these Nonconformist chapels and churches, as well as a large Catholic church, collectively tell a story of the growth of alternative traditions once the Anglican Church started to lose its grip on the hearts and minds of Britain's working class.

The presence of faith communities who oppose the drinking of alcohol is often also revealed by an absence of pubs. Most Nonconformists were teetotallers, and the Methodists, Salvation Army and Church Army all stressed this in their missions. Consequently, pubs were banned wherever they had influence. For example, there were no pubs in Bournville, the model village built just outside Birmingham by the

Quaker Cadbury family (see Chapter 9). Of course, they could not control what happened outside their areas of influence, so vast pubs often sprang up all around Nonconformist strongholds to cater for the demands of the unreformed.

All of our villages, towns and cities are constructs of the human imagination as well as the physical elements of the land, and all have stories to tell. However, each of these stories is part of a much greater story – one that is almost always rooted in the sacred. By doing a little research, asking questions and examining names we can once again become pilgrims in this sacred land.

GAZETTEER

Place names with tales to tell

Where a cross-reference is given please see the main text for the significant story of each.

Scotland
- Edinburgh (see pages 191–3)

Wales
- Llanelli, Carmarthenshire (SA15): means 'Church of St Elli'
- Llangollen, Clwyd (LL20): means 'Church of St Collen'
- Tregaron, Dyfed (SY25): means 'Farm of Caron'

Northern England
- Alnwick, Northumberland (NE66) – (see page 212)
- Thornthwaite, North Yorkshire (HG3) – (see page 218)
- Whitby, Yorkshire (YO22) – (see page 218)
- Wroxeter, Shropshire (SY5) – (see page 189)
- York, North Yorkshire (YO1) – (see page 213)

Southern England
- Baldock, Hertfordshire (SG7) – (see page 214)
- Banbury, Oxfordshire (OX16) – (see page 199)
- Colebourne, Gloucestershire GL53 – (see page 217)
- Fulbourne, Cambridgeshire (CB21) – (see page 215)
- Hackney, London (E8) – (see page 212)
- Ivington, Herefordshire (HR6) – (see page 217)
- Lowestoft, Suffolk (NR32) – (see page 218)
- Mansfield, Nottinghamshire (NG18) – (see page 223)
- Norfolk, East Anglia – (see page 216)
- North Stoke, Somerset (BA1) – (see page 216)
- Scunthorpe, Lincolnshire (DN15) – (see page 218)
- South Stoke, Somerset (BA2) – (see page 216)
- Suffolk, East Anglia (DN17) – (see page 216)
- Thetford, Norfolk (IP24) – (see page 189)
- Tresco, Cornwall (BTR24) – (see page 216)
- Walsingham, Norfolk (NR22) – (see page 189)

Classical cities

All these towns and cities have areas of fine Georgian design and layout manifesting the Georgian belief in the divine nature of order and symmetry.

- Cheltenham, Gloucestershire: almost entirely rebuilt in late Georgian style
- Chester, Cheshire: fine rows of Georgian houses built on the lines of the earlier classical Roman city
- Edinburgh New Town: built to tell a new story (see page 191)

- Tenby, Dyfed: delightful example of small Georgian town landscape and layout
- Tunbridge Wells, Kent: late-Georgian centre

Biblical cities

Each of these towns or cities has a basic layout based on the Biblical model (see pages 194–5).

- Chapel-en-le-Frith, Derbyshire
- Chichester, West Sussex
- Forfar, Angus
- Glasgow
- Lincoln, Lincolnshire
- Llanidloes, Powys
- Norwich, Norfolk
- Rhayader, Powys
- St Andrews, Fife
- Winchester, Hampshire

Sacred market places

Spaces where the omphalos, the central point of the town or city (see pages 195–201), is still marked by a cross or some other sign of the sacred nature of doing business. Where a cross-reference is given, you'll find further details in the main text.

- Bristol (see page 202)
- Devizes, Wiltshire (see page 198)
- Farnham, Surrey (see page 200)
- Fettercairn, Aberdeenshire (see page 198)
- Geddington, Lincolnshire (see page 200)
- Glossop, Derbyshire: war memorial and Methodist campus

- Hay-on-Wye, Hereford: cheese and butter markets and isolated church (see page 200)
- Lichfield, Staffordshire (see page 200)
- Northampton, Northamptonshire
- Salisbury, Wiltshire (see page 201)
- Sandbach, Cheshire: superb examples of standing crosses similar in role to standing stones in stone circles
- Shepton Mallet, Somerset (see page 195)
- Waltham Cross, Hertfordshire: surviving Eleanor Cross

Churches of Bristol (BS1)

The significance of the names of the key Bristol churches can be found in the main text – see pages 201–3.

- All Saints and All Souls
- Christ Church (originally Holy Trinity)
- St Clement's
- St Ewen's (now gone)
- St John the Baptist (no longer used as a church)
- St Leonard
- St Mary le Port (remains)
- St Michael the Archangel on the Mount Without
- St Nicholas
- St Peter's
- St Stephen's

Streets and churches of Canterbury (CT1)

See the main text (pages 203–4) for the significance of the names of each of these.

- St Alphege's
- St Edmund's
- St George's Street
- St Helen's
- St John's Lane
- St Mary's Street
- St Michael's
- St Sepulchre's

Carmarthen (SA31)

Where a cross-reference is given, see the main text for further information on the stories and meaning of each of these.

- Bryn Myrddin (Merlin's Hill): supposed birthplace of Merlin
- Friars Park: reminder that there used to be a friary in the town
- Priory Street: reminder that there used to be a priory in the town
- St Catherine's Street: named after the long-gone chapel of St Catherine, which stood on the hill to the north of the town (see page 205)
- St Mary's Street: commemorates St Mary's church, which once stood here
- St Peter's: the main parish church, which stands to the east of the town

Street and district names

Please see the main text (pages 212–19) for the significance and stories behind each of these.

- Angel Place, Southwark
- Cheapside, London
- Fenchurch Street, London
- George Inn Yard, Southwark
- Grimsbury, Banbury, Oxfordshire
- Houndsditch, London
- King's Head Yard, Southwark
- Mermaid Court, Southwark
- Old Jewry Street, London: site of the Jewish community before their expulsion in 1290
- Tabard Inn Yard, Southwark
- White Hart Yard, Southwark

Pub names

The following were all pilgrim pubs.

Northern England
- Olde Trip to Jerusalem, Nottingham (NG1)

Southern England
- George and Pilgrim, Glastonbury, Somerset (BA6)
- George Inn, Norton St Philip, Somerset (BA2)
- Saracen's Head, Bath (BA1)

7

Reading the buildings where you live

and all our ancestors we've never met
standing behind us like these walls
scrolling back through decades, centuries
bearing our story.[51]

Walk down the high street in almost any town, city or large village in Britain, and you will probably see a fine Georgian façade. It might form the front of what is now a bank, a hotel, a shop or even a private home. Symmetrical, elegant, Greco-Roman, made of either handmade bricks or beautifully cut stone, at first sight it will seem to be the perfect image of the Georgian ideal of order and control in the urban landscape. But look more closely and you may notice that the roof and gable end of the building do not quite live up to the promise of the stylish façade. That is because there is often a much older, much less elegant building hiding behind it. In some places, such as Rye in Sussex, the bricks won't even be real. They will be nailed-on facades of real bricks.

When the Georgian architectural style swept through fashionable Britain in the eighteenth century, not everyone could afford a

The symmetry and order of the Georgian city was an attempt to reflect belief in God as 'architect'.

complete rebuild of their existing home, so they simply stuck a façade over the front. This was a particularly common practice among the owners of coaching inns, who attracted more customers if they could gave the impression of being at the cutting edge of fashionable society but generally did not have the funds for lavish refurbishment projects. Many a Georgian traveller must have been sorely disappointed when he stepped through a classically elegant doorway and into a rickety hallway straight out of the Middle Ages.

In 1787, the Empress of Russia, Catherine the Great, decided to visit her newly conquered territories in the Crimea. This land had been won at great expense after a lengthy military campaign, but it consisted of little more than dozens of impoverished towns and

▶

villages that had been devastated by the war. Catherine's chief adviser (and lover), Grigory Potemkin, felt he had to put a good spin on the region, so builders were instructed to erect gleaming façades in front of the battered buildings. The empress drove past in her carriage, seeing what seemed to be a wealthy and happy land, little knowing that misery and poverty lay behind the façades. From this, we get the term Potemkin façade – meaning something that is not all it seems, yet reveals a far more significant truth.

This chapter will help you understand what our major buildings were designed to tell us – what the builders and owners intended to convey to those walking past or coming inside. The façade, the public face of a building, is an extremely effective visible symbol of power. Consequently, each one tells a story. We stroll past them every day without giving them a second thought, yet their subtle influence on our collective subconscious cannot be overstated.

Not far from you, there is probably a supermarket. It may well have been built in a sort of mock-farmyard style – half stable block with clock tower and half barn – echoing the outbuildings of an ancestral hall. Reassuringly semi-rural yet ruthlessly efficient in parting you from your money, it is a façade of country life that puts you in touch with food production and nature through its architecture. Inside, parts of the supermarket may have been designed to mimic a row of old-fashioned shops – the baker, the butcher, the fishmonger – to give the impression that you are walking through the high street in a market town. Yet, it was the rapacious advance of the supermarkets that killed off exactly those types of shops.

The story being told in supermarkets is one of dislocation and embarrassment – coupled with unashamed ambition. The fake link to the countryside and to the natural cycles of life – emphasised by the inclusion of the clock tower – is designed to reassure you that you are still touch with nature, even though you have no idea where, or how, the food you are buying was grown. This tactic of manipulative reassurance dates back to at least 2500 BC in Britain. Tombs were built in the centres of the earliest stone circles in order to foster a sense of continuity with the ancestor-worship culture of the First Great Cycle. But the builders of the stone circles wholly rejected the earlier culture (presumably viewing it as naive and primitive), so the tombs were fake – they contained no human remains. They were included purely to reassure the locals and to persuade them to sign up to the new religion, just as supermarkets reassure us and persuade us to part with our cash – one could even say, persuade you to be part of their story.

Next, consider the monumental office blocks that now blight almost every large town and city. These buildings – so often brutalist in style – tell us a great deal about the literal facelessness of modern big business and civic authority, with their reflecting windows, their total absence of any decorative flourishes, and their compulsion to proclaim that they are serious places of business. The reflecting windows have an added bonus, too, in that they grant these businesses the secrecy that they seem to crave. Maybe thousands of people are chained to their desks in these buildings? Maybe no one is inside? As we walk past, seeing only our reflections in the windows, we cannot know the truth.

Buildings tell stories. They are highly visible works of art. We walk past them and through them every day. We live in them. Every one of them was designed to say something. It is fun to work out what that something was, but even more rewarding to uncover the stories that their builders and original owners had no intention of revealing. As a general rule, the more pompous the building, the less confident was its builder, even if they liked to think they were in control. Conversely, with modern architecture, the more stark and brutal the design, less secure is the builder, especially with respect to their debt to or relationship with the past.

SIMPLE TO COMPLEX: NARRATIVE
IN THE WALLS

In some cases, it is possible to detect the precise point that has been reached in a great story purely from the buildings that date from that time. For instance, if the people are still happy and confident in themselves, and comfortable with their belief system, their buildings will express this in their elegant simplicity. But when that story starts to head towards collapse, when the people start to lose all confidence, they often try to camouflage their insecurity with ever-grander, more ornate building projects.

Until around 1400, Britain was still an overwhelmingly rural society, so most people had very little opportunity to express themselves through architecture. The only special buildings in most communities – the only ones that could tell a story – were the church and the manor house or castle. In larger towns and cities, the city walls and the homes of wealthy merchants and elite members of the clergy could be added to the list.

A fine example of the progression (or, perhaps more accurately, the decline) through a great cycle – the fourth, in this case – is provided by the cathedral at St Davids, Pembrokeshire. When David (Dewi) founded his church and monastery on this site in the sixth century, the building style was very simple. David used nothing but wood and mud because he did not want the local people to be distracted by glitter and wealth. His sole aim was to bring them closer to God. He chose the spot for pragmatic reasons: it was close to many springs and streams that provided fresh water for baptisms as well as daily life. The simplicity of the building impressed visitors because it reflected the austerity of the monastic life and David's closeness to nature, as well as the presence of God.

When the Normans arrived in the area, they wanted to enhance their power by claiming the spiritual blessing of the local saint, yet they completely disregarded the modest example set by David because they set about building a huge stone cathedral and a glamorous bishop's palace. These buildings proclaimed, 'Here is power ... and we own it.' Before long, though, nature answered: 'How very silly to build two vast stone buildings on a site with over 150 springs. Don't you know anything about subsidence?' For nearly a thousand years, untold sums have been spent shoring up the cathedral and the bishop's palace because they keep sinking into the marsh.

Winchester Cathedral has experienced similar problems for similar reasons. The original Anglo-Saxon church, built in 635, was a small, modest affair, which grew significantly over the next four centuries; but it was the Normans who decided to start constructing the enormous, heavy building we know today. As soon as it was finished, it started to sink. By the early twentieth century, there was a real danger of the whole east end collapsing because the foundations were deep underwater. The cathedral authorities contracted an experienced deep-sea diver, William Walker, to reinforce the foundations with hundreds of bags of cement. The job took six years, with Walker working every day. A statue in his honour now stands in the cathedral.

Some locations were better suited to the Normans' extravagant style – such as Durham and Aberdeen. Nevertheless, all of their cathedrals – monuments to their excessive ambition and determination to proclaim their power – signal the moment when the Fourth Great Cycle changed direction, rejected the simple in favour of the complex, and headed towards inevitable collapse.

Each of these styles – simple wood and mud; and vast, beautiful but unsupportable stone – tells a story about the relationship between humanity, God and nature. But these conflicting stories are not only expressed in Britain's great cathedrals. For example, the little village of Hailes, in Gloucestershire, tells them just as well. Most of the simple but beautifully decorated parish church dates from the fourteenth century, although some parts of it are even older, pre-dating the rise of the mighty Abbey of Hailes in the Middle Ages. The church is still active today, while the abbey is now nothing more than a pile of rubble. Yet, had you visited as a pilgrim in the fourteenth century – to see the supposedly miraculous Holy Blood of Hailes (a phial that was said to contain the blood of Christ) – you might well have walked straight past the little church, seduced by the size, power and grandeur of the abbey. Of course, it was precisely that power and grandeur – not to mention wealth – that led to the abbey's downfall, along with all of the other abbeys and monasteries in Britain, during the Reformation. Meanwhile, the modest church is still standing its ground almost five hundred years later, looking out quietly at the ruins.

However, as we saw in Chapter 5, such churches were themselves eventually considered too grand, too proud, too complex, which was why the Nonconformists built such simple, homely chapels. These modest buildings were explicitly designed to deal a counterblast to the traditional parish church and everything it represented. They marked the beginning of our current great story.

CASTLES

Castles make a very obvious declaration: 'We are here and we are in power. So either go away or do as you are told.' They were built, almost without exception, as a consequence of the Norman Conquest – or, in the case of Scotland, from the intermingling of the Normans with the Scottish nobles. Indeed, the *Anglo-Saxon Chronicle*, written between the eighth and the twelfth centuries, states in its obituary for William the Conqueror that he built castles – buildings that were unknown to the Anglo-Saxons – and that the Normans dominated and terrified the surrounding land from these castles: 'He had castles built and wretched men oppressed.' Later, during the civil war between Matilda and King Stephen, which wreaked havoc on early twelfth-century England, the chroniclers record castles springing up all over the countryside, housing evil and devilish people.

Castles were power statements, erected by a small, elite group of people who had seized the land and were determined to hold on to it against all odds. Initially, they were little more than motte and baileys.

> The motte and bailey was created by earth from the excavation of a defensive ditch being formed into a small hill (the motte), which was topped with a wooden fort, and this then left an area below the motte which was flattened out to the edges of the ditch where the ancillary buildings stood (the bailey). All of this was then protected by a wooden wall above the ditch. The simplest motte and bailey castles were probably erected in little more than a week. Soldiers excavated the ditch and levelled the soil. Then they would slot together the sections of a wooden wall kit (a very early example of prefabrication) – a far swifter and safer process than chopping down trees in the presumably hostile surrounding area and fashioning them into a defensive barrier from scratch. Crude, basic, cold and probably extremely unhygienic, these castles were designed to stake a claim upon land that had very recently belonged to others, most of whom were eager to reclaim it. They were very similar in both design and purpose to the wooden forts built by the US Army in the nineteenth century as it advanced into the lands of the native peoples.

Precisely how many motte and baileys were built is unknown, because so many have disappeared or now lie beneath stone castles or even under parts of towns. Estimates vary from five hundred to a thousand. Some of those that remain – in various states of decay – are clearly labelled 'Motte and Bailey' on OS maps, but many others are not highlighted in this way. However, with a little practice, you should be able to spot the tell-tale small hill, adjacent flat area and surrounding ditch. The mottes are usually no more than twenty metres high and perhaps only a hundred metres around the base. The top of the hill is usually flat – to provide a stable foundation for the wooden fort – while the bailey extends out from two-thirds of its base, leaving the other third as a steep climb for any attackers. You will usually find these early castles (or traces of them) precisely where you would expect them to be: namely, guarding the entrance to a valley, a river crossing or some other strategically important position. Most of them were built between 1066 and 1087, which means that at least one was erected every fortnight, even if the lowest estimate is correct. I once found one when looking for a house for sale and although it was obvious from both the very detailed ground plan and from simply looking at it, it was not marked on any map. It sat above a key river with commanding views up and down the valley.

A good example of a motte and bailey (with later stone additions) is at Berkhampstead, Hertfordshire. This was built by William the Conqueror himself, and was later home to Thomas Becket, Chancellor of England and Archbishop of Canterbury.

By the middle of the twelfth century, most motte and baileys were abandoned as fears of local uprisings diminished. However, by then, the Norman families were starting to fight among themselves. The wealthier families started to build stone castles, with the royal family building the largest of all, such as the Tower of London. These massive new structures had an obvious dual function: they were designed to defend the family's vested interests and to make it absolutely clear that they were to be feared and obeyed.

The classic example of this trend is Old Sarum, to the north of Salisbury. This site had been occupied and fortified in various ways since Neolithic times, but the Normans took this to a whole new level when they started work on a castle and cathedral complex around 1075. The castle was originally a modest motte and bailey, but this was soon converted into a full-blown stone citadel and royal residence. The cathedral grew up literally in the castle's shadow – a physically and symbolically subservient position that the Church could not countenance for long, especially given the abouse and threats that emanated from the castle towards the Church. So, in 1219, the Bishop of Salisbury formally removed the centre of his holy see from Old Sarum, decamped to the plains below, and started work on the magnificent cathedral that still stands today. The rest of the town followed suit, leaving the castle on the top of the hill with nothing to guard. Finally, during the reign of Henry VIII, it was demolished.

Even though no one lived there for centuries, Old Sarum remained infamous long into the nineteenth century. It was the most notorious of several 'rotten boroughs' – places with no residents yet with the right to send MPs to Parliament. These MPs were invariably the lackeys of the local landowners, so they did whatever they were told in the Commons. Such flagrant abuses of democracy led to the Reform Act of 1832, which swept away the rotten boroughs – including Old Sarum – along with much of the rest of the old order.

What happened in Old Sarum gives a glimpse into the battles that were being played out throughout Britain in the Middle Ages. No individuals and scarcely any communities could hope to challenge the power of the Norman monarchy and aristocracy, who literally looked down on the lower orders from their mighty castles. However, the medieval Church could – and did – stand up to these temporal powerhouses. This is exemplified in the humiliation suffered by Henry II after his soldiers murdered the Archbishop of Canterbury, Thomas Becket, in 1170. This assassination shocked Christendom far beyond the boundaries of England, and Henry knew that he had to find a way to placate the Church and its numerous allies throughout Europe. As a result, he made a barefoot pilgrimage to Canterbury for penance and founded several monasteries, including Witham, in Somerset, and Newstead, in Nottinghamshire.

Elsewhere, though, the rule of the castle was virtually unchallengeable, and the huge towers, keeps and walls became symbols of oppression, enhanced by their sheer scale and ominous design. Only very occasionally did the people attempt to usurp this power. In Bristol, the castle started life in the 1080s as a royal motte and bailey before being expanded over the coming decades, eventually to form the second-largest keep in England, after the Tower of London. The local people resented it from the very beginning, and in 1307 they rose in rebellion and declared Bristol to be an independent city-state – on the model of the likes of Venice and Padua, in Italy. They built a wall that separated the castle from the city, isolated the soldiers and defied both the local lord and the king for seven years. However, in 1314, a force of three hundred ships besieged the city and forced its surrender. The great dividing wall was dismantled and Bristol once again fell under the authority of the king. The townsfolk never forgot their brief period of independence, though, and they finally had the opportunity to exact revenge over three centuries later. In 1656, Oliver Cromwell's Commonwealth government gave the city permission to demolish the castle, and the Bristolians lost no time in almost completely obliterating it.

The romanticising of castles is an eighteenth- and early nineteenth-century phenomenon, bound up with a revival of interest in chivalry. This gained popularity in the context of a rising sense of Britain's imperial mission, which viewed colonial adventurers such as the Normans as noble pioneers and defenders of virtue. Long past their sell-by date, the ruins of the formerly great castles were often transformed at that time into new expression of power – the comfortable mansions of the wealthy and status symbols for the emerging city councils and authorities.

Nottingham Castle, famous for its role in the Robin Hood legend, is a fine example of how a castle tells a different story each time it assumes a different function. The original motte and bailey was built in 1067 to assert Norman control in the Midlands and regulate access to the North, where rebellion was rife. Rebuilt in stone by the twelfth century, it became a major royal palace and dominated the town for five hundred years. However, after the Civil War, Parliament ordered

The infamous Nottingham Castle, for centuries, in different shapes and styles, a symbol of power in the city.

its destruction. In an echo of what happened at Bristol, the local people enthusiastically attacked this symbol of royal oppression. When they had finished, just a few sections of the castle remained above and below ground. After the Restoration, though, the local lord erected a splendid Italian-style ducal mansion on the site, and it instantly became a symbol of the reassertion of aristocratic power. However, by 1831, the Industrial Revolution had created thousands of discontented workers in Nottingham, so it was a dangerous place to flaunt an opulent house. Almost inevitably, a mob targeted the mansion and the aristocratic power that it represented during the Reform Act riots of that year. It was left as a shell, but was grandly restored forty-four years later, in more peaceful times. It opened as the new municipal museum – an expression of rising local pride among the newly enfranchised (by the various Reform Acts) middle classes and industrial barons, who wanted to announce that

Nottingham possessed culture, not just some of the most notorious slums in the country. Throughout almost a millennium of history, then, the buildings on this site (and their occasional demolition) have proclaimed who holds power and authority in the city of Nottingham. Similar stories are told by many of Britain's other great castles: Norwich became a jail and then a museum; Carlisle was an army barracks before becoming a museum; while Taunton was rebuilt as a mansion and now houses hotels as well as the town's museum.

However, perhaps the most telling castle story is told every Christmas Eve in Rochester, Kent. Two great Norman buildings face each other in this town – both built by a bishop who was also a warlord. One is the castle, with its huge keep; the other is the cathedral, with its magnificent towers. Every Christmas, the impressive cathedral is ablaze with lights as hundreds of people stream in for Midnight Mass – to celebrate the story of a child born in poverty to save the world. Just over the road, the ruined castle squats in complete darkness, deserted. Temporal power has moved elsewhere, while spiritual power – albeit radically modified over the years – still resides within the cathedral.

TOWN AND CITY WALLS

Of course, town and city walls were functional, protecting the citizens from attack. But they were also symbols of both power and spirituality. This is exemplified in the walls that encircle Caernarfon, Gwynedd. As we saw in Chapter 5, legend says that Helen, the mother of Emperor Constantine the Great, was born in the Roman city that lay just to the south of present-day Caernarfon. In the early fourth century, Constantine founded a new capital city on the banks of the Bosporus, in modern-day Turkey. Named Constantinople, this was the greatest city in the Western world for over a thousand years.

Its huge defensive walls, built in the sixth century, were designed to be beautiful as well as practical. Banded with multicoloured layers, they have withstood innumerable sieges and battles, and they remain impressive to this day. However, in addition to being the greatest city in Europe, Constantinople was the heart of the Orthodox Christian world – the first Roman city to be built as a Christian city. So it possessed unsurpassed temporal *and* spiritual power – to such an extent that its influence spread all the way to North Wales. Caernarfon's walls – erected in the late thirteenth century – are made up of layers of coloured stones, just like Constantinople's. It seems likely that this was done in honour of the local girl – Helen – without whom there would have been no Constantine and no Constantinople.

Naturally, every town wall had to be fitted with gates to provide points of exit and entry. Once built, such a gate was topped by either a church or statues of appropriate guardians, including the Trinity, saints and even kings and queens. Many town walls were dismantled in the seventeenth century, but old maps can reveal where they and their various gates once stood. The names and locations of the gates usually give numerous clues to the sacred and secular layout and self-image of the town. For instance, as we saw in Chapter 6, the gate church of St Leonard in Bristol was built to remind locals never to trade in slaves again. Poignantly, the church was demolished in 1771, at the height of the slave trade with Africa and the Americas.

Norwich's city walls are a good example of how these features both serve as a boundary and possess considerable religious significance. Of its ten major medieval city gates, six had religious dedications. Just outside five of these – including those dedicated to saints who were widely associated with healing, such as St Giles and St Mary Magdalene – were leper hospitals, run by monks. Some of the other gates were named after saints who were not generally linked to care for the sick – such as St Benedict and St Augustine – but these still expressed the profound monastic influence on such places. (Without the monasteries, there would have been no hospitals in medieval England.)

PUBLIC SPACES

In a feudal society, such as medieval Britain, public spaces – including market places, village greens and fairgrounds – were protected from abuse or misuse by sacred tradition and custom. These were important sources of alternative authority under feudalism, and meant that ordinary people were not *wholly* subservient to the local lord or the Church. The sense of relative freedom that people enjoyed within such spaces sometimes led to them being breeding grounds for revolt.

The greens in many of Britain's villages have remained largely unchanged over the past six or seven hundred years. They are usually encircled by the community's major buildings – the church, pub, village hall and shops as well as the homes of prominent families – and still often provide a focus for village life. Meanwhile, in towns, the green's various roles were assumed by the market place. This was not necessarily a square: for instance, the market areas of both Wigtown, Dumfries and Galloway, and Chipping Sodbury, Gloucestershire, were on long, wide streets. In Edinburgh, Market Street runs into the High Street, and both of them, plus the space around St Giles Cathedral, housed the city's market.

In Hay-on-Wye, Memorial Square now occupies the former site of the green. Created in the early nineteenth century by the energetic and reforming Archdeacon Bevan, it is named after the war memorial that stands in its centre and therefore serves as the town's omphalos. Today, the famous Thursday Market takes place in the square itself and the adjacent Cheese Market, and up Market Street to the Butter Market. The whole space is framed by the castle to the south and the natural slope of the land to the north. It is a classic

© Topfoto

Many of Britain's village greens have remained unchanged for centuries. Once the scene of Maypole dancing and livestock fairs, today they are more likely to be the venue for the village fete.

example of a public space that is not controlled by either the Church or the lord of the manor – something that both have (sometimes grudgingly) acknowledged is essential to keep the peace.

Market places were often much larger than they are today. The simple reason for this is that, over the centuries, market stallholders have eventually built shops. In a town's market square or street, look for unusually narrow buildings that have been wedged between more substantial structures; or for buildings that protrude into the street, beyond the frontages of most of the other houses. For example, on Broad Street in Ludlow, Shropshire, there are three rows of very narrow houses and shops, all of which have intruded into the original market space. Each house is the width of the stall site that was allocated to a medieval trader. Exactly the same thing can be seen in Edinburgh.

BUILDING A NEW WORLD WITH GOD, THE DIVINE ARCHITECT

As we have seen throughout this book, medieval towns, cities and buildings all expressed humanity's intimate relationship with God through their dedications to the saints in their churches and hospitals, their incorporation of the sign of the cross in their street layouts, and the care they took to honour His presence and guidance even in their centres of commercial activity: the market places. All of these elements collectively acknowledged that each person belonged firmly within a much greater, dynamic, sacred narrative.

However, by the eighteenth century, this sense of humanity's place in a cosmic story had been undermined by centuries of religious dispute and warfare. The philosophers of the Enlightenment argued that God had created the universe and established sacred patterns in nature, but then He had left us to our own devices. We had got it wrong many times in the past, but if we now followed His sacred patterns to the letter, we could make the world run smoothly. People rejected the power of saints, and they even denied a special role to Christ. They still believed in God, but not the personal God of the Middle Ages. Instead, He was viewed more like an architect, a scientist, someone concerned with facts and figures.

Melvyn Bragg elegantly captures this shift in thinking and perception:

> The Garden of Eden, which in medieval interpretations had been full of allegorical and psychological meanings, was now seen as a particular place on the planet, though there were complaints that not enough information had been provided as to where exactly it was. Seventeenth-century authors tried to remedy that with numerous suggestions as to the precise location. The Bible was being tested in a similar way to that in which the scientists were testing the weight of air or the content of various seeds.[52]

This shift – from God as storyteller to God as architect – was much more than a minor development in theological interpretation. It signalled the abandonment of the personal in favour of the distant (or even absent) God, who was a scientific planner not a passionate friend, companion or judge. 'Man' was now the measure of all things, while God was reduced to a useful adjunct – an absentee landlord who had left management of the world to us. Indeed, many people – pioneers in everything from agriculture to town planning – started to believe that they were destined to *improve*, rather than merely manage, the world God had given us. While some of these innovators' schemes certainly did improve people's lives, many of them also carried the whiff of self-satisfaction. This reached its height in the Victorian period, when almost everybody agreed that Britain's empire-builders, scientists and industrialists were enhancing life not only here but throughout the world. Even the Church bought into this spirit of self-confidence (or smugness), as is reflected in the hymn that begins 'God is working His purpose out as year succeeds to year', written by Millicent Kingham in the late nineteenth century, when the British Empire covered a third of the globe.

Interestingly, Britain's architects, builders and designers displayed this change in people's personal relationships with and attitudes to God long before Enlightenment philosophers wrote about it. The first signs came in late Elizabethan garden designs, which regimented plants in serried ranks and cut and shaped hedges into intricate patterns. Central to such a garden design was a small hill that allowed the owner to gaze at his little piece of paradise on earth, and to see himself as god of all he surveyed. A wonderful example is the garden at Little Morton Hall, in Cheshire. (See Chapter 9 for much more on garden design.)

By the late seventeenth century, this type of order and symmetry was becoming the norm in buildings, too, with Greco-Roman temples often providing the templates. St Paul's Cathedral is perhaps the most dramatic expression of this in both church and state architecture, because this has always been as much of a civic building as a place of worship. Having received the commission to replace a vast, rambling medieval cathedral that was destroyed in the Great Fire of London of 1666, Sir Christopher Wren set out to create a building of complete symmetry, soaring arches and domes, and proportions that spoke clearly of the Great Architect. He succeeded. St Paul's is an astonishing building that employs the classical style in a revolutionary way, enabling this huge church to project a sense of the sacred as well as the grand.

Mereworth Castle, Kent, built around 1723, is a similarly impressive building, albeit on a much smaller scale. It fuses Greek and Roman temple design in a way that was first perfected in Vicenza's Villa Rotunda, built by the greatest exponent of classical revival design, Andrea Palladio. Palladio went on to create some of the finest sixteenth-century Italian villas – half temple, half house – and his principles were religiously followed by the architects who designed so many of Britain's country houses in the late seventeenth and eighteenth centuries. These were temples to success, so it should come as no surprise that perhaps the finest of all – Stourhead, in Wiltshire – was commissioned by one of the country's foremost bankers, Henry Hoare.

Throughout the rest of the eighteenth century, and even into the Regency period at the beginning of the nineteenth, architecture continued to reflect the shift in Britain's great story. This was exemplified in the astounding work of John Wood the Elder. When he set out to develop Bath from the 1740s onwards, Wood not only cast God in a new role: he rejected His son, Christ, altogether. For John Wood designed Bath as a purely pagan city. His greatest work, the Circus, was modelled on contemporary interpretations and reconstructions of what Stonehenge would have looked like in its heyday. So there are the three entrances to the circular street (just as the Georgians thought there were three entrances to the stone circle), the Druidic role is symbolised by the sculpted acorns that adorn every house,[53] and pagan imagery is used in the beautiful panels that form a continuous frieze between the ground and first floors of the three terraces. Wood had a very romantic – and, to some extent, anti-Christian – understanding of the Druids, in that he believed they had been in touch with Greek philosophers and mystics, and even Egyptian priests. This led him to evoke a lost world of symbolism and power by incorporating versions of Stonehenge's trilithons – those magnificent 'doorways' of two uprights and one lintel – within his classical Greek-style buildings. The trilithons are represented in the shape of the ground floor of each house, while the three storeys boast, from the ground floor upwards, Doric, Ionic and Corinthian pillars. Wood therefore combines the stories of an imagined heroic British past, the power and sacred architecture of Greece, and the emerging strength of imperial Britain – all expressed in one of the most harmonious of all urban developments.

Whereas much of Wood's inspiration came from classical Greece, many Georgian architects looked to the other great power of antiquity: Rome. The idea was to announce to the world that Britain's growing empire was already on a par with the greatest the world had ever seen. There was a sacred element to this, too, because the British felt they had a divinely ordained right – or even duty – to establish their empire. It is no accident that so many Georgian buildings look like temples, at least from the outside. Inside, there were no shrines to a god or goddess. Instead, those in the vanguard of the British commercial and imperial revolution celebrated themselves and their achievements. So, for example, St George's Hall in Liverpool is a monument to British culture, while the British Museum celebrates the power that allowed Britain to acquire objects from other – and implicitly lesser – cultures around the world. The city designs of Bath and Edinburgh New Town give pride of place to the residents themselves and the commercial ventures they run. Many classical-style banks, town halls and post offices tell the same story: we are the heirs of the great empires; we are rational beings made in God's image who are now managing the world on His behalf; and we have the talent and ability to make a perfectly symmetrical world of order and purpose.

Or, at least, *almost* perfectly symmetrical. Jewish, Christian and Islamic religious architecture had always shared a common feature. Each of these traditions was familiar with the biblical story of the

Tower of Babel – a building that challenged the power of God and led to disaster.[54] To avoid such a fate, the builders of every church, synagogue and mosque incorporated a deliberate mistake into its design, such as a subtly asymmetrical corner or a stone that was left unfinished rather than cut perfectly straight. The perfection-seeking architects of the seventeenth and eighteenth centuries were very familiar with hubris, so it is hardly surprising that they continued this tradition. For example, St Paul's Cathedral has an unfinished set of three stones over the doorway that leads down to the crypt. On this occasion, the deliberate mistake served the purpose it had fulfilled for well over a millennium – as a reminder that only God is perfect and only He ultimately controls this world and the next.

However, the architects of secular buildings – often men who had rejected such notions of the divine – were careful to incorporate flaws, too. In Bath I always take visitors to see the classical building façade that runs along the south side of Wood Street, where there is a deliberate mistake on one of the capitals above the first-floor pillars: whereas all the others have five flutes, this one has four and a half. This was no doubt included to remind all architects and indeed passers-by to avoid hubris. But at a deeper level, it was an acknowledgement that even Georgians – people born into a scientific, industrialising, enlightened world – understood that they were still part of a great, sacred story – notwithstanding the fact that that story had changed radically over the previous couple of centuries.

HOW CIVIC ARCHITECTURE TELLS THE GREAT STORY

Town halls

The main buildings around a town's market place tell many stories. They often include a significant civic building, such as a town hall or a museum. Town halls especially often evoke the growing self-confidence of nineteenth-century urban communities, with the grandest usually found in old industrial powerhouses, such as Halifax, Manchester, Bolton, Newcastle, Birmingham and Glasgow. They date from a period when ordinary people were starting to demand more democracy, and their local politicians were increasingly 'self-made men' – scions of wealthy industrial families or even, towards the end of the century, working-class intellectuals. These people were proud of both their own achievements and their town or city. The town halls in which they made their speeches were the sacred spaces in a secular world – the modern equivalents of medieval cathedrals.

These civic buildings – along with others, such as libraries, local higher education colleges and even some schools – were statements about new power and new confidence, yet many of them deliberately harked back to medieval religious styles, as if they were unsure

Manchester Town Hall, a classic example of the new religion of civic pride in the nineteenth century.

whether they stood for progress or continuity. Manchester Town Hall was designed by a Liverpudlian Quaker architect, Alfred Waterhouse, who lovingly recreated a magnificent medieval palace. The building bursts with civic pride, and its façade is filled with statues of great figures from the city's past – with barons standing alongside bishops and saints. It is civic religion incarnate. Such a medley of religious and secular imagery and influence can be seen in many other town halls, too. Just as the builders of the stone circles incorporated tombs – comforting reminders of the natives' old faith – nineteenth-century architects included reassuring echoes of the past while celebrating the present and taking the townsfolk on a journey into what was surely going to be a bright future.

> Manchester Town Hall regularly doubles as the corridors and rooms of the Houses of Parliament when film companies want to recreate the real thing. (They are not allowed to film within Westminster.) Alfred Waterhouse was a great exponent of the Victorian Gothic revival style, as were the architect and interior designer of the reconstructed Houses of Parliament, Charles Barry and Augustus Welby Pugin.

Big business asserts itself

Banks and post offices also tend to cluster around main squares, and they also tell a story. In the eighteenth and nineteenth centuries, banks echoed the confident statements being made by the town halls: they loudly proclaimed that they were local success stories. However, many of them proved to be anything but. They were extremely vulnerable to crises caused by wars or even just rumours circulated by rivals, so they often went bust, as the City of Glasgow Bank did in 1878. The fragility of the early nineteenth-century banking world is well captured by Elizabeth Gaskell in her novel *Cranford*, where the collapse of the local bank leaves Miss Matty almost destitute. The vast majority of local banks that managed to survive were eventually swallowed up by the huge national and international corporations we know today. Nevertheless, their names can often still be seen carved into the pediments of the buildings now occupied by the likes of Barclays and Lloyds.

The façades of these buildings – through elaborate statuary and ornate carvings – announce that their wealth is linked to the bounty of the land, often featuring sheaves of wheat or cornucopias of fruit. They also employ the Greco-Roman temple design to lend an air of historical authority to their temporal – often all-too-temporal – business dealings. Some even boast statues of classical philosophers, or the Virtues, to emphasise their trustworthiness. Another favourite statue is of a lightly clad classical-style woman – apparently in a bid to project both virtue and a sort of sexuality. Presumably, the idea was to persuade successful Victorian men that they would be able to attract such women if they deposited – and therefore protected – their wealth in the bank.

The North of Scotland Bank building on Castle Street, Aberdeen – designed by Archibald Simpson and built between 1839 and 1842 – employs all of these subtle marketing devices. This huge building has a classical Greek temple-style portico, topped by a statue of a Greek goddess who is pouring out a cornucopia of fruits and flanked by a lion. The message is obvious in this temple to money: success, wealth and strength. In Brecon High Street, Powys, the HSBC bank is housed in a magnificent late nineteenth-century building that is similarly bursting with symbols of wealth and status. Tellingly, it is situated almost directly opposite the parish church of St Mary: a new place of worship for a new religion. Lloyds on Corn Street, central Bristol, has one of the most elaborate façades of any bank building. Created in 1857, this building was originally the home of the West of England and South Wales District Bank. On the ground floor, the main cities of the old bank – Newport, Bath, Bristol, Exeter and Cardiff – are depicted through their coats of arms, their main products and their rivers. On the first floor, classical female statues representing wealth, peace, justice, plenty and integrity are surrounded by the coats of arms of the smaller towns where the bank had a presence.

Every eighteenth- or nineteenth-century bank façade offers reassurance along with the promise of wealth and success. They like to announce that they are stern defenders of finance (look for the common use of castle motifs), but they also have a spiritual dimension through the use of Gothic arches and their semi-ecclesiastical appearance. Two good, if contrasting, examples can be found in Castle Street, Liverpool. The Adelphi Bank mixes Renaissance classicism with Nordic and Eastern European flourishes and features scenes of 'brotherly love' on its bronze doors, presumably to reassure investors that the bank cared for the well-being of the whole community. Further down the street is the National Westminster Bank, housed in the old Parr's Bank building, which adopts a far less subtle approach: it simply seeks to awe the customer through its sheer scale, grandeur and classical lines.

Of course, the ultimate assertion of sacred financial power in a building can be found in the Bank of England on Threadneedle Street, London: modern Britain's foremost Temple to Mammon. Vast, overpowering, almost gaunt – rejecting decoration as mere whimsy – it embodies solidity and seriousness. However, it also projects itself as a holy place – a place where money is sacred – something that would once have been considered shameful, but not now. It can stand to the east of St Paul's Cathedral with its head held high.

Post offices, meanwhile, are celebrations of communication. The pride in design that led to the famous red pillar box is often repeated in Victorian post office buildings, which pull off the impressive trick of coupling business with glamour. They give the sense that they are gateways to the world. Their dual function – part shop, part despatch centre – can sometimes still be seen where they have stagecoach doors to one side, perhaps with the large iron door guards that stopped the carriages' wheels from smashing the stonework or the wooden doors themselves. You might also still find a pub near a main post office, an old coaching inn, because that is how the postal service began in the late eighteenth century. Sadly, though, many post offices have now closed after a series of economy drives, and the old-fashioned ones have often been replaced with modern buildings of almost no physical significance whatsoever. An exception is the magnificent BT Tower in London, which still draws the eye, more than forty years after it was erected. It is a dramatic statement of the power of communication, giving the impression that the whole world is in reach of its signals, even when it is shrouded in mist.

The Victorian art of dropping in

The Victorians prided themselves on their religiosity. Yet, it was during the Victorian era – for the first time in British history – that architects and builders abandoned the idea of telling the sacred great story in the whole layout and structure of their towns. Instead, they opted for what might be called a 'dropped-in story'.

The vast Victorian housing developments – such as Bethnal Green in London; Moss Side, and Platt Fields in Manchester; and the Gorbals in Glasgow – pay homage not to God (at least not directly) but to the glories of the British Empire and the royal family. Through their street names, they express an ironic devotion to power and wealth in some of the poorest areas of Britain (see Chapter 6). By the mid-nineteenth century, at the peak of Britain's imperial adventure, this story was itself becoming semi-sacred – a greater story of Britain's divinely ordained pre-eminence in the world. There was still a place for the more traditional, faith-based greater story, but it had to compete for space with this increasingly powerful new story. Consequently, it had to be parachuted into the huge industrial housing estates in the form of elaborate Gothic churches. These buildings often stood on streets that honoured great nineteenth-century battles, rather than saints, and alongside pubs with names like the Imperial and the Empire, rather than St George and the Dragon or the Cross Keys. Other pubs looked to Britain's folkloric past and adopted such names as the Green Man and the Robin Hood. Still others started to celebrate working-class heroes by calling themselves the Weavers' Arms, the Miners' Arms or even the Joseph Arch (the leader of the first attempt to unionise Britain's farm labourers). Finally, some echoed the streets that honoured the royal family, with names like the Queen's Head and the Prince Albert. When Inner City, Salford – the district on which *Coronation Street* was based – was demolished in the 1960s, the only Victorian buildings to survive the wrecking ball were the churches and the pubs. Nothing else was thought to be sufficiently characterful or beautiful to save. (Or perhaps the only groups who were strong enough to resist the local council and the developers were the Church and the brewers.)

Many of the Victorians' most beautiful churches still solemnly represent the sacred in some of our most deprived urban areas. For example, in Gorton, Manchester, the stunning church of St Francis now stands alone among the sixties and seventies boxes that have replaced row upon row of grim back-to-back terraces. Similarly, in the centre of the Langworthy housing estate, Salford – where residents dare park only behind a double layer of high fencing, with a permanent guard to buzz them in – there is St Paul's with Christ Church. This Victorian church has a beautiful little garden, the only such green space on the whole estate. Meanwhile, the church itself is full of art – from its stained-glass windows to its statues – and offers the locals a place of peace and reflection.

However, the East End of London has the most extraordinary examples of this practice of dropping beautiful churches into slum areas. In the early 1830s, James Blomfield, the Bishop of London, launched a campaign to build churches in the poorest parts of the capital. By the time he retired, in 1856, two hundred had been founded. In Bethnal Green, which Blomfield described as 'one of the most desolate parishes' in the diocese, just two ancient churches – St

Matthew and St John – served a population of over seventy thousand in the 1830s. Blomfield added ten more – each of them also dedicated to an apostle – so in the end Bethnal Green honoured all twelve. Particularly beautiful examples of these East End churches – specifically designed to uplift the downtrodden, at least on a Sunday – are St Philip's, St James the Great and St James the Less, St Peter's and St Bartholomew's.

THE AGE OF THE TRAIN

The Victorians had to deal with novelty as well as poverty. They had to create buildings – and therefore façades for buildings – that had never ever existed before. Perhaps the most important of these were railway stations, bridges and tunnels. The advances in technology that were showcased by the railways were as exciting to the Victorians as the latest tablet computers, mobile phones and MP3 players are to people today. They were immensely proud of their technical skills, yet they had no precedent on which to base their designs, because no mass transportation system had ever existed before. Consequently, the architects and engineers borrowed and reinterpreted old symbols of power and faith, and fashioned them to meet the contemporary needs of the railway companies.

The principal stations, such as London Paddington, Glasgow Central, Liverpool Lime Street and especially Bristol Temple Meads, were built as castles, cathedrals or some combination of the two. Even simple country stations were exclamations of pride: the earliest ones tended to look like Gothic estate cottages. They expressed the exuberance of people who found themselves in a new world that was still searching for its identity. In the process, these people created what has come to be known as 'railway architecture', which reached its pinnacle in St Pancras, London. The architect of that station, Sir George Gilbert Scott, designed something that was part

Gothic castle, part lakeside chateau, yet still evoked the romance of journeys.

The long Twerton Tunnel leads into Bath on the main line from Bristol. This once formed part of the Great Western Railway, known affectionately as 'God's Wonderful Railway', so great was the pride felt by the builders and staff for this historic line. It was one of the very first railway tunnels, completed in the 1830s, and its façade was designed in the Gothic revival style – the height of fashion at the time. So it resembles the great gate of a medieval castle or the western entrance to a fine twelfth-century cathedral. Bramhope Tunnel, West Yorkshire, built in 1849, goes as far as including a turret tower on its northern end in order to recreate the image of a Norman castle, while many people have compared Paddington to a cathedral since its completion in 1854. Not all tunnels looked to the Middle Ages for their inspiration: for example, the entrances to the Severn Tunnel, Gloucestershire, and the Summit Tunnel, West Yorkshire, have façades that resemble elegant Georgian doorways. Irrespective of which period they echo, though, all of these iconic structures could be seen as tributes from humanity to God in the sheer skill and effort that went into their construction.

Building the railways demanded enormous engineering skill. But the magnificent Victorian viaducts (such as the one that soars through the clouds from Broadbottom into Glossop, Derbyshire), huge engine sheds (such as those in Derby), whole railway villages (such as the wonderfully preserved one in Swindon) and cathedral-like, glass-ceilinged mainline stations are much more than pragmatic, ingenious solutions to engineering problems. They are architectural exclamations of the wonder of science and technology. Moreover, they announce the emergence of the force that has done more to shape the British landscape ever since: the desire for – almost worship of – speed. Over the past century, our ever-increasing reverence for speed has led us to bury vast areas of our countryside under motorways, container ports and, most recently, multi-runway airports.

THE STORY BENEATH OUR FEET

Two great, distinctive features of Victorian town design – now often overlooked – are Britain's parks and sewerage systems. We will stroll around some parks in Chapter 9, but we cannot postpone our descent into the sewers any longer.

In 1817, people living in slum settlements beside a river delta in north-east India started to exhibit symptoms of an unidentified illness. It killed many of them – including ten thousand in a single district – and then started to spread: east to China and the Philippines; and west to Persia, Europe and eventually the Americas. By then, it had a name – *Cholera morbus* – from the Greek for 'bile' and 'flow' (in reference to the extreme nausea that it provoked) and the Latin for 'death'. From the 1830s onwards, cholera devastated the British Isles in a series of horrific epidemics: in the summer of 1849, over 33,000 people died of the disease in just three months, 13,000 of them in London. Finally, in 1855, the Victorians discovered that these epidemics were caused by people washing in and drinking infected water. Armed with this knowledge, they set about building the greatest sewerage system in history – first in every major city and then in most towns and even villages.

The Victorians' sewage-pumping stations reflected their pride in this achievement: they were among the most beautiful buildings of the nineteenth century. The ornate Papplewick pumping station in Nottinghamshire opened in 1884 complete with a tree-lined cooling reservoir in the shape of a classical decorative lake and a central fountain. Such stylish, temple-like buildings help to tell the Victorians' great story of combining public philanthropy with technology, scientific research and engineering to improve the world and save lives. Along with the Natural History Museum in London, they are among the greatest physical expressions of the Victorians' unstinting faith in science and in humanity's potential to study, understand, reveal and then resolve its own problems.

Papplewick pumping station, a superb example of nineteenth-century pride in improving health, harnessing new technologies and building beautiful industrial plants.

DARK SATANIC MILLS

It was William Blake, in his short poem 'Jerusalem', who coined the telling phrase 'dark satanic mills'. Most people assume that he was describing the textile factories that were springing up all over Britain in the early nineteenth century. However, given his highly unorthodox, dissenting Christianity, it could be argued that Blake was actually referring to the mill churches built by powerful industrialists to instil respect, order and morality among their workforces. Every great mill town of Lancashire had at least one of these churches, as well as schools that served a similar purpose for the younger workers.

The mills themselves – especially the early ones – were certainly dark places, both literally and metaphorically. Built just a few decades after the height of ornate Georgian elegance, these places told a very different story: the vast majority of them embodied the utilitarian principle to the utmost. They were almost purely functional, their only concession to decoration being found in the manager's office or on a grand entrance designed to impress visitors. The rest was uniformly bleak. These were the battery-hen sheds built for human beings.

Thankfully, from the middle of the nineteenth century, and especially following the first three Factory Acts (1847, 1850 and 1856), some improvements started to be made. These related not only to the welfare of the workers (Parliament limited the working day to ten hours ... for children) but to the appearance of the buildings themselves. Sometimes the architects displayed Byzantine or Italian Renaissance influences, following the examples set by John Ruskin in his book *The Stones of Venice* (1851–3). This great work shaped the notion of good architecture for decades to come, and featured a powerful dual attack on utilitarian design and capitalist production methods:

And the great cry that rises from all our manufacturing cities, louder than their furnace blast, is all in very deed from this – that we manufacture there everything except men; we blanch cotton, and strengthen steel, and refine sugar, and shape pottery; but to brighten, to strengthen, to refine, or to form a single living spirit, never enters into our estimate of advantages.[55]

MANY STYLES, MANY PHILOSOPHIES

The first three decades of the twentieth century saw a confusion of styles, some inherited from the Victorians, others innovative: Gothic revival, art nouveau, classical, functional, Arts and Crafts.

John Ruskin inspired many to reject the mass-produced uniformity of the industrial age and seek a return to beauty and to the skills of the individual craftsman or woman. The most outstanding expression of this was the Arts and Crafts movement, founded by William Morris (1834–96). Morris had trained for the priesthood of the Anglican Church but rejected that and instead studied architecture and painting. In 1861 he founded his own company to create beautiful decorations for homes and design homes fit to house them. His was an unashamed return to what he and colleagues such as Sir Edward Coley Burne-Jones saw as the excellence of medieval art, which had been destroyed by capitalism and mass production. Burne-Jones was a painter but is perhaps best remembered for his beautiful stained glass windows.

The influence of the Arts and Crafts movement was felt throughout Britain, from homes to churches and from tapestry to book making. It offered a vision of a different way of being contemporary and it also brought back for many a sense of beauty and of the sacred in the world of human endeavour.

The First World War created a sense of desperation among those who survived, leading to the flapper generation, who seemed to live to party. Their somewhat frenetic desire for colour and flare was reflected in the extraordinary industrial architecture of the time, such as Fort Dunlop, Birmingham, and the Hoover Building, west London. These buildings possessed an excitement and vitality that endured until 1939, when the second great conflagration of the century snuffed out all such vigour for decades to come. By contrast, the domestic buildings of the same era often attempted to create a romantic image of Britain's legendary bucolic past. The middle classes moved out from the city centres to sprawling mock-Tudor suburbs and then commuted back in every day on new train, bus and tram systems. This new way of living was most fully realised in the garden cities, such as

Welwyn, in Hertfordshire. Such places attempted to recreate some of the community spirit and comfortable scale of the traditional village for people who were sick and tired of urban life.

Before the Second World War, the British Empire was still at its height, despite its redesignation as a 'commonwealth' in 1931 (for the 'white' colonies, at least). Consequently, the façades of many new buildings continued to reflect the sense of Britain as heir to imperial Rome. However, from the late 1920s onwards, some banks and civic buildings started to follow an alternative trend. The banks of this period are often gigantic, bearing down on both the street and their customers. Some of them feature heavy statues of muscular men and women, frequently wielding tools, including sickles and hammers. These celebrations of labour and industry echo the Soviet Realist style of the era, and they were built in response to (and possibly in support of) the Russian Revolution of 1917. By contrast, on other façades dating from the same period, you may well see the fascisti – a bundle of sticks bound together around an axe – a symbol of power since the days of the ancient Roman Republic and adopted by Benito Mussolini and his Fascist Party. This symbol was much imitated by power-hungry organisations throughout Europe, including Britain.

THE DEATH – OR MURDER – OF A GREAT STORY

After the Second World War, Britain was physically and economically broken. Little of any significance was built until the late 1950s, at which point a new generation of town planners – the majority of whom were disciples of the brutalist school of architecture – were given free rein to display their almost visceral hatred of anything old. The end result was the deep scarification of vast swaths of our urban environment.

Most of the last forty years of the century was a tale of destruction, imitation, pastiche and brutalism. This was an era of featureless glass boxes – especially in post-1960 civic architecture – with a complete absence of delight in decoration or detail. If a building was large, it was invariably overblown and pompous, rather than grand. Utilitarianism was back, and it was even more omnipresent than it had been in the industrial towns of the first half of the nineteenth century. Local traditions (and wishes) were ignored as many historic urban areas were bulldozed. With them went the sacred stories that had been woven into the fabric of their street layouts, buildings and open spaces.

The entire inner city of Worcester is a classic example of how the arrogance of 1960s planners destroyed centuries of sacred stories in just a couple of years. The old street pattern was swept away and replaced with featureless shopping centres, more 'car-friendly' streets and bleak open spaces. All of these were plonked down with no regard to aesthetic beauty or any sense of place and time to produce one of the most depressing city centres in Britain. The still-magnificent cathedral and a few other old buildings have been left stranded in the midst of this concrete mess.

Meanwhile, in Edinburgh, the destruction of the lower façades on Princes Street in order to accommodate modern shopfronts was a triumph of consumerism and banality over beauty and meaning. Similar council-approved vandalism occurred throughout Britain, destroying the uniqueness of each high street and leaving us with a series of grey, uniform city centres. Everywhere seems to have its own ugly sixties or seventies shopping centre, but my personal *bête noire* is the Viking Shopping Precinct in Jarrow, Tyne and Wear. The Arndale Centre in Manchester comes a close second.

THE BEGINNING OF THE END OF THE FIFTH GREAT CYCLE?

At the end of the 1960s, a few voices started to be raised against all of this brutality. Over the next thirty years, their numbers swelled and they acquired a powerful – if sometimes controversial – champion in the form of the Prince of Wales. His attacks on the banality of so much modern architecture raised the hackles of architects, but prompted others to speak out as well. It is partly because of his intervention that many places are rediscovering, recreating and re-envisioning what they had almost lost entirely. There is a new delight in decoration and in proportionate scale that considers the wider context. Liverpool is a fine example. The old Albert Dock area has been rebuilt and redesigned to become a place of real beauty and elegance, attracting new residents, new businesses and even new art galleries, such as the Tate. The refurbished grand old Georgian and Victorian riverside buildings, aided by creative new developments, have generated new income but also a sense of genuine pride in the city. The old port of Edinburgh, the town of Leith – with its mixture of grand sixteenth–eighteenth-century and rather less beautiful nineteenth-century buildings – has undergone a similar process of sensitive redevelopment that has celebrated the environment, buildings and stories of this once run-down area. Now formally part of Edinburgh, Leith's new story speaks of the surge in pride that increasing independence has generated among the citizens of Scotland's capital.

As yet, Bristol has not enjoyed such a renovation, but it has belatedly rediscovered its civic pride. The city was a prime target for the Luftwaffe in the Second World War because of the important docks at Avonmouth, to the west, the aircraft factories at Filton, to the north, and even the Wills tobacco factories and warehouses. (The Germans believed that cigarettes were vital to British morale.) Then, in the thirty years after the war, developers and planners continued the work of the bombers: they flattened many of the surviving old buildings and thoughtlessly changed the street layout. Over the past decade, however, some of the old sacred patterns and meanings have been rediscovered. Thankfully, when they are found, they are now cherished. One church, St Stephens, hopes to trace a map of the old city on the floor of the nave, so that people might walk through it as a form of meditation.

Part of this nationwide process has been a new celebration of streets. The closing of some roads to traffic has revived the hearts of many towns and cities by recreating the sense of space that public areas traditionally provided in the crowded confines of Britain's urban areas. For the first time in maybe a century, people can sit, relax, enjoy, talk and look around, rather than merely move. In 2003, the northern section of Trafalgar Square was closed to traffic. Cars and buses were diverted around the western and eastern edges of the square, and pedestrians were invited to stroll across the new piazza in front of the National Gallery, or stop for a coffee in the alfresco café. They now have an unimpeded view to Nelson's Column, London's principal omphalos, the capital's central sacred pillar. Meanwhile, in Bath, the new Southgate development (which celebrates the city's history as it was named after the south gate of the medieval city wall) was opened in 2010, replacing an old, tatty 1960s bus station and utilitarian shops. All of its Georgian-style streets are pedestrianised, and they have been given new sacred names, such as St Lawrence Street. It has already proved a great success, tempting people to sit and enjoy, rather than rush.

Sadly, pedestrianisation under a roof never seems to be quite so geomantically successful. The ubiquitous Arndale Centres, which sprang up across the country in the 1970s and 1980s, were perhaps the nadir of the shopping mall, but even larger, more recent developments, such as Meadowhall in Sheffield and Westway in London, share the same basic design shortcomings, even though they camouflage them with a little more style. Malls might provide a variety of places to sit, but they lack the diversity of buildings – churches, offices, houses – and gardens that traditional shopping streets always had. These enclosed ghettoes of consumerism offer little in terms of communal space for reflection or enjoyment. Their goal is to entice you in, persuade you to part with your money as quickly as possible, and push you out again. They all employ security guards to drive away groups of young people who linger too long and treat the mall like a traditional omphalos by sitting, chatting, flirting and teasing passers-by. As a result, today's youngsters have to find somewhere a little less central, and probably a lot less safe, to do what teenagers have done since the dawn of history. These mock streets and centres are poor imitations if the real thing and while they attract ever more cash and customers, the real hearts of our towns and cities – the high streets and their satellite roads – are dying. In the years since the Second World War we seem to have lost something of the plot. We have lost confidence in our own great story, or perhaps our belief that there is any sort of story.

We seem to be at the point in the Fifth Great Cycle when there is a lack of overall direction. Some of the recent developments outlined above are clearly trying to restore our relationship with the landscape and the past while attempting to curb the destructive forces of power

The Eden Project – a biblical name linked to the new beliefs and values of ecology. It is one of the most innovative examples of trying to tell a new story.

and control. Others – such as the glut of malls – seem to indicate that those destructive forces are as strong as ever. Which path we take is very much up for grabs.

However, occasionally, creative minds still have the ability to produce flashes of wonder and beauty. New bridges – such as the Millennium Bridges that span the Thames and the Tyne – Cardiff's Opera House, Manchester's Imperial War Museum and the Eden Project's magnificent domes stand as symbols of new vision, imagination and – perhaps as important – fun at the end of a long period of awfulness and tedium. Each of these wonderful structures works precisely because it was built to tell a story.

It is too early to be certain, but perhaps this signals a return to us wanting a greater narrative in our lives, albeit probably in a different form to any we have known in the past. We have lost so much – architecturally, narratively and ideologically – so we need to dig deeper to rediscover the old stories and create a new or renewed vision of our place in the world. Then we may be able to look at the world around us as a cosmos of wonder and awe, and see ourselves as more than mere functionaries in a soulless universe.

GAZETTEER

Castles, churches and abbeys

Scotland
- St Machar's Cathedral, Aberdeen: a stern, granite masterpiece of early medieval art and faith

Wales
- St Davids Cathedral, Pembrokeshire (SA62): vast Norman and medieval cathedral built on site of humble church and monastic community of St Dewi (David) and constantly under threat of sinking

Northern England
- Durham Cathedral (DH1): best Norman cathedral in Britain
- Newstead Abbey, Nottingham (NG15): former abbey then Georgian country house associated with Lord Byron
- Nottingham Castle (NG1): fragments of the famous castle but rebuilt since the seventeenth century; the various rebuildings tell many stories
- St Francis, Gorton, Manchester (M12): superb example of Victorian church dropped into the centre of what were slums and is still a very poor and poorly designed area

Southern England
- Berkhampstead, Hertfordshire (HP4): excellent motte and bailey with later stone castle
- Bristol Castle, now site of a park (Castle Park) with a few fragments, central Bristol (BS1)
- Hailes Abbey, Gloucestershire (GL54): fragments left only
- Hailes parish church, Gloucestershire (GL54): good wall paintings and it has survived while the great Abbey is now a few ruins
- Mereworth Castle, Kent (ME18): good example of Georgian country house
- Old Sarum, Salisbury, Wiltshire (SP4): dramatic ancient castle and cathedral site
- St Paul's Cathedral, London: Sir Christopher Wren's most famous building
- Winchester Cathedral, Hampshire (SO23): medieval cathedral built on site of simple Saxon cathedral and once so flooded it needed a deep-sea diver to work on the foundations
- Witham Abbey, Somerset: built by Henry II as penance for the killing of Thomas Becket – only the village church survives but is most distinctive

Town and city walls

- Bristol: fragments and built to create a divine circle around old Bristol
- Caernarfon, Gwynedd: built to imitate the walls of Constantinople because of link to the Emperor Constantine

- Chester, Cheshire: fine example of walled city
- Norwich, Norfolk: stories associated with every one of the old – now mostly gone – gates

Shopping areas and public spaces

Scotland
- Market Street/High Street/St Giles Cathedral courtyard, Edinburgh (EH1): a long wide area now partly invaded by buildings which took over the site of stalls
- Wigtown, Dumfries and Galloway (DG8): old market town with fine wide market street

Northern England
- Broad Street, Ludlow, Shropshire (SY8): good example of market place and medieval encroachment
- Little Morton Hall, Cheshire (CW12): fine knot garden
- Meadowhall, Sheffield (S9): modern shopping centre
- Viking Shopping Precinct, Jarrow, Tyne and Wear (NE32): what not to build

Southern England
- Chipping Sodbury, Gloucestershire (BS37): means a market place and still has very wide main street for the market
- Circus, Bath (BA1): built as a version of Stonehenge
- Southgate, Bath (BA1): redesigned from disastrous 60s buildings on site destroyed by bombing in World War Two

- Stourhead, Wiltshire (BA12): superb gardens and home to the medieval market cross of Bristol
- Trafalgar Square, London (WC2N): ritual centre of London and omphalos
- Westway, London (W10): classic example of consumerism as new cult
- Worcester city centre: how to destroy a beautiful and historic centre

Town halls and civic buildings

All these town halls tell a story of civic pride and belief. Please see pages 248–50 for stories.

Scotland
- Glasgow

England
- Birmingham
- Bolton
- Halifax
- Liverpool
- Manchester
- Newcastle
- St George's Hall, Liverpool

Commercial buildings

Scotland
- City of Glasgow Bank (G2): a good example of Victorian bank as shrine
- North of Scotland Bank, Castle Street, Aberdeen (AB11): an example of a bank as shrine

Wales

- HSBC, High Street, Brecon, Powys (LD3): late 19th century cornucopia representing wealth through banking

Northern England

- Adelphi Bank, Castle Street, Liverpool (L25): classic example of 19th-century bank as religion
- National Westminster Bank, Parr's bank building, Castle Street, Liverpool (L25): wonderful example of symbolism

Southern England

- Bank of England, Threadneedle Street, London (EC2): classic symbol of money as the new deity of the eighteenth century
- BT Tower, London (W1T): wonderful example of what could be built that is exciting in the 60s
- Lloyds, Corn Street, Bristol (BS1): one of the most extravagant of early 19th-century banks – covered with symbolism

Urban developments

Tackling the mistakes of the past and sometimes the mistakes of the present.

Scotland

- Gorbals, Glasgow

Northern England

- Inner City, Salford
- Moss Side, Manchester
- Platt Fields, Manchester

Southern England

- Welwyn Garden City
- Bethnal Green, London

Railway architecture

Scotland

- Glasgow Central Station (G1): the magnificence of 'railway architecture'

Northern England

- Bramhope tunnel, West Yorkshire (LS17): castle with turret
- Derby engine sheds (S42): cathedrals of the industrial age
- Lime Street Station, Liverpool (L1): local pride manifest in stone
- Summit tunnel, West Yorkshire (OL14: a fine example of imaginative railway architecture
- Viaduct between Broadbottom and Glossop, Derbyshire (SK14): an example of the heights of Victorian architecture and skills

Southern England

- Paddington Station, London (W2): the new railway 'cathedral'
- St Pancras Station, London (NW1): the greatest example of railway architecture of the 19th century
- Severn Tunnel, Gloucestershire (SN4): tunnels as doorways in Georgian style
- Swindon engine sheds: huge sheds still standing as testimony to the strength of the railway age
- Temple Meads Station, Bristol (BS1): Old Temple Meads is a mock medieval manor house with the current mid-nineteenth century station a masterpiece of gothic
- Twerton Tunnel, Bath (BA2): tunnel entrance as a castle

Recent construction and redevelopment projects

Scotland
- Leith, Edinburgh (EH6): rejuvenation of the old

Wales
- Opera House, Cardiff (CF10): design as statement

Northern England
- Albert Dock, Liverpool (L70): revitalised old dock side

- Imperial War Museum, Manchester (M17): design as symbol
- Millennium Bridge, Gateshead (NE8): how to make a dull stretch of river come to life

Southern England
- Eden Project, St Austell, Cornwall (PL24): one of the most imaginative modern buildings in Britain
- Millennium Bridge, London (EC4): new and beautiful

8

Walking on the dead

What is the turning?
First we must see
A world that's unreal
We're sure is reality.[56]

In St Francis's famous *Canticle of the Creatures*, written around AD 1220, the saint praises everything that God has created – from the sun and the moon to animals, birds, trees, water … and death. For Francis – and indeed everybody else, until very recently – had no problem discussing the reality of death. They viewed it as an essential element in their sacred stories.

In all five of Britain's great stories, death has been a fundamental part of life, and it has left a deep impression upon our physical and psychological landscape. Partly, this has happened because each of the first four great cycles collapsed through plague or disaster that wiped out much of the population. However, it is also the result of every individual's story ultimately ending in death, and the fact that this has been honoured over the millennia.

© John Gay/English Heritage. NMR/Mary Evans Picture Library

Highgate Cemetery in London is one of the great nineteenth-century cemeteries, which took over from the more traditional churchyards. It is a famous burial place for people of all faiths, as well as atheists like Karl Marx.

DEATH ALL AROUND

Stand almost anywhere in Britain and you will see some sign of our preoccupation with death – and therefore also our preoccupation with life and its meaning. Death may be the taboo subject of our generation – just as sex was for the Victorians – but we are never far from reminders of it. A distant church spire; a burial mound; an obelisk marking a battlefield; a village war memorial; a park bench dedicated to a beloved relative who used to enjoy feeding the ducks – all of these represent the eternal paradox of life in death and death in life. The same is true of bouquets of flowers or teddy bears left by a roadside to commemorate someone killed in a traffic accident. These replicate the old wayside shrines – and the comfort they afforded the bereaved – that could be seen throughout Britain until the Reformation removed them from the landscape.

Yet, while we commemorate death in these very specific, small-scale ways, we ignore it on a much larger scale. Much of our physical landscape is built upon death: the corpses of untold billions of sea creatures whose bones and shells form the limestone on which so many of us stand, and out of which many of our great buildings have been constructed. Our energy needs are met primarily by death: oil, gas and coal are all formed from plants and trees that died millions of years ago. Across Britain, there are hundreds of plague pits dating from the sixth century onwards. We walk over them in blissful ignorance because they are no longer marked as places that contain the bodies of thousands of our ancestors. Death is something we literally bury and then usually ignore. Even the foot-and-mouth pits of the early 2000s – the final destination of some six million cattle – are unmarked, recalled by almost no one, save for the desolate farmers and their families. Many of these people have now given up farming and left the places where they witnessed so much death – unable to deal with it on a daily basis.

HOW OUR ANCESTORS BURIED THEIR DEAD

As the Anglican Church's Book of Common Prayer says, 'In the midst of life, we are in death.' If you want to understand a culture's concept of the sacred and its great story, you need to explore its attitude towards death. The best way to do this is to examine how that culture buried its dead.

Prehistoric death and its sacred and narrative significance

The oldest identified burial in Britain dates from roughly twenty-five thousand years ago. It was of a young man who was laid to rest in

Goat Hole Cavern at Paviland, on the Gower Peninsula in South Wales. His body was arranged as if sleeping, or perhaps to replicate the foetal position, and it was painted with red ochre. We do not know if this was done to give him the semblance of a living hue, or whether it had a sacred connotation. However, it seems clear that the people who laid him so carefully in that cave respected death and believed in some sort of life after it.

We next meet death in the British landscape in the form of the long barrows – the focal points of belief and ancestor worship in our First Great Cycle. As we saw in Chapter 3, for two millennia, the dead were regarded as integral to their communities, possibly even as deities in their own right. It was thought that they protected the hilltop settlements and farms, guarding the boundaries from attack from the wild lands below. But when Britain's hilltop communities collapsed around 3000 BC, they abandoned these ancestral tombs. The dead had failed the living, so they were stripped of their mystical, sacred power and left as just piles of dry bones, sealed inside their tombs.

At least some long barrows seem to have been built to enhance natural features in the landscape, as if the people of the First Great Cycle wished to build upon what nature had provided, in order to tell its story better. For example, in the Peak District, the long barrows follow the contours of the land at Perryfoot and the distinctive ridge line of the hill at Rockhurst. This would make sense for communities who felt that the land had given them place, purpose and meaning. If the land is seen as a gift from the ancestors, then it is only natural to bury those who have recently become ancestors in such a way as to celebrate the landscape. So the long barrows symbolise not just respect for the dead but an intimate relationship between human beings and the local landscape. In the Orkney Islands, this is reflected in the fact that the long barrows are spread out fairly evenly across the archipelago, with a couple on each of the bigger islands and one on almost every smaller island.[57] It seems that they were specifically created to cater for these distinct island communities, much as individual parishes were five millennia later.

The attitude to death changed sharply once stone circles replaced long barrows as the principal places of worship in the Second Great Cycle. These great monuments probably had some role to play when somebody – especially somebody important – died, but they were not primarily places of death. As we have seen, they were used much more often as places of business. Burials took place *around* them, not *in* them. The dead were moved outside the community's most sacred

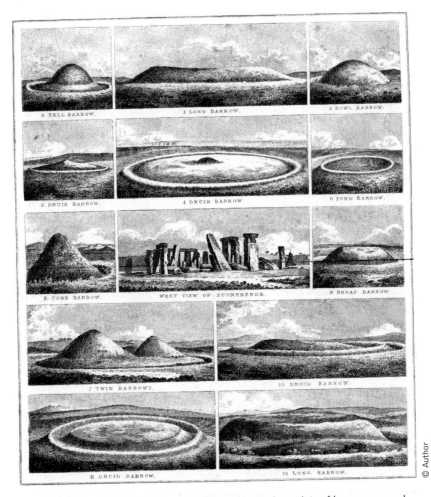

This fascinating eighteenth-century illustration shows the variety of barrows around Stonehenge. Few now remain in anything resembling their original form.

space, which leads one to conjecture that their place inside must have been taken by something else. Perhaps, then, this was the point when Britons started to worship divine beings that were credited with much more power than mere ancestors.

The greatest ancient British landscape of death can be found in the vicinity of Stonehenge. Hundreds of burial mounds are clustered around the great stone circle, all seemingly seeking a plot close to this epicentre of ritual and power. However, none actually lies within its bounds. By around 2000 BC, it seems that burial sites had become primarily status symbols. Families or tribes displayed their wealth by claiming plots as near as possible to the powerful sacred centres. They were supplicants to whichever chief controlled access to such sacred places and to the divine forces that were held to live within them. The dead were no longer the focus; they were part of the living's devotion to something greater.

It was around this time that the first cemeteries started to house the dead. Dozens of people might be buried in a single location, close to settlements and sacred sites, but not within either. Eyam Moor, in the Peak District, has vivid evidence of this. Deep holes, hidden for most of the year beneath heather and gorse, mark the sites of huts that must have comprised a sizable village. There are also several modest stone circles, with the stones often less than a foot high. Close to both is a field of over twenty burial cairns, piles of stones that were revealed when the earth that once covered them was eroded away. Although this ritual burial area was set apart from the village, it clearly would still have formed a backdrop to daily life – in much the same way as village cemeteries do today.

Similar grouping of the dead can be found in the two famous sets of round barrows at Priddy, in the Mendip Hills, Somerset. Dating from the Bronze Age, they stand on two ridges, separated by a shallow valley, with nine on one side and eight on the other. Near by are four huge henges or circles – each almost two hundred metres across – lying side by side. Nothing like this is known anywhere else, so the clustering of barrows might simply reflect the immense spiritual power that was accorded to this place. There is another theory, though. One cannot help noticing that the lines of barrows look like war graves, so perhaps this was a cemetery – or rather two cemeteries, one for each side – that was created after a great battle. Either way, once again, the tombs were sited very near, but not within, a major sacred centre.

Whereas rituals and celebrations probably took place in the fore-courts of long barrows, round barrows seem to have been much more functional. They were simply where the dead were laid to rest. End of story – unless offerings were made on the anniversary or other special occasions. There is no evidence that parties were ever held near them. This is yet more evidence that the people of the Second Great Cycle had a very different attitude towards their dead. Long barrows, with their ancestral emphasis, reflected the importance of lineage. Cemeteries were more about locating the dead within a much larger sacred picture. Whereas ancestors looking down from a great ridge are godlike, dead relatives buried in a cemetery near a sacred power centre are no more than adjuncts to the divine force that dwells within that centre. They still have a place, but it is no longer a central one. Bronze Age cemeteries were concerned more with disposal than divinity, setting the pattern that we still see in parish churchyards and municipal cemeteries today.

As we saw in Chapter 3, when the Second Great Cycle collapsed, there seems to have been a long period – perhaps six hundred years – when almost nothing sacred, not even burial of the dead, took place in Britain. Certainly, there is no evidence of it in the landscape. Part of the return to nature that characterised this period might well have been the introduction of cremation, with the ashes scattered in rivers. Whether the dead were disposed of in this or some other way, they were no longer laid to rest in cemeteries close to settlements and stone circles.

Then, around 300 BC, suddenly a whole new form of burial emerged – chariot or carriage burials in the uniquely square barrows of the Iron Age. The most dramatic example of this is Arras Cemetery, near Driffield, East Yorkshire. More than 250 barrows lie side by side, with several of them containing the remains of a chariot in the square tomb. Quite why so many barrows are clustered here – and why they have such an unusual design – has yet to be explained, because elsewhere there is very little evidence of what happened to the dead until the arrival of the Romans.

That arrival signalled the start – in Britain, at least – of digging graves and burying the dead in the ground – something we have continued to do ever since. This begs the question: why, up to the first century AD, did people bury their dead *above* ground? (Almost all barrows – be they long, round or square – were constructed on top of the ground, rather than in it.) The answer may well be that the communities who built these graves viewed them as *homes* for the dead, not tombs. Today, when Christians bury a body, they see the ceremony as disposal of a temporary case that once housed the eternal spirit but is no longer needed. There is no reason to believe that our prehistoric ancestors viewed dead bodies in the same way.

The Romans

Although the ancient Romans were often fearless warriors, they were all terrified of the dead – not of death itself, it should be noted, but *the dead*. No Roman could countenance burying anyone within the confines of a village or town. To the Roman mind, the dead should not dwell among the living, so their cemeteries were placed well outside their communities. The Appian Way – the main southern approach to Rome – is still lined with tombs from the imperial era, built close enough for Romans to be able to visit the graves of their dead ancestors, but firmly outside the city walls. In Britain, Roman cemeteries could be as far as three miles from town. Examples have been excavated in Brougham, near Penrith in Cumbria, the East End of London, and Ilchester in Somerset.

Sometimes, a church was built directly on top of an old Roman cemetery, particularly if an early Christian martyr was known to be buried there. For instance, the church of St Stephen, in St Albans, stands some way outside the old Roman walls, on the site of a Roman cemetery. It is dedicated to the first Christian martyr, which probably symbolises respect for Alban – a British-born soldier in the Roman army in the third century who was said to have sheltered a Christian priest from persecution. When the authorities arrived to apprehend the priest, Alban dressed in his cloak and said he was the man they sought. He was put to death, and is regarded as Britain's first Christian martyr. It seems likely that his body was buried in the local cemetery that now lies below St Stephen's before being disinterred and moved to the site of the cathedral, where he has been venerated for over fifteen hundred years.

Similarly, in the village of Northover, outside Ilchester, Somerset, stands the church of St Andrew, which was built long before 1066. Roman burials have been found in the churchyard, and Richard Morris speculates that the church was probably constructed directly on top of a site that was considered sacred because a local Christian martyr or saint had been buried there when the area was still pagan.[58] The same may well be true of many other ancient churches that are situated close to Roman settlements.

CHRISTIANITY'S SCANDALOUS VISION OF DEATH

When they first started to establish themselves in the Roman Empire, the early Christians scandalised polite society with their attitude towards death. For them, death was not something to be feared and pushed outside the city walls. Instead, they considered the dead to be fellow denizens in the Kingdom of God, spirits that remained in communion with the living as part of the family of the Church. As a result, they took to burying their dead right beside their churches, in the very centre of their communities. Christians wanted to gather all of the faithful, living *and* dead, in one place so that whenever the living held their rituals, the dead were there with them, both literally and spiritually. They were certain that death was not an end but a transition to a more wonderful, deeper relationship with God, so they welcomed rather than feared it. Ever since, this belief has had an enormous impact on our sacred landscape.

Almost every village and town in Britain, and many city districts, still have a peaceful, quiet, green graveyard near their centre. If, in a couple of thousand years' time, archaeologists were to excavate a churchyard with no knowledge of the beliefs and rituals that went on there, they would conclude that we worshipped our ancestors. This visceral link with the past is a key element of the importance of churches to communities to this day. So the churchyard is still much more than just a place to put the dead. It is a statement about their significance to us.

The very shape of a churchyard reveals a great deal about its history. If it is circular, rather than rectangular, then it is probably very old – possibly dating back to pre-Christian times – and it may once have been the homestead of the local chieftain. Many Welsh, Scottish and Cornish churchyards are circular, and *llan* and *kirk* (in Wales and Scotland, respectively) both originally referred to such sites, before the word was also applied to the adjoining church itself. A circular layout – symbolising the 'all-embracing arms' of God – was popular in early Christian church sites, but this was an adaptation and reinterpretation of the traditional circular shape of pre-Christian Iron Age homesteads.

As we have seen with the location of St Michael's churches, north was considered the direction of evil forces, and churchyards reflect this notion, too. In almost any old churchyard, the earliest graves occupy the most desirable plots – to the south of the church. Then there is a distinct chronological order to the siting of subsequent graves: first the east side of the graveyard is filled, then the west, and finally, when space is at a premium, the north. Most of the northern graves date from no earlier than the nineteenth century, by which time the old traditions were being forgotten or dismissed as superstition.

Some old churchyards still have the remnants of a 'preaching cross'. In the medieval period, anyone was allowed to preach at these tall stone pillars, but this often caused trouble because wandering friars tended to be much more outspoken than the local clergy.

Preaching crosses were especially loathed by Protestants because they were topped by images of saints and especially the Virgin Mary. However, a few survived the Reformation. For instance, there is a superb Celtic example in Eyam, Derbyshire, and a beautiful fifteenth-century one at Derwen, Denbighshire. The latter's octagonal pillar is topped with four fine carvings: the crucifixion on the west side; a battered Virgin and Child on the south; the coronation of the Virgin on the east; and an impressive St Michael, with raised sword and scales to weigh souls, on the north.

In a village churchyard near where I live, there is just one old tomb to the north of the church. It commemorates a girl who died in the 1830s, within the first year of life. Her grave is not even entirely within the bounds of the churchyard – half of it is in the surrounding earth wall. The fact that her tomb stands alone in the north of the graveyard, and not even wholly within it, probably means that she was not baptised and so should not have been buried in consecrated ground at all. However, it seems that the parish priest took pity on her grieving parents and was more generous than official Church teaching dictated and provided a place for her just within the encircling embrace of God.

Direction also plays an important role in the orientation of the graves: almost all Christian graves face east. As we saw in Chapter 5, east was considered the direction of paradise, as well as being the direction in which each new day began. Christian theology associated daybreak with the Day of Resurrection, when the dead will join the living and enter the Kingdom of Heaven. This image was beautifully captured by Archbishop Cranmer in the sixteenth century, when he described these two groups as 'the quick and the dead'. (Interestingly, although they are overtly secular, most municipal cemeteries also bury the majority of their dead in an east–west direction. However, they also usually have sections for Jewish and Muslim burials, which follow their own traditions. For instance, in Manchester's Southern Cemetery, the Jewish graves face Jerusalem and the Muslim ones face Mecca.)

If you frequent graveyards, you will soon notice that none of the headstones date from before the seventeenth century. This is because ordinary people in the Middle Ages knew that their bones would be dug up after fifty years or so. The disinterred bones were then either stored in a charnel house (after the Latin word for 'flesh') or burned on a 'bone-fire' and the ashes scattered: hence the word 'bonfire'.

The change in people's attitudes towards the sanctity of graves was a consequence of the collapse of the Fourth Great Cycle around the time of the Reformation. Throughout the medieval period, the Catholic Church taught that anyone who paid their tithes and dues, did not commit suicide and followed the teachings of the Church was guaranteed a place in heaven. In return for this devotion, the Church, through its priests and saints, would intercede on behalf of the faithful. This is most vividly expressed on the west fronts of some of the great medieval cathedrals – where most people enter. Carvings depict the Day of Judgement, with the good ascending to heaven and the bad condemned to hell. This could be viewed as an early form of advertising: 'Enter the church and we will carry you to heaven; stay outside and you will be damned for eternity.' Good examples of such decoration are at Lincoln and Wells cathedrals.

It is often thought that the medieval world was dominated by an overriding fear of hell and damnation, but that was not the case. Hell and heaven were certainly vividly depicted both within and outside medieval churches in carvings, paintings and even plays. However, few ordinary people worried about hell, because the vast majority of them were faithful sons and daughters of the Church

▶

and believed that it would carry them to salvation and heaven. They were all part of something much bigger and much more stable than they could – or indeed needed to – understand. The deal had already been done. The Church held the keys to heaven and would unlock the door for anyone as long as they obeyed a few simple rules. Even if you sinned, you could get in via the back door – Purgatory. And you could knock years, or even centuries, off the time you would have to spend there by buying indulgences.

This trust in the power of the Church to ease the path to heaven explains why medieval gargoyles, paintings and carvings tend to be humorous rather than devilish. Hardly anybody was terrified by the idea of hell, because hardly anybody thought they would end up there. The world of evil had been contained and was now under the control of Christ. This is borne out by the fact that no one in Britain was executed for witchcraft until the late fifteenth century, when the Black Death and the rise of the Renaissance thinking was finally starting to undermine the old medieval Catholic story.[59]

As we have seen, the traditional contract between ordinary people and the Church was smashed to pieces (literally, in the case of statues) with the arrival of the Protestant Reformation. In Britain after the 1530s, the saints had gone, the priest was no longer a magician and even the Church itself was now just a collection of people, rather than a supernatural body with great power over what happened to you after you died. Suddenly, every Christian was on their own, obliged to forge a personal relationship with God. The Church could not guarantee a place in heaven for you; you had to earn it yourself.

One aspect of this change was that it was no longer enough simply to be buried in consecrated ground. Protestants needed to ensure that their personal saviour knew precisely where they were on the Day of Judgement. So they or their families started to commission headstones that spelled out who they were and also included the names of their mother, father, husband or wife and children, their parish and sometimes even their job and address. Gravestones therefore mark a profound shift in the belief system of most ordinary Britons. From the sixteenth century onwards, people felt a little more alone and a little less secure.

Another aspect of this growing insecurity was a significant deterioration of explicit faith. Visit any old churchyard – or read the seventeenth- and eighteenth-century monuments on the walls of any church or even many Nonconformist chapels – and you will find that fewer than one in five graves makes any reference to God, Jesus or salvation. By the nineteenth century, this proportion had dropped even lower.

Of course, ordinary people's increasing knowledge of and faith in science had a large part to play in this, but so did their growing awareness of other religions. Britons, at the centre of a worldwide empire, had such a breadth of existential choice that the standard Christian faith was bound to wane … and it did. New and often bizarre forms of belief arose, including the conviction that God had chosen the British to rule the world because of their moral and spiritual superiority. (To their credit, most mainstream churches vigorously argued against this.) The British-Israelites took this even further by claiming that the Anglo-Saxons were the Lost Tribe of Israel and thus enjoyed a special and most blessed relationship with God.

THE SECULARISATION OF DEATH

It was in this existential context of doubt, choice, diversity and novelty that the municipal cemetery came into being. Ever since Christianity had first arrived in Britain, virtually everyone had been buried in a parish churchyard (although see 'Outcasts', pages 288–9). Then came both a legal and a psychological change: by law, burials had to take place largely outside the main cities and towns.

This was a necessity because the industrial urban areas were massively overcrowded and the parish graveyards simply could not cope with demand. Initially, from around the mid-eighteenth century, parishes tried to solve the problem by buying more land and extending their graveyards. For instance, in Endell Street, just off Long Acre in London's Covent Garden, there is a tiny park that sits about two metres above the road. This was the overflow graveyard for St Martin's in the Field, the local parish church. Its elevated level is due to the tens of thousands of bodies that were buried here.

Before long, though, there was no more city centre land to buy; then the cholera outbreaks of the 1830s and 1840s made matters even worse. Many churchyards were full, literally, to overflowing. Bodies were not buried deep enough and the rotting corpses started putrefying and leaking into water courses, which of course led to even more disease. In 1846, Parliament finally took action: it ordered that most of the old urban churchyards should be permanently closed, and instructed that large municipal cemeteries must be built on the outskirts of Britain's towns and cities. Of course, in terms of location, this almost exactly replicated Roman burial practice. However, it was prompted not by fear of the spirits of the dead, but by fear of the diseases that were being spread by their rotting corpses.

Some of the new cemeteries celebrated death in their architecture. The little houses for the dead in Edinburgh's Calton Old Burial Ground and Glasgow's Skyline Necropolis, both dating back to the eighteenth century, are particularly impressive. In the following century, the grand designs of Arnos Vale in Bristol, the park-like features of Cathays Cemetery in Cardiff, and the studied discipline of the vast Southern Cemetery in Manchester all indicate that some people, at least, were not yet willing to treat burial merely as the disposal of potentially hazardous waste. Others attempted to disguise a cemetery's function through landscaping – as, for example, at Keynsham in Somerset, which resembles parkland more than a graveyard. Sometimes, an existing parish churchyard was incorporated within a much larger and more regimented cemetery, as at Hathersage, Derbyshire, reputed to be the burial site of Little John. Here, the original graveyard has been extended down the hill. It becomes ever more

Glasgow Necropolis, with its numerous grandiose monuments, is a stunning 'celebration' of death in the eighteenth and nineteenth centuries.

controlled and functional in design as you descend and the dates on the headstones near the present day.

The traditions of Christian Britain were not abandoned entirely in these places. For instance, most municipal cemeteries have a chapel, and the Victorian ones are often very beautiful. However, these chapels serve only one purpose – they are there to mark some-one's death. No one is married or christened in them. God is not worshipped in any meaningful way in them. In a sense, then, they could be seen in a similar light to the fake tombs that were built in the middle of stone circles – as reassuring references back to a belief system that still offers some comfort to the bereaved, not places of great sacred significance in their own right.

The rise of the municipal cemetery coincided with the loss of belief in a grand sacred story. It was the Victorians who first fundamentally challenged belief in *any* divine power and purpose, and as a result they were the first not to treat the sacred as a given. The new cemeteries acknowledged this new reality because you could now be laid to rest in a dignified ceremony irrespective of what you did or did not believe. As long as there was a rather vague assertion of Anglican (or Presbyterian, in Scotland) faith, you would be granted a plot. And everyone knew that there would be no pastoral follow-up – as these places were not under the jurisdiction of parishes – so there was no danger of being found out later. The organised lines of graves and the bureaucratic management of these cemeteries robbed death of some of its social and sacred depth. Instead, they reflected the widening gap between communal faith and private life.

By the late nineteenth century, in Highgate Cemetery, north London, Karl Marx and other atheists were being laid to rest by friends and family without any nod to religion whatsoever. Meanwhile, extraordinary tombs filled with pre-Christian or non-Christian imagery started to be erected around the country. A quite astonishing example is the small-scale but almost full-blown pagan temple in the churchyard at Madron, Cornwall.

LIVING CHURCHYARDS

In recent years, much attention has focused upon the environmental significance of churchyards. For centuries, these sacred places have not been farmed, built upon or, until very recently, sprayed by pesticides. They therefore offer a glimpse of the old meadowlands from which they were carved. Moreover, the separation of the sacred churchyard from the temporal outside world reflects a similar delineation between the medieval town and the countryside. The town was a refuge, a sanctuary, a place of civilisation and religious expectation, often protected by walls from the rest of the world.

The Living Churchyards Project was established to preserve these sacred spaces so that rare and endangered species might be encouraged to grow within them. Over a thousand churches have agreed to cut some designated areas of their churchyards only once or twice a year, thus enabling a wide variety of plants to thrive. Others have planted native species or have attracted animals and insects through the creation of ponds and wet areas.

These living churchyards are the most recent expression of the notion that, within church walls, everything is protected and holy before God. The scheme, which was originally aimed almost exclusively at rural Anglican parishes, is now spreading to other faiths: for example, Leicester's Muslim and Hindu communities are enthusiastic participants. It is also having an impact in urban areas' municipal cemeteries. Much of the work is undertaken by volunteers, and their highly impressive results speak volumes for a continuing commitment to nurturing the sacred in the natural environment.

OUTCASTS

While the sacred aspect of burial started to be rejected by some people in the late nineteenth century, it had been denied to others for hundreds of years before then. Both criminals and suicides were traditionally buried not in parish churchyards but beside crossroads – and not the sacred crossroads in town centres, but out in the countryside. While it is perhaps obvious why criminals were not interred in the consecrated ground of the village or town churchyard – even though this does rather go against the Christian notion of forgiveness – the ostracism of suicides is rather more complex. It rests on the idea that life itself is a gift from God. The corollary of this is that God – and only God – has the right to decide when that gift should be withdrawn. So, if someone ended their own life, they were challenging one of God's inalienable rights and insulting Him. Christians have started to view suicide in a different way only relatively recently.

In part, at least, the traditional attitude towards suicides may have been a convenient theological construct to allow people to bury them far from the community. Of course, whenever someone takes their own life, it is a tragic and often violent event – not the sort of thing that people usually want to commemorate close to home. Small, close-knit communities undoubtedly found suicides frightening and disturbing, so it is hardly surprising that they buried them far away, both physically and emotionally. A crossroads was the preferred site because it made it difficult for the unquiet spirit, confronted by a multiplicity of routes, to make its way home.

While the bodies of suicides were taken outside the community after death, criminals were often transported beyond the town or village boundary to meet their death. Marble Arch stands on the spot that was used for London's public executions for over four hundred years: the Tyburn gallows. Condemned men and women were brought here all the way from Newgate Prison in the City. Far from all of them were criminals: many Catholics were burned at the stake or hanged, drawn and quartered for their faith at Tyburn in the sixteenth and seventeenth centuries. Elsewhere, executions were routinely held on hilltop gallows, with the victim left hanging once he or she had died, visible for miles around. (There are innumerable Hanging and Gallows hills throughout Britain.) Even more gruesome displays of convicted criminals took place on city gates, where heads and bodies were put on spikes and left to rot, sometimes for years.

Tyburn's public executions ceased in 1783, but every jail built before the 1960s was equipped with an execution yard, to carry out the death sentences that were still passed by Britain's courts until 1964.

ASHES TO ASHES, BODIES INTO SMOKE

As early as 1769, an illegal cremation took place in St George's Burial Ground (now St George's Gardens), Bloomsbury, London, when the body of the eccentric aristocrat Honoretta Pratt was burned in an open tomb. Later, a proud epitaph was attached to the tomb. It said that Honoretta had wanted to be cremated because the noxious fumes arising from decaying bodies was injurious to health. She hoped that she had set an example that others would follow, and had thus made a positive contribution to general health. However, in spite of the devastation wrought by the cholera outbreaks of the mid-nineteenth century, cremation was not legalised until 1885. In that year, another woman – Jeannette C. Pickersgill, a well-known scientific figure of her time – became the first person to be legally cremated in Britain.

The Victorians were so reluctant to endorse cremation primarily because of the Creed, the core statement of traditional Christian belief. According to the version of the Creed that is still recited in many churches today, Christians should believe in their bodily resurrection. With no body, no matter how decayed, how could they expect to rise on the Day of Judgement? Cremation therefore seemed to be an attack on a core Christian belief, and it generated a huge debate about life after death. The fact that it was practised by Indians made many people even more suspicious of it: at the height of empire, the theory was that India should be learning from Britain, not vice versa.

This deep-rooted Christian problem with cremation helps to explain why British crematoria have so little explicit religious symbolism on their walls and in their architecture. Even the main gathering place, where the coffin stands throughout the ceremony, looks more like a public meeting hall than a chapel.

Today, many people have totally rejected the tradition of lying for eternity next to a church as a symbol of their communion with God by requesting that their ashes be scattered. This is usually done in a place of deep personal significance. Sometimes the ashes are buried, not in a uniform plot in a municipal cemetery, but in a dedicated woodland burial site, where a tree will grow alongside others, creating a habitat for wild animals and a place of personal reflection for mourners.

My parents' ashes are buried in a place they both loved, high on a hillside on the Malvern Hills. My father was a vicar, he had given his life to the Church, and once he was dead my mother wanted him to be freed from that context. This is an example of the independent thinking about death that characterises our era. At the moment, most of us assume that this will be the permanent state of affairs, but no doubt it will change at some point in the future, just as every other strain of thinking about death has changed with each great cycle.

THE DORSET CURSUS

While the preceding pages have traced this shifting understanding of death, a common theme has run through most of the last six thousand years: the need to respect and honour the dead. Perhaps the only partial exception to this rule occurred in the fearful Roman period, but even then the dead were respected: they were just not trusted to behave themselves in the presence of the living.

There is one place in Britain where it is possible to see almost the whole history of this respect for the dead. To the west of Blandford Forum, in Dorset, lies an extraordinary landscape of death. Here, the dead have been honoured, feared and/or contained for perhaps five millennia. Running for nearly seven miles across the top of the downs is Britain's largest Neolithic monument – a narrow raised walkway that curves from hilltop to hilltop, dipping down to cross streams and the valley on its way. It is called the Dorset Cursus – a name bestowed by archaeologists in the last century, who thought it might have been a racetrack. No one knows for certain what it was for, but it almost certainly had a ritual aspect, and it is just one of several astonishing features of this strange landscape. Scattered over the hills and down in the valley are burial mounds created between the third and the first millennia BC. There are also traces of henges, now just circles of grass, surrounded by shallow ditches and embankments to create mini-amphitheatres.

Three villages of note lie in the valley. Almost nothing survives of Knowlton – even its church is in ruins – but what remains of that church stands inside a henge, mute witness to the continued reverence for divine forces across generations and even belief systems in this valley. It is the only church we know to have been built within such a pre-Christian sacred place, and this speaks of a very powerful relationship with much older beliefs. The other two villages share the first name of Gussage (meaning 'the place where water rushes out'). They are distinguished from each other by the dedications of their parish churches. Gussage St Michael is dedicated to the archangel who will balance the souls of the dead in the scales of justice on the Day of Judgement. Gussage All Saints celebrates its dedication day on 1 November each year – the day after Hallowe'en and of enormous significance with respect to Christian attitudes to the dead. For the pre-Christian people of Celtic Britain, Hallowe'en was a date of dread. The old year was dying and the new one had yet to be born. It was believed that on this night a gap opened between the spirit world and our world that allowed the dead to walk on the earth. Genuine fear of these spirits persisted long into the Christian era, but Gussage All Saints countered it by urging its parishioners to put their faith in the power of all the saints to overcome evil.

The names of these villages illustrate how Christianity appended its own stories and traditions on to those that were already ancient when it first arrived, perhaps fifteen hundred years ago. Of course, it might be pure coincidence that the churches carry names associated with the dead; and that a church was built inside a prehistoric henge; and that the tombs of even earlier people overlook them all from the hills of the cursus. But it cannot be denied that this has been a sacred place for a very long time. And throughout that time, rituals, symbols and traditions have been developed to help the living come to terms with the dead.

MONUMENTS TO DEATH IN
THE LANDSCAPE

Many an OS map, if looked at carefully, will show the sites of former villages. Historically, there were all sorts of reasons why a village might be abandoned – a shifting coastline, a river that changed its course, a Highland laird who wanted the land for his sheep – but one of the most common, certainly in the Middle Ages, was death. As we have seen, plague swept through Britain for centuries – from the first recorded outbreak in the sixth century, which may well have killed most of the Romano-British population, through the Black Death of the mid-fourteenth century, to the Great Plague of London of 1665 and beyond. The worst of these was the Black Death, which probably destroyed more British villages than any other force in history. Its impact is chillingly captured in an entry in the Bishop of Durham's rent rolls for the year 1352 – four years after the Black Death arrived in Britain – which simply says, 'No tenant came from West Thickley because they were all dead.'

Sometimes, as in the case of West Thickley, a deserted village is literally a sign of death. At other times, it might symbolise the death of a community because a landlord was determined to clear the area or because all of the young people headed for the cities or even abroad. Once they had gone, never to return, and the older members of the community died off, nobody was left. The same process continues to this day, as can be seen in the rapid decline of Welsh hilltop farms and Scottish crofting communities. This is another form of death – the death of a way of life.

More recent – and much more hopeful – symbols of death in the landscape are the new woods that are growing all over the countryside. Woodland burials are becoming increasingly popular as people start to give more consideration to their impact on the environment, but they also hint at the birth of a new great story – a reunion with nature. As the drift away from formal religion continues, these organic monuments to death will continue to grow and shape the landscape; and they will become sacred, if they are not already, because of the way in which they honour the dead.

BATTLEFIELDS AND MASSACRES

While deserted villages can symbolise death in several different ways, battlefields are much more straightforward: they mark the point were dozens, hundreds or even thousands of people lost their lives, usually in a single day. And there are hundreds of them all across Britain. However, only a few of the most significant – such as Culloden (1746 defeat of Bonnie Prince Charlie) and Bosworth Field (1485 defeat of

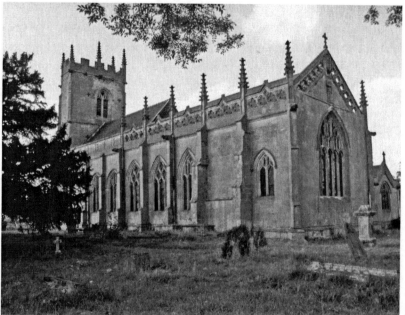

© Topfoto

A terrible sacred place. The church was built by Henry IV in 1403 to honour those killed in the Battle of Shrewsbury. The site is still called 'Battle', as is the church.

King Richard III by Henry Tudor) – are marked on the ground itself. (Others are marked on maps.)

One of the most extraordinary battlefield memorials is just outside Shrewsbury, at a place called Battle. Here, in 1403, Henry IV fought the rebel Henry 'Hotspur' Percy. Around ten thousand men perished that day, including Percy himself. As an act of repentance, Henry IV erected the church of St Mary Magdalene on top of the mass grave of many of the soldiers who died. Yet, this church does more than remember those who fell in battle: it positively celebrates one of the weapons that killed them. The gargoyles on the roof are in the form of cannon being loaded by soldiers. This strange, haunting church is one of the few places where the horror of war is commemorated right on a battlefield, and it remains a chilling place for that reason.

Henry Percy's body does not lie beneath the church built at Battle. Initially buried in a dignified ceremony by his nephew, his corpse was disinterred on Henry IV's orders, salted to preserve it, sent up to Shrewsbury, skewered on a spear, and exhibited in the town's market place. Later, it was quartered, with the four pieces sent to Chester, London, Bristol and Newcastle. His head was impaled on the north gate of York's city walls.

A few generations later, on 4 May 1471, during the Wars of the Roses, the army of the House of York decisively defeated the forces of the House of Lancaster just outside Tewkesbury. Many of the Lancastrians' high command – including the heir to the throne, Edward, Prince of Wales – died during the battle. When it became clear that the Yorkists were winning, many Lancastrian nobles sought refuge and sanctuary in the great abbey church of Tewkesbury. Nevertheless, two days later, they were seized, taken outside the abbey and executed after a summary trial. This brutal act horrified people throughout Britain, as it violated the traditional right of sanctuary. The abbey was reconsecrated a month later in a bid to restore a sense of sacredness.

Not all massacres occur on the battlefield, of course. Writing at the end of the eighth century, Bede tells of the massacre of twelve hundred monks at the ancient monastery of Bangor-is-y-coed, near Wrexham. And, as we saw in the Introduction, some 150 Jews took their own lives in Clifford's Tower, York, in 1190, rather than allow themselves to be torn apart by an anti-Semitic mob.

One of the last massacres to take place on British soil occurred in Manchester in 1819. Led by radical Nonconformist ministers, a crowd of some sixty thousand people marched through the centre of town to protest against the harsh economic conditions in the aftermath of the Napoleonic Wars and the lack of political representation for ordinary working men. When they reached St Peter's Fields, where the main city library stands today, the local authorities panicked and ordered a squadron of dragoons – mounted soldiers – to disperse the crowd. At least fifteen people died and perhaps seven hundred were injured when the soldiers set about the protesters with their sabres. This massacre of men, women and children caused outrage throughout Britain. The tragedy was named Peterloo in an ironic reference to the Duke of Wellington's recent triumph – supposedly over the forces of repression – at Waterloo. Some of the troops who had defeated Napoleon just four years before were now being used to suppress the British people themselves. A red plaque – rather than the more familiar blue – commissioned by the city council in 2007, now marks the spot of the massacre.

War memorials are now a feature of almost every village, town and city in Britain. The movement began with the Boer War, gathered strength in response to the horror of the First World War (when out of 18,000 parishes in England only 36 did not lose someone killed in the war) and have gone on ever since. Their role is part religious – they usually have a cross – and part secular, a place where the community can gather, regardless of belief. In the late 1980s, serious thought was being given to what to do with them, as the memories of the First World War, and survivors of the Second World War, were dying. However, the remarkable renaissance in the one-minute silence on Remembrance days, and the wars in Iraq and Afghanistan, have brought renewed significance to these profoundly important new sacred sites.

ELEVATING THE MEMORY OF THE DEAD: THE RISE OF THE OBELISK

While footsoldiers who die in battle are often not commemorated in any way in the British landscape, the same cannot be said for their generals. Since at least the end of the seventeenth century, Britain has produced a very specific form of monument to its dead heroes: the obelisk. The name comes from the Greek word for 'dagger', in reference to the way that they stand like upright knives in the landscape. They were very popular in antiquity, and pilfering them from classical sites became an obsession for the Georgians and especially the Victorians: the obelisk on the Thames Embankment, known as Cleopatra's Needle, was taken from Egypt in the 1870s.

Such vast monuments, usually commemorating a war or a successful general or great local figure, can be found on hilltops and in city centres right across Britain, where they serve a dual function: as symbols of death and as celebrations of particularly significant lives. For instance, on the highest point of the Blackdown Hills in southern Somerset, just above the town of Wellington, there is an enormous obelisk dedicated to the Duke of Wellington, whose family lived there for generations. Although started in 1817 to celebrate his victory over Napoleon at Waterloo, it was not finished until 1854, two years after his death. It is fifty-three metres high and can be seen from many miles around. Another great figure of the age, Captain James Cook, is commemorated by an obelisk on Easby Moor, North Yorkshire. Built in 1827, it stands sixteen metres high and celebrates a local lad made good.

These could well be considered sacred objects. After all, the people whom they celebrate certainly had an impact on the way our great story developed, and they are designed to inspire reverence for those people. However, they could also be viewed as the first symbols of a post-Christian, Enlightenment world of death. They do not contain the remains of the dead person; nor are they erected on consecrated ground. They honour death without the need for religion. Whether that makes them truly secular or just a new form of sacred is open for discussion.

DEATH IN LIFE AND LIFE IN DEATH

Today, we do not seem to know what we think about death, nor how to commemorate it. Yet, there is always uproar whenever a local council seeks permission to sell an old churchyard to property developers; and over the past twenty years a wholly new tradition of public shrines to the dead – such as those that were created in the aftermath of the Hillsborough disaster and the death of Princess Diana – has emerged. Both of these facets of our own great story seem to indicate that we still feel a need to honour and display respect for the dead, even those we never knew personally.

How we deal with the dead, what we think they are and whether we believe in life after death all tell us as much about life as they do about death. This is encapsulated in one of the most common epitaphs carved on gravestones over the last four to five hundred years:

Just as you are now, so have I been;
Just as I am now, so shall you be.

GAZETTEER

Cemeteries, burial grounds and commemorative sites

Scotland
- Calton Old Burial Ground, Edinburgh (EH12): spectacular eighteenth-century graveyard
- Skyline Necropolis, Glasgow (G4): the classic necropolis (see pages 285 and 286)

Wales
- Bangor-is-y-coed, near Wrexham (LL13): site of the massacre of hundreds of monks in the seventh century
- Cathays Cemetery, Cardiff (CF24): a vast cemetery
- Derwen, Denbighshire (LL21): has a fifteenth-century preaching cross
- Goat Hole Cavern, Paviland, Gower Peninsula (SA3): site of oldest known burial c.25,000 years ago

Northern England
- Arras Cemetery, Driffield, East Yorkshire (YO25): a unique collection of square Iron Age burial mounds
- Bosworth Field, Leicestershire (LE17): battlefield but now controversial
- Brougham, near Penrith, Cumbria (CA10): Roman cemetery
- Clifford's Tower, York (YO1): site of mass suicide of Jews in 12th century (see page 296)
- Easby Moor, North Yorkshire (DL10): Neolithic burial sites

- Eyam parish church, Derbyshire (S32): has a superb Celtic preaching cross
- Eyam Moor, Peak District (S33): Neolithic graveyard
- Hathersage, Derbyshire (S32): old graveyard turns into new rigid cemetery
- Lincoln Cathedral, Lincolnshire (LN2): fine carvings of the Day of Judgement on the west wall
- Perryfoot, Peak District: distinct burial mound siting
- Rockhurst, Peak District: distinct use of geography to highlight tomb
- Southern Cemetery, Manchester (M21): twentieth century and multi-faith
- St Mary Magdalene, Battle, near Shrewsbury, Shropshire (SY1): church built to seek forgiveness for massive loss of life in fifteenth-century battle (see page pages 294–5)

Southern England
- Arnos Vale, Bristol (BS4): vast Victorian cemetery
- Bath Abbey (BA1): built above the Roman remains and with a 'west front' story
- Blackdown Hills, Somerset (EX14): obelisk dedicated to the Duke of Wellington (see page 297)
- Cleopatra's Needle, Thames Embankment, London (WC2N): famous Egyptian obelisk
- Dorset Cursus, near Blandford Forum, Dorset (DT11): longest prehistoric site in Britain (see pages 291–2)

- Gussage All Saints, Wimborne, Dorset (BH21): part of ancient sacred landscape (see page 292)
- Gussage St Michael, Wimborne, Dorset (BH21): part of ancient sacred landscape (see page 292)
- Hanging Hill, Upton Cheney, Bath: example of execution site within view for miles around
- Highgate Cemetery, north London (N6): the classic nineteenth-century cemetery
- Endell Street, off Long Acre, Covent Garden, London (WC2E): remains of seventeenth and eighteenth century burial ground closed in the 1840s because of cholera
- Madron, Cornwall (TR20): extraordinary tomb temple
- Marble Arch, London (W1H): site of London's execution place of Tyburn (see page 289)
- Northover, near Ilchester, Somerset (BA22): site of Roman cemetery and ancient church on site of possible buried Roman saint
- Priddy, Mendip Hills, Somerset (BA5): outstanding examples of mass graveyard of Bronze Age
- St George's Burial Ground (now St George's Gardens), Bloomsbury, London (WC1): site of first cremation in the eighteenth century
- Stonehenge, Wiltshire (SP4): the most sacred landscape in Britain and site of hundreds of ancient tombs (see pages 275 and 276)
- Tewkesbury Abbey (GL20): site of a massacre in the fifteenth century
- Wells Cathedral, Somerset (BA5): post-Black Death tomb with rotting corpse symbolism as well as elaborate tomb cover

Participants in the Living Churchyards Project

Each of the following has a fine example of a living churchyard where the ecology has been carefully preserved and protected (see pages 287–8).

Northern England

- Cheshire: St Thomas's, Mellor (SK1); St Mary's, Acton (CW5)
- Cumbria: St Cuthbert's, Kirkby-in-Furness (LA17); St Aidan's, Barrow-in-Furness (LA13)
- Lancashire: St Peter's, Bolton (BL1); St John's, Great Marsden, Nelson (M2)
- Lincolnshire: St Giles's, Lincoln (LN2); St Peter and St Lawrence's, Wickenby (LN8)
- Norfolk: Parish churches at Sisland (NR14) and South Walsham (NR13)
- Shropshire: Parish churches at Hope Bagot (SY8), Westbury (SY5) and Hopesay (SY7)
- Yorkshire: Parish churches at Sheriff Hutton (YO60), Low Moor (BD12), Bradford (BD1), Mirfield (WF14), Kirklees (HD1) and Hutton Buscel (YO13)
- Halam Parish church, Southwell, Nottinghamshire (NG22)

Southern England

- Cornwall: Kenwyn church (TR1); the United Beniface of St Genny's church, St Genny's (EX23); St James's, Jacobstow (EX23); St Werburgh's, Warbstow (PL15); St Gregory's, Treneglos (EX22)
- Essex: The diocese of Chelmsford has gone further than most in

supporting the project (CM1). The churchyard at Witham (CM8) is especially fine

- Gloucestershire: Lydney parish church (GL15)
- Hereford and Worcester: Colwall Green parish church (WR13)
- Oxfordshire: Stanford-in-the-Vale parish church (SN7)

- Somerset: Aisholt parish church (TA5)
- Sussex: Holy Trinity, Hurstpierpoint (BN6); St Pancras, Arlington (BN26)
- Warwickshire: Parish churches at Stoneleigh (CV8), Brailes (OX15), Hillmorton (CV23), Rugby (CV21) and Great Wolford (CV36)

9

'And the Lord God planted a garden eastward in Eden'[60]

The Earth's deep measured song
Season sung, its Evensong
Of twilight blackbirds and human voices
Telling us this land is
From age to age what it was
Beyond our reckoning.[61]

What we build, how we farm and where we develop are clearly expressions of our beliefs and values. These activities are the mainframe of the stories we have been exploring throughout this book. In building a church, creating a town or laying out fields, we make our mark and tell our great story. Throughout all of this, there has always been tension between being part of nature and being apart from nature. Moreover, a split has developed between rural and urban – between the natural environment and the built environment. Each great cycle – from simple to complex to collapse – relates in one way or another to this tension.

As we saw in Chapter 6, the tension between the countryside and the city is a major theme in the Bible, and it has persisted ever since Christianity rose to pre-eminence in Western culture. Precisely because of this tension, the way in which we design, use and understand gardens – be they domestic plots behind our houses, parks or grand estates around stately homes – reveals as much, if not more, about Britain's great stories as any building or town layout.

TRACES OF THE FIRST GARDENS

Quite when gardens – rather than plots of land for growing food beside houses – came into being is not clear. It has been suggested that Neolithic people cultivated them, and some sites on Dartmoor seem to indicate that there were gardens in Britain by the Bronze Age. However, there is no doubt that the Romans had them, and this is the first period when gardens start to reveal something about people's beliefs and sense of the sacred. At the huge Fishbourne Palace in West Sussex, archaeologists have excavated the detailed ground scheme for a vast and complex garden of hedges, bushes, flowers and borders. The museum on the site has displays and images of what the garden would have looked like in its heyday, and outside the northern half has been replanted.

This was a classic walled garden, symmetrical and ordered, with areas for quiet reflection complete with statues to inspire thought, as well as a pathway for strolling through the scents and sights of a lovely flower garden. Despite the natural wonders it contained, though, Fishbourne epitomised the Romans' self-imposed separation from nature. It attempted to assert humanity's control and power over nature – the same misguided philosophy that would eventually lead to the collapse of the Roman Empire itself when all of its agricultural land was exhausted. Here, nature did what we told it to do, and its beauty was at our disposal, for our amusement. It was paradise, to use the word in its original sense. 'Paradise' comes from a Persian word meaning, simply, 'walled garden' – as opposed to the wilderness (or often the desert, given its origin) that lay outside. Control versus wildness has always been one of the fundamental aspects of gardening – as if we are playing God by trying to make nature obey us.

Of all our sacred historical landscape features, gardens are the most difficult to spot in the modern environment because we always eventually lose that fight with nature. Projects such as the Lost Gardens of Heligan, near St Austell, Cornwall, remind us just how swiftly a garden will disappear within nature's embrace once it is left to its own devices ... and how hard it is to restore back to its original state. The design of Fishbourne could be determined only after discovery of a piped water system, which had been laid out throughout the garden to keep the plants alive.

THE MONASTIC GARDEN

We have had no such luck in identifying Celtic or Anglo-Saxon gardens from the post-Roman period, but we do know that the first monasteries had medicinal-herb gardens that often served as centrepieces for their cloisters. By the late eighth century, these monasteries – such as Lindisfarne in Northumbria, Iona in Scotland and Bangor in North Wales – and their gardens were well established.

These monastic communities took their inspiration for gardening directly from the Bible. Genesis makes it clear that humanity was not only a part of creation but the co-creator, along with God, of the world. God's final creative act, according to Genesis, was not to make human beings but to make the garden that would be their home. This image of Eden gave early Christians (as well as Jews and Muslims) a sense of creating order out of the raw materials of creation. Thus, gardening – taking what existed and making it even more wonderful and useful – was a divine act in which they were full participants. This was why monks viewed their gardens as places where they could commune directly with God and the rest of creation. Their gardens were symbols of order but also of their – and the rest of humanity's – role in the sacred construction of a more beautiful world.

A large number of common plant names were coined by monks in the Middle Ages, and it is fascinating how many of these have sacred associations – such as St John's wort, and marigold, Madonna lily and Lady's mantle – all of which were named in honour of the Virgin Mary. Other plants – such as the strawberry – came to symbolise purity and were therefore often found in paintings of the Virgin. It was believed that God gave us each and every flower and plant for a special physical (including medicinal) or spiritual purpose. Consequently, everything in a garden was seen as part of the great, cosmic story. Even the collection of herbs was linked to this: medieval monastic herbals advised that they should be picked only at certain times of the day or night, depending on the phases of the moon and the influence of the planets. The monks followed these guidelines because they accepted that they were part of something infinitely greater than they could fully understand, but they also knew that they benefited from being part of this great whole. For instance, they did not know why certain herbs assisted healing, but they knew that they did.

Indeed, the medicinal qualities of many plants were seen as sacred in their own right. One of the chief functions of medieval monasteries was to provide infirmaries and free treatment for the poor, with most of the medicines grown in their own herb gardens. These gardens were situated within the 'close' – the sacred space enclosed by walls that was the holiest and most special part of any community. In these areas, the monks cultivated sage, rue, fennel, horehound, wormwood, lovage, white lilies, poppies, mint, catmint, mandrake, parsley, coriander, lettuce, onions, shallots, daffodils, beetroot, sorrel, marigolds, peonies, celendine, rosemary, acanthus, orache, smallage and clary, among many other plants.

A typical monastic garden was subdivided into areas for specific uses – such as the physician's garden, the cook's garden and so forth. Meanwhile, the *giardini sacristi* was reserved for specially sacred plants. Monasteries and churches let wild flowers grow here, and then used them to decorate the church during festivals and local events, such as weddings. Among the plants found in these sacred gardens were old roses, such as *Alba maxima*, maiden's blush, blush damask, *Rosa x alba* (the 'white rose' of the House of York), *Rosa gallica officinalis* (known as the 'apothecary's rose'), *Rosa mundi, Rosa eglanteria* and *Rosa phoenicia.* Monastic writers such as Benedict of Aniane and Walafrid Strabo provide a vivid picture not just of the use of herbs and flowers but of their symbolism in medieval times. For example, it was they who first linked roses to the blood of Christ and white lilies to the Virgin Mary – powerful symbols that were still in play in the Renaissance, half a millennium later (see Chapter 6).

Most of these beautiful and useful gardens disappeared when the monasteries were dissolved by Henry VIII in the mid-sixteenth

© The Art Archive

Old roses, such as this *Rosa gallicaofficinalis* (the 'apothecary's rose'), were common in monastic gardens and were used to decorate the church.

century. However, a number of them were taken over by cathedrals or parish churches. The monastery gardens had been planted in raised beds, and it is still possible to see traces of them in some cathedral and church grounds. Gloucester and Peterborough cathedrals have rebuilt their original herb gardens, as has St Peter's Abbey, in Shrewsbury. Other good examples of sacred gardens can be seen today in the churchyards of St Mary's, South Walsham, Norfolk, and St Lawrence's, Beckenham, Kent. A few monastery sites – such as Haverfordwest Priory, in Dyfed – also have displays of their old garden layouts.

THE GRAND HOUSE AND GARDENS

From 1066 onwards, Britain's castles and great houses had gardens that were usually used for food production, as in the kitchen gardens behind the grand houses on The Strand, in London, each of which stretched all the way down to the river. There were also formal walled gardens, specifically designed as places where ladies could sit in peace amid grass lawns, floral borders, and clipped trees and shrubs. These gardens were often depicted in books of hours, the private prayer books of the fourteenth and fifteenth centuries. In these beautifully illustrated books, much of the imagery refers directly to the Garden of Eden, with the central woman usually being a composite of Eve and the Virgin Mary!

From the Restoration onwards, with the rise of the landed gentry and the diminishing need to live in a fortified manor house or castle, the number of private gardens increased exponentially. Whereas the monastic gardens were developed in the context of a Catholic world-view – of a beneficial universe created by God and filled with the sacred – the British private flower garden was essentially a Protestant invention. It became primarily a place of pleasure and leisure. Some kitchen elements were retained, but the medicinal function was largely abandoned and forgotten. Now, the garden emphasised the notion of home, control and order, but only in the private sphere. The householder was a little god, theologically in control of his own fate and increasingly living a life of conspicuous display. This new class of merchants and landowners had the means to do this because of the former monastic lands and buildings that they – or their forefathers – had acquired after the dissolution of the monasteries. The sacred had been made domestic, and these people placed themselves at the centre of their picture of the universe. The most obvious manifestation of this new philosophy in a garden landscape is the 'knot garden'. Here, plants are trained to form a perfectly geometric pattern, with the quartered sections all visible from the small hill that allowed the God-like owner to survey his domain. A wonderful example of this vision of control and order can be found in the grounds of Barnsley House, Gloucestershire, which complements its stunning knot garden with formal, identical lines of topiary trees that stretch into the distance.

By the end of the seventeenth century, the designers of British formal gardens were finding inspiration in the French and Italian

© Mary Evans Picture Library

This early illustration of the regimented ranks of plants and trees in the gardens at Versailles shows the sixteenth- and seventeenth-century fashion for controlling and 'ordering' nature.

styles that culminated in the astonishing Palace of Versailles, built by King Louis XIV (r. 1643–1715) – the ruler who epitomised order and control at the time. Everything in the palace and especially its formal gardens was regimented and symmetrical, almost to the point of obsession. British landscape architects viewed this as entirely admirable and attempted to replicate it. Rivers were diverted to form formal lakes and ponds; trees were planted in ramrod straight lines; clipped hedges marched forth from the terraces that encircled the great houses; flowers grew only in their designated areas, which were usually perfectly square beds.

The great British gardens and estates of the seventeenth century clearly expressed the early modern world-view that humanity was in total control and that nature existed for our delight and use. The landscape was straightened, moulded and flattened – as if the mighty boot of humanity had stamped down and left its imprint.

RETURNING TO NATURE ... VIA CHINA

Then, at the beginning of the eighteenth century, the tide began to turn. Ironically, just when Britain was becoming an empire and imposing its ruthless order and control around the world, the reins were loosened at home. Landowners began to search for ways to be part of nature, not apart from nature. It was as if creating an empire, not to mention increasingly vast buildings and cities, needed to be balanced by letting nature back into the picture.

The first stirring of this alternative view was expressed by the poet Alexander Pope. In 1723, he wrote about creating his garden in London and expressed his desire to respond to the 'genius of the place'. In other words, he wanted to work with what nature had provided, rather than erase that and build his own creation from scratch. This was a conscious revolt against the formal garden and the control-and-order mentality of the previous century:

Consult the genius of the place in all;
That tells the waters or to rise, or fall;
Or helps th' ambitious hill the heav'ns to scale,
Or scoops in circling theatres the vale;
Calls in the country, catches opening glades,
Joins willing woods, and varies shades from shades,
Now breaks, or now directs, th' intending lines
Paints as you plant, and, as you work, designs.[62]

This was a highly significant moment in the history of Britain's sacred landscape, because, for the first time in well over a millennium, a spiritual tradition other than Christianity started to play an important role. The quest to identify the spirit – or genius – of the place in early Georgian England was partly inspired, astonishingly, by the Daoist view of nature. At the start of the eighteenth century, snippets of this ancient philosophy started to filter into Europe via the published writings of Jesuit missionaries, who were working hard to convert China to Christianity at the time. Lancelot 'Capability' Brown was deeply influenced by these books and soon started to incorporate the philosophy in his designs for many of Britain's grandest gardens (see below).

The vision the Jesuits revealed to Europe – a continent, it should be remembered, that was obsessed with order and control at the time – is best described as naturalism: going with the flow of nature rather than fighting against it. One of the most influential Jesuit books, written by the missionary Louis le Comte and translated into English in the 1690s, was *Journey through the Empire of China*. Le Comte noted: 'The Chinese so little apply themselves to order their Gardens and give them real Ornaments, do yet delight in them, and are at some cost about them: they make grotto's in them, raise pretty little Artificial Eminences, transport thither by pieces Rocks, which they heap one upon another, without further design, than to imitate Nature.'[63] Just a few decades after this book was published, everybody wanted a 'natural' landscape in their garden – or rather a landscape that was manufactured to appear natural. Gone were the rigid rows of topiary, the tight formations of flowers and the geometric knot gardens. In came flowing water, long vistas through woods, twisting paths through meadows and grassland, and even true wilderness areas in forests, at lakesides and on hilltops. Stourhead, Wiltshire – with its lakes, temples, grottoes, rolling hillsides and woodlands – is the classic example of Daoist philosophy put into practice in an English country garden.

When Western writers first attempted to describe Chinese yin/yang gardens, they faced two significant problems. The first was the sheer scale of these gardens and the amount of planning and construction that went into them. The second was the fact that the end result looked natural. All of these writers were used to formal gardens laid out in geometric patterns – 'organised naturalness' – so the 'planned disorder' of Chinese gardens tested their powers of description to the extreme.

At its most basic level, yin/yang brings this planned disorder to gardening. Yin represents order, while yang stands for chaos, so a Chinese garden – and especially a Daoist garden – attempts to capture both of these elements in its design. Also fundamental to a yin/yang garden is the contrast between hard and soft. This might be achieved by having a stream flow around a solid rock; or by planting fragile reed-beds next to a stone pagoda; or by building a bridge over running water.

Yin and yang are the two elemental forces in the Chinese view of the cosmos and everything within it. They are totally opposed to each other; yet, because each contains a speck of the other, neither can overcome the other. Their eternal struggle generates the dynamic of life – known as chi, qi, life energy, or life breath.

Yin and yang are found in all forms of life, but some are predominantly yin and others predominantly yang. For example,

▶

water, cold, clouds, women, winter, the north, river valleys, vegetables and the earth itself are all predominantly yin, while the
heavens, fire, steam, men, summer, mountains, birds, dragons and
the south are predominantly yang. Each has destructive and con-
structive aspects, so neither is seen as wholly good or wholly evil.
Such a rigid dichotomy does not exist in Chinese philosophy, in
marked contrast to the dualism that so bedevils Western thought.

One of the best models of the interaction between yin and yang
is the seasons. Autumn marks the growth of yin power, culminat-
ing in its dominance in winter. Then, at mid-winter, yin's decline
begins, leading towards the growing yang of spring, which reaches
its peak in mid-summer. But, of course, the seeds of yang's collapse are already sown by that point, and the cycle moves
inexorably towards autumn and the next growth of yin power.

Yin and yang are not viewed as gods or even as divine forces.
They simply describe the way the cosmos is. Their interaction
causes life to begin and their eternal struggle spurs it on.
Humanity has a unique role to play in this struggle because we –
and we alone – are believed to have the wisdom and skills to
ensure that yin and yang remain balanced. Conversely, we also
have sufficient power to disrupt that balance and bring disaster or
disorder to the world. Too much yin and the world will grow cold
and rivers will flood. Too much yang and deserts will spread and
water sources disappear. Humanity therefore needs to ensure that
balance is maintained or – if it has been lost – restored.
Gardening thus becomes not just a pleasant activity but an aspect
of our role in the cycle of cosmic harmony. It becomes a sacred
responsibility.

Feng shui, the Eastern art of geomancy, is fundamental to
everything from the design of cities to the creation of gardens in
East Asia. It literally translates as 'wind water', and teaches that
the whole landscape is alive with the forces of yin and yang, which

▶

must be taken into account when building anything. It determines good directions and bad, and advises on the scale and colour of both buildings and plants. Most significantly, it teaches that the forces generated by human activity must balance and work in harmony with existing, natural forces. It is the methodology through which yin and yang are applied – or revealed – in a garden.

The nature of the landscape

Alongside respecting yin and yang, the Daoist garden seeks to draw out or respond to the innate nature of the landscape – its water, trees and other plants. This concept of an innate nature is profoundly Daoist. Chuang-tzu, the great fourth-century BC philosopher and wit, explains it well. He contrasts the innate nature of a wild horse with the way in which humanity tries to improve or innovate:

> Horses have hooves so that their feet can grip on frost and snow, and hair so that they can withstand the wind and cold. They eat grass and drink water, they buck and gallop, for this is the innate nature of horses. However, when Po Lo [a famous horse trainer] came on the scene, he said, 'I know how to train horses.' He branded them, cut their hair and their hooves, put halters on their heads, bridled them, hobbled them and shut them up in the stables. Out of ten horses, at least two or three die. Then he makes them hungry and thirsty, gallops them, races them, parades them, runs them together.[64]

Substitute trees, bushes, flowers or landscape for horses, and you can see how Chuang-tzu's allegory applies equally well to gardening. Daoists believe that the very best in nature is natural. Humanity's role is simply to enhance it through skill, care and learning from nature itself – for example, by appreciating that emptiness is more natural than filling a space to overflowing.

Despite the enormous influence that Daoist thought has had on gardening in Britain since the early eighteenth century, we have not yet fully learned these lessons. Here, gardeners still focus on what they put into a garden. In true Daoist gardens, the space between the plants, the absence of human impact, is just as important – if not more so.

CAPABILITY BROWN

The greatest eighteenth-century landscape designer was Lancelot 'Capability' Brown. Almost single-handedly, he convinced landowners to abandon the formal, serried ranks of trees and bushes that had been the hallmark of most grand gardens since the sixteenth century.

© The Bridgeman Art Library

Luton Hoo gardens. This formal part of the garden reflects the 'controlling-nature' approach to gardens and contrasts with the Daoist-inspired 'natural' landscape Capability Brown created in the wider park.

Instead, Brown created romantic, wild landscapes, with little temples, vistas through shady woodland and rolling hills broken by the occasional copse or even a folly, such as a mock-ruined castle. His work was usually described as 'improvements' rather than 'design'.

Whenever Brown met a lord or lady who was anxious to join his list of esteemed clients, he would first survey the estate and then give the concerned aristocrat his verdict. Invariably, when asked if he could create one of his masterpieces on their land, Brown would reply, 'It has capabilities' – hence his nickname. Across the country – from Blenheim, to Stowe, to Warwick Castle – he redesigned the great country estates and created the rural, 'natural' landscapes that remain such a delight to this day.

GOING WITH THE FLOW

One evening, Brown was seated next to the Bishop of Oxford at dinner. The bishop reputedly leaned over and said, 'You know, Mr Brown, I do hope I die before you.' As can be imagined, Brown was taken aback by the bishop's comment, but eventually he asked, 'Why would that be, My Lord?' The bishop replied, 'Because I would quite like to see heaven before you improve it, sir.'

This apocryphal tale gives some sense of the threat that Brown – and other landscape designers who had been bitten by the naturalist bug – posed to the Established Church. Or, at least, the threat that was perceived by many members of that Church. They viewed naturalism as little more than a revival of paganism, celebrating nature, rather than God. Meanwhile, other members of the establishment disdained it for a different reason. Many a determined military colonialist thought of it as weak-kneed and faintly ridiculous – not the sort of philosophy on which to build an empire. These men – and the vast majority of them were men – still adhered to a scientific worldview that rested on the principles of control and order.

However, despite the antipathy of these two strands of the establishment – or possibly because of it – naturalism struck a chord in the hearts and minds of the British people. The growing lack of interest in conventional religion and the frustrations of an increasingly urban lifestyle combined to make this naturalist philosophy very attractive. It inspired the development of cottage gardens among the poor as well as the vast 'natural' landscapes of the gentry. And it prompted people to take long rambles in the countryside – possibly the first time in history that walking was viewed as a pleasurable activity, rather than a means to an end – which eventually led to the network of footpaths, national parks, walking groups and guidebooks that are such features of British culture today. The novelty of this activity is reflected in the story of an English Methodist minister who was on holiday in Portugal in the late nineteenth century. Just as he did at home, he spent much of his time wandering across the vast, open landscape before circling back and returning to his lodgings. None of the locals could believe that anyone would spend the whole day walking around in circles purely for pleasure, so the authorities arrested him, on suspicion of being a spy.

THE PARK

As we saw in Chapter 3, the grand landscaped park arrived in Britain with the Normans. These vast new estates – fenced-off areas of woodland and meadow – numbered some three thousand by the start of the fourteenth century. There was an element of farming to them, but that was not their chief purpose. Primarily, they were places of escape, areas where a mighty lord or even a king could cast himself as a wild hunter leading a band of comrades in the eternal battle between men and beast. They were early theme parks of aristocratic irresponsibility that offered the nobility temporary freedom from the dynastic struggles, leadership issues, church–state relations and other headaches that made ruling medieval Britain such a chore.

For the bulk of the Middle Ages, park landscaping went no further than erecting fences around these areas. Nevertheless, their sheer scale makes them very easy to spot. Look at any sixteenth- or seventeenth-century county map and you cannot miss them. For example, John Speede's 1612 map of Somerset has seventeen such parks: green circles and squares indicate the parkland itself, while an illustration of a wooden fence often marks its boundaries. These were the places that became the grand landscaped estates of eighteenth-century England, the grounds that Capability Brown and his disciples 'improved'. Meanwhile, in Scotland, such estates were expanded during the Clearances to create the great sheep runs and hunting estates of modern Scotland – at the expense of the people who were forced off the land and out of their villages, of course.

All of these great estates were symbols of the elite and manifestationsof their power and sense of belonging and entitlement. They were still little more than that when the nobility commissioned Brown to 'improve' them in the eighteenth century. However, Brown's activities almost immediately gave them an entirely new role, significance and relevance for everybody, not just the aristocracy. By designing his gardens with respect for nature itself, Brown started to write a new great narrative of open spaces that was soon adopted by the lesser gentry and then, most dramatically, by the town and city planners of Victorian Britain.

THE DEMOCRACY OF THE GARDEN: THE URBAN PARK

Thanks to the National Trust, National Heritage organisations and numerous independent family trusts, we can now visit Brown's masterpieces with relative ease. While that is certainly worth doing, precisely the same story is told every day in any local park.

Of course, there had always been open spaces in built-up areas –
the village green and the market places of towns and cities. In
London, there was also Hyde Park north of the Thames and Vauxhall
Gardens to the south – both of which were places to walk, ride and
court (or, in the case of in the latter from the seventeenth century
onwards, pick up ladies – or gentlemen – of the night). However, it
was the rise of the cramped, crowded and insanitary towns and cities
of the nineteenth century, together with the Victorian sensibility, that
provided the impetus for what we know today as urban parks and
gardens. Moreover, there was a ready-made template for how these
should be designed, in the form of Capability Brown's natural remod-
elling of the English landed gentry's country estates. What was good
enough for the aristocracy was deemed good enough for the aspiring
middle classes and indeed – in the spirit of philanthropy that characterised the age – the working people. Along with the building of
town halls, the development of urban parks is therefore one of the
clearest signs that democracy was on the rise in Victorian Britain. Most
people now agreed that even the poorest worker needed occasional
access to beauty, nature, green spaces and, if possible, cleaner air – all
of which could be provided by a park.

Most public parks and gardens fall into one of two categories: the
natural park or the order-and-control garden. Reflecting the esteem
in which Brown was held when most public parks were built in
Britain's towns and cities, the former style is far more common. It usually has a little wildness about it – as is exemplified in Glasgow's
Sighthill Park. There will be wandering paths, little bridges over cul-
verted or open streams, small woods, fields of long grass and bushes,
as well as more formal sections with flower beds and perhaps a small
artificial pond or lake. If you can manage to ignore the traffic noise
and the buildings that rise above the trees, you could almost be walking through the grounds of a grand country house. Sometimes, you
might literally be doing this. As Britain's urban areas grew, they
absorbed many of the landed gentry's neighbouring estates. Once the
noble family had fled to more salubrious, deeper countryside – far

from the slums and the fumes – the municipal authorities would take over the site and turn it into a public park. One example is Platt Fields in Manchester. Here, the original manor house still stands in isolated splendour on the edge of a park that has been surrounded by terrace houses and bordered by a major trunk road for at least 130 years.

Other natural parks were created when councils stopped industrial developers from building new factories on the edges of towns and cities and then designated the area parkland. Birchfields Park – which lies just half a mile from Platt Fields – was created from open countryside in this way. In both parks, the intention was to provide space for games – sport was viewed as healthy – as well as areas to wander and simply 'be in nature'. That telling phrase reveals just how crucial Daoist philosophy was to the development of Britain's urban parks and gardens – even though the local councillors probably had no direct knowledge of it. All they knew was that they liked what they had seen in other cities, whose authorities had been inspired by the estates of the landed gentry, who had been convinced to change their attitude to the landscape by Capability Brown, who had read the Jesuits' descriptions of Chinese gardens, which were built with the respect for yin and yang that is the bedrock of Daoism. The meandering path, especially, is a feature that comes straight out of Chinese gardens and ultimately from the Daoist belief that a path should follow the contours of the land. When recreated in British urban parks, it is an undeniable manifestation of the great story of being part of nature that has recurred in each of our great cycles of history.

The other style of urban park harks back to the model of order and control that reached its peak at Versailles. The most formal kind has flower beds in rigid, geometric patterns; plants in straight lines; perhaps a floral clock or a floral representation of the town's coat of arms. The paths will be dead-straight avenues bordered by equally spaced trees of uniform height. A prime example can be found in southern Manchester, just a mile or so from Platt Fields: Whitworth Park, a small, carefully designed space that sits beside one of the city's art galleries. Here, you can see the determination to impose order on nature that has heralded the collapse of every great story. It is also manifest in the studied perfection and rigid geometry of London's St James' Park and Glasgow Green.

One peculiarly British type of formal park can be found in seaside towns. They nearly always have a floral clock amid their uniform flower beds, straight paths and carefully clipped hedges. Perhaps they were created in a rather pathetic attempt to assert 'mankind's' control over of nature. If so, they fail quite dismally, because the notoriously uncontrollable and powerful sea rages just the other side of the esplanade. While humanity might be able to dictate which flowers grow where, it is certainly unable to tell the sea what to do.

Public gardens – as opposed to parks – also primarily subscribe to the order-and-control model, although they often throw in a bit of naturalism too, as if they cannot quite make up their minds what they want to be. The Marie Louise Gardens, just off Palatine Road in Manchester, are a good example of this internal contradiction. However, gardens are almost defined by their usefulness – hence the monasteries' medicinal gardens and cottage gardens for growing fruit and vegetables – so nature is never allowed free rein in them. If that were to happen, as any keen gardener would tell you, the garden would produce nothing but weeds.

OUR GARDENS

The struggle between what nature – or God – provides and what we make ourselves is neatly captured in a late nineteenth-century cartoon that appeared in *Punch*. It shows a small, beautiful garden with an old man leaning on his spade. Peering over the old stone wall is a vicar, who looks at the man's lovely garden and says, 'Isn't it wonderful what God can do?' The gardener replies, 'Ahh, but you should have seen the mess it was in when He had it all to Himself!' Walk

© Mallett Gallery, London. UK/The Bridgeman Art Library

The Victorian dream of a cottage garden – nature as fruitful, with a dash of wild, but ultimately useful.

down any suburban street today and you will see dozens of attempts to tidy up God's handiwork.

The most obvious sign of this used to be the neatly trimmed privet hedge, for decades the symbolic and physical border between the suburban home and the outside world. The neater and higher the hedge, the more likely the people behind it found the rest of the world alarmingly chaotic – lacking the order that they had created in their domestic environment. This symbol of Middle England was borrowed from the Islamic gardens of Spain, where the privet hedge was used to create the straight, geometric lines that honoured God as the Great Architect yet emphasised that we, his followers, were now in full control of nature. Increasingly, though, Britain's privet hedges have disappeared, either to make way for more parking spaces or simply to create 'low-maintenance' gardens. The fad for gravel, decking or even concrete – with just the occasional potted plant to break up the monotony – is the latest reincarnation of the order-and-control model. These are gardens designed for busy people who want instant gratification and effortless control.

A khalifa is appointed by a mighty king or emperor to rule in his stead over an area, and Islam teaches that each of us is a khalifa of God. This may sound like a licence to exploit the world, but nothing could be further from the Islamic philosophy. Instead, we are expected to reflect on the authority granted to us by God, but also on His mercy, love, compassion and wisdom. Our role is to care for God's creation with the same tenderness He would display Himself. The Islamic garden needs to be understood in this context, for it is not just for the enjoyment of human beings. A much-loved saying of the Prophet Muhammad is: 'If anyone plants a tree or sows the land and people, beasts or birds eat from it . . . he should consider it as a charity on his part' (Bukhari and Muslim). A garden that discourages animals, birds and insects is not a true Muslim garden.

Islam also brought a love of numbers and geometry to garden design. The ban on images in the Qur'an is absolute, so traditionally Islam has forbidden the depiction of any human – and indeed often any animal – form (although this has started to be relaxed in recent years). This led Islamic designers to experiment with abstract patterns copied from plants and flowers as well as geometric shapes. They created dozens of exquisite designs, each of which has theological and philosophical significance. The octagon, perfected by the Moghuls in India between the thirteenth and sixteenth centuries, is a prime example of this. Here, two squares are overlaid to create a stylised circle, with the squares symbolising humanity and the circle the unity of God.

Thankfully, other private gardens still celebrate nature, rather than attempt to control or even obliterate it. The classic cottage garden usually features an abundance of flowers in addition to its useful herbs and vegetables, not to mention a pond, fruit trees, bushes and even wild areas that provide habitats for frogs, birds, hedgehogs, foxes and maybe even badgers. There will generally be no straight lines, only plenty of curves. Here, Daoism provides the model and helps us understand who we are and how we fit into the natural world.

The pond, if there is one, provides a calm, reflective centre – an 'empty' space in the true Daoist tradition. Look at a traditional Chinese room and you will see that it is empty in the middle, with all of the furniture placed around the edges. The same principle works well in a garden. If not a pond, the empty centre might be a small hill, which forms a simple yet powerful focal point; or just an open space, defined by encircling bushes or trees.

THE NATIONAL PARKS

A new form of park came into being in Britain in the late 1940s, primarily in response to the demands of weekend walkers who gained the freedom to explore the countryside through ever-expanding car ownership. Our national parks were inspired by those of the United States – such as Yellowstone – which were founded in the late nineteenth century after intensive lobbying by the Transcendentalist Movement – a group of ostensibly Christian romantic poets who were also deeply influenced by other religions. These American wildernesses were the first such parks in the modern world, although Mongolian Buddhists had created national parks as far back as the twelfth century (and, of course, in Britain we had something similar in the Normans' great hunting estates). The likes of Beatrix Potter – who helped found the National Trust – were impressed by the American model and campaigned for something similar to be adopted in Britain.

Eventually, they succeeded, and huge swaths of land between our major conurbations – such as the Peak District, which lies between the urban sprawls of Manchester, Leeds, Derby and Stoke–on-Trent – were designated as national parks. They have been dedicated to our enjoyment and to healthy activities ever since. Their creation reflects the fact that the average Victorian city dweller could walk only to his or her officially approved recreational area – the local park – whereas their grandchildren could drive into the countryside and then traipse all over it, irrespective of whether they were breaking the law by doing so. The great 'mass trespass' of 1932 at Kinder Scout in the Peak District was the most obvious signal that something had to be done about this. In this great act of civil disobedience, perhaps five hundred determined walkers took to ancient pathways and demanded the right to walk along them; five were arrested. As we have seen, pilgrimage had not been part of British life since the Reformation, but this mass demonstration had an echo of the old pilgrimage spirit about it. For the first time in almost four hundred years, people were renewing their sacred link with the landscape by walking along its pathways. Even once the national parks had been created, campaigners continued to lobby Parliament for the 'right to roam' throughout the countryside, including on private property. This right was finally guaranteed in law in 2004.

The national parks are the epitome of the naturalist model, even though they still have to wrestle with the realities of farming and local economic use of the land. Urban dwellers travel to them in their millions to rediscover their sense of their place in nature, and to mitigate the smog, strain and stain of city life.

THE GREEN BELT TIGHTENS AROUND THE URBAN SPRAWL

The national parks were not the only means to protect the countryside from advancing urbanism. In addition, there was the notion of the green belt, a ring of land around major conurbations that was supposed to announce 'This far but not further' to the industrialists and developers. Increasingly, though, Britain's green belts have come under pressure from roads, housing estates and out-of-town shopping centres. On the whole, they still just about manage to keep the large cities in check, but it is a different story around smaller towns. Here, identical white-roofed trading estates seem to spring up with little or no control, and they are threatening to destroy the boundaries between urban and rural.

TOWN AND COUNTRY MERGE INTO ONE

Bournville, now firmly within Birmingham but originally built on its semi-rural outskirts, is a delightful example of a workers' suburb that was designed to fuse an urban industrial environment with nature. Founded in 1879, it was a much more pleasant place to live than most working-class communities of the time, and it had the added advantage of being within easy walking distance of the Cadbury's chocolate factory. The whole concept reflected the Cadbury family's Quaker beliefs and principles.

A couple of decades later, the garden cities movement was another largely successful attempt to resolve the dichotomy between urban and rural by merging one into the other. The vision was generally good, and it is once again finding favour with ecologically minded town planners today: create a city with integrated open, green spaces, lots of trees and a sense of fusion between town and country, and hopefully people will be happier and more productive. However, only two garden cities were founded before the Second World War: Letchworth, in 1903, followed by Welwyn Garden City in 1920. After the war, Milton Keynes (founded in 1967) followed the good example set by the garden cities by planting masses of trees in its early development stages with the result that it is now an astonishingly green town, especially along the roadsides. All of these places quite skilfully employ the naturalist principles championed by Capability Brown 150 years earlier.

Sadly, though, these are isolated success stories. More often than not, attempts to create a rural–urban fusion have ended in near disaster. This was the case when huge numbers of people were shifted out of the slums of Glasgow, Liverpool, Bristol and Manchester and deposited in sprawling post-war developments that had been built from scratch in the countryside, such as Skelmersdale (for Liverpool), Hattersley (for Manchester) and Hartcliffe and Knowle (for Bristol). The concept probably seemed flawless to those who dreamed it up: take poor people out of unhealthy and often bombed-out inner-city slums and give them clean air, sports fields and views of open countryside and babbling brooks. However, in reality, it was ill-conceived and poorly implemented. The idea took no account of these people's need for continuity, family and community, and it stuck them miles away from potential places of employment. Whereas they had been able to walk to work in the city (or at worst catch a cheap bus or tram), they now faced an expensive car journey each day – if they even had a car, which most of them did not. These new towns therefore became black spots of unemployment, which inevitably led to mounting pressure, family break-up and community disintegration. The final insult was to call these experiments in social engineering 'estates', as if they were somehow recapturing the rural beauty of the old hunting grounds of the nobility. Instead, they have often become isolated, depressed areas, cut off from the energy of towns and cities, and left to decline and decay.

TWO STORIES LEADING TO ONE RESULT?

The introduction of national parks, green belts and even some public parks means that vast areas of land are now under public control and protection. Of course, this concern for the environment is laudable as it has helped to preserve some of our most important, fragile and beautiful landscapes. However, as extensive as these areas are, they make up only a tiny proportion of the total land area of Britain. Moreover, they allow irresponsible developers to justify their activities in *unprotected* areas: after all, how can anyone complain that a new housing estate is being built on a green-field site in rural Derbyshire when the Peak District is just down the road? Similar arguments have been voiced wherever protected areas have been established – from African game parks to Native American reservations. As soon as you venture outside the pristine landscape, you are confronted with urban sprawl.

Over the past hundred years, then, the two conflicting stories that emerge in every great cycle have been running in parallel. The story of order and control is manifest in the ceaseless expansion of our towns and cities, the building of ever more factories, the development of the motorway network and so forth. Meanwhile, the creation of the national parks indicates that many of us still yearn to locate ourselves within nature, to be a part of it, not apart from it. Maybe these two stories were quite evenly matched before the Second World War, when militant ramblers from Manchester demanded the right to walk on Kinder Scout, but they are not now: the forces of order and control are winning, as can be seen every time the M25 is widened or a new runway is added to an airport.

Throughout history, soon after order has achieved apparent victory over simplicity, a great cycle has collapsed. We are heading for a similar collapse now, unless we do something to stop it.

MORE SACRED THAN A CHURCH

In 'Garden Thoughts', the English poet Dorothy Frances Gurney wrote:

The kiss of the sun for pardon,
The song of the birds for mirth,
One is nearer God's heart in a garden
Than anywhere else on earth.

The relationship between God, nature, our gardens and ourselves is complex. We often feel more spiritual in a garden than we do in a church, perhaps because gardens are our way to try to recapture Eden. That might explain why far more people visit National Trust gardens – and, indeed, garden centres – than sit inside a church each Sunday.

Gardens also offer a form of sanctuary from the urban landscape that surrounds so many of us. The Georgians and the Victorians delighted in planting thousands of trees along their streets, creating gardens in town squares, beautifying their cemeteries – all acts that brought nature into *public* spaces. By contrast, over the last hundred years, we have kept our increasingly tenuous link to nature to ourselves, behind our privet hedges and garden fences. It is hard to think of a major new public park that has been built in the last fifty years. School playgrounds and playing fields have been sold off to fund building improvements. Shopping malls are constantly nibbling at the edges of urban parks. The end result is that we have largely lost our communal link to nature – the brave new world that the Victorians hoped they were creating.

However, there are some causes for optimism. Particularly in industrial cities and towns, allotments allow people to grow food for themselves and develop a communal appreciation of nature with others. Side by side, scores of individual owners tend to their little plots, but they all belong to a greater whole that they administer among themselves. Here, the communal and private aspects of gardening complement each other to tell the great story of working with nature, not against it.

The Sacred Land Project is contributing to this story by working with community groups to create new gardens on old dockland sites, disused railway lines and the grounds of former religious buildings.

For instance, one group in Bristol has created gardens to commemorate the children who died in the great cholera epidemics of the 1840s. In Norfolk, members of the Sikh community are creating a garden around the tomb of their last maharajah.

For some people, of course, the garden will always be nothing more than an extension of their ironed, vacuumed, immaculate back room. Such gardens are invariably pristine, their straight lines and uniform borders signalling that the owner is not entirely comfortable with the abundance of nature. But most gardens are not like that. They are places to meet, share and even contribute to the wonder, glories, triumphs, decay, death and rebirth of the natural world. In this way, perhaps they hold the key to how we might avert the tragedy that has engulfed every previous great story.

Maybe our gardens, parks and national parks preserve a trace of what we have lost elsewhere in our world: namely, a sense of being part of something much greater, much more significant and ultimately much more sacred.

GAZETTEER

Early gardens

- Dartmoor, Devon: many ancient settlement sites some with possible gardens
- Fishbourne Palace, West Sussex (PO19): best example of a Roman garden in Britain
- The Strand, London: once the site of many palaces running down through gardens to the river

Monastic gardens

The following have remains of, or have recreated, monastic gardens.

Scotland
- Iona, Scotland (PA76)

Wales
- Bangor, North Wales (LL57)
- Haverfordwest Priory, Dyfed (SA61)

Northern England
- Lindisfarne, Northumbria (TD15)
- Peterborough Cathedral (PE1)
- St Mary's, South Walsham, Norfolk (NR13)
- St Peter's Shrewsbury (SY2)

Southern England
- Gloucester Cathedral, Gloucester (GL1)
- St Lawrence's, Beckenham, Kent (SE6)

Great estates

- Barnsley House, Gloucestershire (GL7)
- Blenheim, Oxfordshire (OX20)
- Lost Gardens of Heligan, St Austell, Cornwall (PL26)
- Stourhead, Wiltshire (BA12)
- Stowe, Buckinghamshire (MK18)
- Warwick Castle (CV34)

Parks

Scotland
- Glasgow Green (G1)
- Sighthill Park, Glasgow (G4)

Northern England
- Birchfields Park, Manchester (M14)
- Marie Louise Gardens, Palatine Road, Manchester (M20)
- Peak District National Park
- Platt Fields, Manchester (M14)
- Whitworth Park, Manchester (M15)

Southern England
- Hyde Park, London (W2)
- St James' Park, London (SW1A)
- Vauxhall Gardens, London (SW1P)

Town in the countryside

- Bournville, Birmingham
- Letchworth Garden City, Hertfordshire
- Milton Keynes, Buckinghamshire
- Welwyn Garden City, Hertfordshire

Conclusion
Where does the story go now?

God is dead – Nietzsche
Nietzsche is dead – God
I'm not feeling very well either[65]

Over the past five thousand years, four great stories have collapsed in Britain, leaving tantalising traces in the sacred landscape of today. On each of these occasions, a new great story filled the void and we recovered. However, the fifth collapse, if it comes, might be more permanent; this time, it might be the point when people lose the ability to believe in *any* great story. Today, we live for the moment, shop till we drop, and, most importantly, opt out of any attempt to construct a grand narrative that might help to explain our place in the cosmos. We have chosen to believe in a small story, rather than a great story. In a sense, we have elevated our cynicism about all faiths and beliefs to a level of truth.

However, we cannot live – and certainly cannot make sense of our predicament – without a great story. As Carl Jung said, without the myths and legends that give us a place, a role and a meaning, we would be 'crushed by the sheer awe-fullness of the universe'. A transcendent great story is essential because it takes us beyond the point where all secular belief systems – such as atheism, Marxism, nation-alism and fascism – must stop. It links us to the universe and thereby gives life a meaning and a purpose beyond simply existing. And, although it deals with what lies beyond material existence, it is man-ifest here, on this planet – in the places where we live, in the soil that nourishes our crops, in the rivers that provide our water. This is because the transcendent has to become immanent – it has to be here, with and around us – in every great story. If we cannot relate our story to the land, trees, birds, animals and water, then it is not true … or at least not true enough.

In their time, Christianity, Islam, Hinduism, Buddhism and Judaism have all claimed to be 'the one true story'. More recently, communism, fascism, nationalism, secularism, capitalism and democracy have made similar claims. All have been adopted and championed by millions of people. However, all have then declined, or are currently in the process of declining. I believe the reason for this is simple: they never include all life in their great story. Some view only human beings as sacred, valuable or blessed; others teach that only those who fully commit to their philosophy are blessed. As a result, a kind of ideological utilitar-ianism now underpins our society. We have reduced and almost lost sense of the divine and have elevated humanity to take its place. Unfortunately, though, as we have proved time and time again, that is a role we are singularly incapable of filling.

Since the Enlightenment, many people have chosen science as their great story – putting their faith in it completely. But they have often been left hungry for a way to address their doubts and anxiety, and they still have no definitive answer to the question of what life is all about. I would argue that a great story has to be about communal, not just individual, well-being; and about the whole of creation, not just human beings. If it is not, then we push nature to the brink because we do not view animals, plants, rivers, the sea and the earth as parts of us, just as things that we can use. This has led to catastro-phe in the past, and it will do so again unless we broaden our understanding of what constitutes our community.

Furthermore, for a great story to endure, it must celebrate as well as warn and mourn. And it must embrace change. Many people see the great religions as models of unchanging continuity, but they are not. They have succeeded in becoming the oldest human organisations in the world because they have worked out how to change and adapt in such a way that they appear timeless. Significantly, the earliest book that is still in constant use today is the three-thousand-year-old Chinese text, the *I Ching* – which translates as *The Classic of Change*. By exploring and playing with change, this book has remained relevant for more than one hundred generations. Many of today's environmentalists – who so often campaign to keep things *exactly* as they are – would be well advised to read it.

THE BEGINNING OF THE END OR A NEW BEGINNING?

Of course, many people believe that the world is heading towards an inevitable environmental apocalypse. They may well be right. As William Temple, the Archbishop of Canterbury during the Second World War, said, 'We are just three meals away from barbarism.' You only have to look at the panic, fighting and selfishness that ensue when petrol is rationed to know that he was right. Moreover, as we have largely sacrificed the local and now rely on multinational companies to supply our fuel, food and even our information, we are highly vulnerable to collapse if any part of that vast, complex system breaks down.

However, we are in a different position to all of those people who stood on the brink of collapse at the end of the previous four great cycles: because, this time, we know what happened to them. We know that if we ignore the fragility of the land, we will eventually exhaust it and make it worthless, as the Romans did. We know that a pandemic can lead to physical and spiritual collapse, as the Black

Death did. We know that we have only ever succeeded by working with, rather than against, nature. Armed with this knowledge – and by casting a critical eye over the vast changes that are being wrought in the world's landscape, the spiralling growth of urbanism, the cult of individualism that leaves so many people feeling alone – we ought to be able to take steps to mitigate, and possibly even avert, collapse.

First, we must rediscover that all of the land is sacred. It is easy to romanticise other places – China, India, Egypt, for example. It is far more difficult – some might say ridiculous – to view the place where you live and work in the same light. Yet, if we do not have a sense of walking on holy ground every day, if we do not re-establish respect and even awe for all of nature, then we may not be able to avoid the fifth apocalypse. That is why this book has offered guidelines on how to read the landscape; why it has sought to recover the sacred in every-thing, from the names of plants to the layouts of our towns and cities. In our fields, farms, villages, buildings, rivers and mountains, we can find clues that aid our understanding of ourselves and our place in the great story. Without that depth of understanding, we simply will not be able to comprehend the changes and the dangers we are facing.

The previous four great cycles collapsed because they eventually abandoned the simplicity of being a part of nature for the complex-ity of being apart from nature. Two of those stories – and our own – were shaped by a combination of Greek and Roman beliefs and the Bible. Perhaps it is time to complement them with a third tradition, before it is too late. We have already encountered this in Chapter 9: Daoism, which teaches that humanity must be part of the flow of nature. This philosophy might just enable us to sidestep the type of catastrophe that proved unavoidable for our ancestors. After all, it has guided one of the world's largest and greatest civilisations for over two thousand years, so it would be surprising if it had nothing to teach us about human nature and the natural world. Crucially, because it comes from a different culture, it also allows us to look at our existing beliefs, practices and traditions from a new perspective, and possibly acknowledge their flaws for the first time.

One of those flaws concerns Western exclusivity, such as that offered by fundamentalism – be it religious or secular – which denies the validity of any alternative view. Another is our abandonment of community in favour of individualism, epitomised by the fact that we have a Convention on Human Rights but no Convention on Human Responsibilities. A third is the notion that science and faith cannot exist happily alongside each other. That concept was invented for propaganda reasons in the early 1890s, when the anniversary of Columbus's discovery of America was drawing near and writers wanted to present him as a modern hero battling against medieval (religious) superstition. Actually, nobody in the 1490s – including his deeply religious patrons – thought that Columbus would fall off the edge of the world if he sailed west.

So many of our Western beliefs are either redundant or serve only to bolster a false sense of superiority. We must abandon these completely, and not just as concepts, but in their material forms – in the ways we behave and in the things we buy and create. In their place, we need to embrace hope, possibility and change. Of course, we can eulogise these concepts in speeches and books, but it would be far better to incorporate them into our everyday lives – through what we build, how we lay out our urban areas, how we farm and how we care for the rest of nature. We need to rediscover that we have a sacred responsibility to protect, nurture and love all life on earth. If we can do that, the fifth great collapse might never happen.

Notes

1 The book covers England, Scotland and Wales. I apologise for the omission of Northern Ireland, but I felt I would not be able to do it justice here. Ireland as a whole has its own extraordinary sacred landscape, and it demands a book of its own. I can only hope that someone with the necessary knowledge will be inspired to write it.

2 Taken from Jay Ramsey's poem *Summerland*.

3 Lo Kuan Chung, *The Romance of the Three Kingdoms*, written in the late fifteenth century. Various English translations are available.

4 *Uncivilisation: The Dark Mountain Manifesto*, pp. 5–6.

5 Revised edition, London: Granta, 2003, p. 220.

6 Taken from Jay Ramsey's poem *Summerland*.

7 Taken from Jay Ramsey's poem *Summerland*.

8 See Timothy Darvell, 'Before the Flood: Early Hunter–Gatherer Societies to 13,000 BC,' in his *Prehistoric Britain* (2nd edn), London: Routledge, 2010.

9 Francis Pryor, *The Making of the British Landscape*, London: Allen Lane, 2010, p. 57.

10 For example, Romans 9:21.

11 See examples cited by Francis Pryor in *Britain BC*, London: Harper Perennial, 2004, pp. 155–7 and 168–73. Other examples are cited in Darvill, pp. 102–6 and 134–5.

12 See Oliver Rackham, *Woodlands*, London: HarperCollins, 2010, pp. 52–3 and pp.89–96.

13 See Mark Edmonds, *Ancestral Geographies of the Neolithic: Landscapes, Monuments and Memory*, London: Routledge, 1999, pp. 69–73.

14 A more mundane explanation maintains that Rollright is simply Anglo-Saxon for 'the land belonging to Hrolla' (presumably a local ruler).

15 Barry Cunliffe, *Iron Age Britain*, London: English Heritage, 1995, p. 99.

16 The oldest history of Britain, written by the sixth-century monk Gildas, is a

diatribe against the corruption of Roman Britain and casts the Anglo-Saxon invasions as God's punishment.

17 *The Anglo-Saxon Chronicle*, translated and edited by Michael Swanton, London: J.M. Dent, 1996, pp. 55, 57.

18 Oliver Rackham, *Woodlands*, London: Collins, 2010, pp. 117–21.

19 Genesis 24:60.

20 Taken from Jay Ramsey's poem *Summerland*.

21 Genesis 2:18–20.

22 Genesis 28:18–19.

23 Francis Bond, *Dedications of English Churches*, Oxford Oxford University Press, 1914, p. 17; James Rattue, *The Living Stream*, Woodbridge: The Boydell Press, 1995, p. 71.

24 Everyman edition, London: Dent, 1959, p. 38.

25 Nigel Pennick, *Celtic Sacred Landscapes*, London: Thames and Hudson, 1996, p. 81.

26 In Jay Ramsay (ed.), *Earth Ascending: An Anthology of Living Poetry*, Exeter: Stride Books, 1997, p. 68 (published as part of the Sacred Land Project).

27 Ruth 1:16.

28 Keith Thomas, *Man and the Natural World*, London: Allen Lane, 1983, p.20.

29 These are just three yews among many. In recent years, the Ancient Yew Tree Group has scrupulously recorded fifteen hundred ancient yews throughout Britain.

30 Taken from Jay Ramsey's poem *Summerland*.

31 William Shakespeare, *Henry V*, Act 3, Scene 1.

32 James Rattue, *The Living Stream*, Woodbridge: The Boydell Press, 1995, p. 64.

33 Matthew 16:16–17 and 18:18.

34 A beautiful carved façade on a fine building in Manchester's Albert Square commemorates this event.

35 I admit to some bias here, because one of these windows can be found in the Palmers' Chapel.

36 Author's translation.

37 Two of the few parish churches to have retained their original rood screens are at Pennant Melangell, in central Wales, and Pawlett, in Somerset.

38 Very few pre-Reformation churches had pulpits, although an exception was in Cold Ashton, Gloucestershire, a private retreat church for a wealthy prior who taught his novices there.

39 A fine medieval stone altar survives in Stratford Tony, Wiltshire.

40 John 20:1–10.

41 Unitarians were specifically excluded from this. They were finally granted tolerance in the Unitarian Relief Act of 1813.

42 Berwick-on-Tweed has a fine example of a nineteenth-century Church of Scotland church with stained glass.

43 Although Lloyd George himself was born into a Nonconformist – Baptist – family.

44 Taken from Jay Ramsey's poem *Summerland*.

45 To complete the set of British patron saints – albeit barely – St David provides the name of a small street that runs down the western edge of St Andrew's Square.

46 It has now been converted into government offices.

47 The four streets leading to the centre of Chichester are even named after the four cardinal points of the compass.

48 Just one saint associated with sailors was scarcely enough for a city that was so dependent on the sea, so another church was built and dedicated to St Clement in the Middle Ages. It was demolished sometime in the seventeenth century.

49 Sometimes the sheer scale of the capital can lead to confusion, with the names of some of its boroughs having no link to the original Roman settlement. For example, Southall, in west London, was named because of its position in relation to its neighbour, Northolt.

50 Chipping – as in Chipping Norton, Chipping Sodbury, Chipping Campden, *et al.* – means the same thing.

51 Taken from Jay Ramsey's poem *Summerland*.

52 Melvyn Bragg, *The Book of Books*, London: Hodder & Stoughton, 2011, p. 115.

53 Of course, we know that the Druids arrived in Britain long after Stonehenge was abandoned. See Chapter 3.

54 Genesis 11:5–8.

55 Quoted in Tristram Hunt, *Building Jerusalem*, London: Weidenfeld & Nicolson, 2004, p. 166.

56 Taken from Jay Ramsey's poem *Summerland*.

57 Barry Cuinliffe, Robert Bartlett, John Morrill, Asa Briggs and Joanna Bourker (eds), *The Penguin Atlas of British and Irish History*, London: Penguin, 2001, p.23.

58 Richard Morris, *Churches in the Landscape*, London: Phoenix Books, 1997, pp. 31–3.

59 See H.R. Trevor-Roper, 'The Diabolical Religion', in *The European Witch-craze of the Sixteenth and Seventeenth Centuries*, London: Penguin, 1990.

60 Genesis 2:8.

61 Taken from Jay Ramsey's poem *Summerland*.

62 Epistle IV to Richard Boyle, Earl of Burlington.

63 'Memoirs and Observations Made in a late Journey through the Empire of China' by Louis Le Comte, Jesuit, published by Benjamin Tooke, London 1699.

64 Opening of chapter nine of *Chuang Tzu*, translated by Martin Palmer and published by Penguin Classics, 2005.

65 Graffiti (in three different styles of handwriting) on the wall of a Cambridge men's toilet in the 1970s.

Index

Page numbers in italic refer to illustrations